NW

WASHOE COUNTY LIBRARY

3 1235 01576 6939

D1772976

DATE DUE

ILL NOV 15 2002	
NOV 16 2002	
DEC 0 3 2003	

DEMCO, INC. 38-2931

RECEIVED

JUN 29 2000

NORTHWEST RENO LIBRARY
Reno, Nevada

BY

WILLIAM B. SECREST

Barbed Wire Press

PO Box 2107, Stillwater, OK 74076
A Western Publications Company

Library of Congress Cataloging-in-Publication Data

Secrest, Bill
    Dangerous trails : five desperadoes of the old West coast / by William B. Secrest.
        p.   cm.
    Includes bibliographical references (p.) and index.
    ISBN 0-935269-17-7
      1. Outlaws—California—Biography. 2. California—History—1850-1950. I. Title.
F866.S48 1995
979.4'04'0922—dc20   95-30908
                                                                  CIP

Cover design by Kelly A. Reed

Copyright © 1995 by William B. Secrest
All rights reserved.

Published by Barbed Wire Press, P.O. Box 2107, Stillwater, Oklahoma 74076. 1-800-749-3369.

Manufactured in the United States of America. First Edition.

Contents

Acknowledgments	IX
Introduction	XIII
1. The Bullet-Riddled Ballad of Cherokee Bob, 1833–1863	3
2. A Bad Seed: The Deadly Charles Mortimer, 1834–1873	49
3. The Nephew of Joaquin Murrieta: Procopio, 1840–1892(?)	100
4. The West's Most Inept Outlaw: Milton Harvey Lee, 1847–1916	132
5. The Strange and Bloody Saga of Abe Majors, 1882–1957	173
Notes	211
Sources	243
Index	253

LIST OF ILLUSTRATIONS

Map of the West Coast 2
Sheriff John Boling 11
San Quentin in 1859 11
The village of San Gabriel 19
The Dalles, Oregon, in the early 1860s.......................................31
Mayor Elias Whitman of Walla Walla 35
Walla Walla, Washington..35
Florence, Idaho, in 1896...37
Cherokee Bob's grave about 1926..47
Charles Mortimer 51
John "Black Jack" Bowen 59
Old San Quentin cell 59
The cornerstone-laying celebration
  for the new San Francisco City Hall in 1872 79
Carrie Spencer...79
Sacramento police detective Leonard Harris.............................89
Charles Mortimer after his arrest for the Gibson murder........89
A California hanging..95
Procopio...100
Narcisso Bojorques..109
Rancher John Rains 109
San Quentin in the late 1860s 113
Street scene in Livermore, California 113
Sheriff Harry Morse 117
Reward proclamation for the capture of
  Sol Gladden's killer 124
Procopio and his daughter, Margarita, about 1887 129
John Herbert 143
Harvey Lee 143
San Quentin mug shot of Harvey Lee 146

VII

Charles Williams 159
Portland police detective Joe Reilly 159
Milton Harvey Lee on entering the
    Oregon State Penitentiary 161
Oregon State Penitentiary, about 1899 165
Harvey Lee in 1916 171
Lloyd Majors 175
Abe Majors and his brother, Archie 175
San Jose, California 181
Bert Willmore and Abe Majors 184
Folsom prison 184
The fight in the Utah hills 193
A 1909 photograph of the Utah State Penitentiary, 1909 199
San Quentin mug shots of Abe Majors taken after his Los
    Angeles burglary conviction 207

ACKNOWLEDGEMENTS

That a nonfiction work of this kind requires diligent research and a great deal of help goes without saying. Backtrailing outlaws is always difficult, particularly if they are little-known criminals whose freedom depended on not leaving a trail. Always itinerants and on the move, they left scant documentary evidence of their passing, and their trails become even more obscure with the passage of time. Still, much of their story can be found.

In attempting to document the lives of Cherokee Bob, Charles Mortimer, Procopio, Milton Harvey Lee, and Abe Majors, many people came to my aid—in Georgia, Utah, Nevada, Oregon, Washington State, Mexico, and California. Some provided veritable reams of material, while others provided a single clue that often proved just as valuable. Together we have put to paper the first biographies of a handful of the most desperate men in the early West.

My first thanks must go to my good friend John Boessenecker of Foster City, California. Few people are more versed in early outlaw history, as his two books, *Badge and Buckshot* and *The Grey Fox* (with Mark Dugan), will attest.

Together, John and I have roamed the plains of the San Joaquin and prowled the corridors of libraries, museums, and courthouses while researching our separate projects. His input and sharing of material added much to this final work.

My brother, Dr. James Secrest of Mariposa, California, provided important data on Cherokee Bob in that area, while Robert Ellison, of Minden, Nevada, expertly researched Talbot's brief sojourn in that state.

Sieglinde Smith, Todd L. Shaffer, and Priscilla Knuth, of the Oregon Historical Society, Portland, were most helpful, as was James Clark, reference archivist of the Oregon State Archives at Salem.

For years Mrs. Sibylle Zemitis and the staff in the California Room of the California State Library at Sacramento have aided me in a variety of ways. I am also greatly indebted to Joseph P. Samora, Laren W. Metzer, Nancy Zimmelman, and Sidney Nelson of the California State Archives who have been most helpful over the years in providing documents and records for my use.

Kip Davis provided much of the photographic work for this project, and many times he demonstrated his skill in getting the most from a faded old mug shot or an underexposed negative.

I also extend my grateful thanks to the following people who helped with the individual chapters.

"Cherokee Bob": Kathy Best, Atlanta, Georgia; DeAnne Blanton and Richard F. Cox, National Archives, Washington, D.C.; Robert Scott Davis, Jr., Hanceville, Alabama; Carlo M. De Ferrari, Tuolumne County Historian, Sonora, California; Guila Ford and Elisabeth Jacox, Research Assistants, Idaho Historical Society, Boise; F. Glover, Reference Librarian, Sutro Library, San Francisco, California; David W. Hastings, Chief of Archives, Washington State Archives, Olympia; Eileen A. Ielmini, Archivist, Georgia Historical Society, Savannah; the late Howard Kaseberg, Walla Walla Valley Pioneer and Historical Society, Walla Walla, Washington; Mrs. Lorrayne Kennedy, Archivist, Calaveras County Museum and Archives, San Andreas, California; Lee Mortensen, Librarian, Nevada

Acknowledgements

Historical Society, Reno; Mrs. Sarabelle O'Daniel, Monmouth, Illinois; Robert A. Olson, Laguna Hills, California; Gayle Palmer, Washington State Library, Olympia; James Snyder, United States Department of the Interior, Yosemite National Park, California; and Virgil Talbot, Colcord, Oklahoma.

"Charles Mortimer": Christian de Guignè, San Mateo, California; Jack DeMattos, North Attleboro, Massachusetts; Russell Estep, Belmont, California; Mike Hendrix, Director, Siskiyou County Museum, Yreka, California; K. Hueston, Reference Librarian, Siskiyou County Library, Yreka, California; Francis M. Jarvis, clerk, Pine Grove Cemetery, Lynn, Massachusetts; Richard C. Kaplan, Reference Archivist, Massachusetts State Archives, Boston; Nadine Mitchell, Reference Librarian, Lynn Public Library, Lynn, Massachusetts; and Henry F. Scannell, Reference Librarian, Boston Public Library, Boston, Massachusetts.

"Procopio": Lori Davisson, Arizona Historical Society, Tucson; William P. Frank, Assistant Curator, Western Manuscripts, The Huntington Library, San Marino, California; Maria Kelly, Albuquerque, New Mexico; Dra. Luz Maria Martinez Mautid, Veracruz, Veracruz, Mexico; L.I.C. Victor Flores Monroy, Hermosillo, Sonora, Mexico; Richard Nelson, San Quentin Museum Association, San Quentin, California; James Officer, University of Arizona, Department of Anthropology, Tucson; Pbro. Teodoro E. Pino, Archdiocese de Hermosillo, Sonora, Mexico; William Roberts, University Archivist, Bancroft Library, University of California, Berkeley; and Manuel Rojas, Calexico, California.

"Milton Harvey Lee": Sharon Christenson, Custodian of Records, Oregon Department of Corrections, Salem; Alice Davidson, San Jose Public Library, San Jose, California; Dorothy De Dontney, Santa Clara County History and Genealogical Society, Santa Clara, California; Barbara Dickenson, San Jose County Library, San Jose, California; M.C. Guerra, Deputy County Clerk, Santa Clara County Superior Court, San Jose, California; James D. Hofer, County Archivist, County Archives, San Bernardino, California; Darryl Lucas, Deputy County Recorder, San Jose, California; Leslie

Masunaga, Archivist, San Jose Historical Museum, San Jose, California; Alden Moberg, Oregoniana Librarian, Oregon State Library, Salem; Chris Shovey, San Bernardino Public Library, San Bernardino, California.

"Abe Majors": Paul Jennens and Val E. Wilson, Research Center, Utah State Archives, Salt Lake City; P. Maiden, Deputy Clerk, Superior Court, Los Angeles County Records Center, Los Angeles, California; Michael Schimmel, Reference Librarian, Fresno County Library, Fresno, California; and Linda Thatcher, Collections Management, Utah State Historical Society, Salt Lake City.

And my wonderful wife who makes my avocation possible by her tolerance, patience and love. Thank you all.

INTRODUCTION

Curiously, the wreckers throughout history are more often remembered than the builders. In California, for example, few people can recite the accomplishments of Peter Donahue or John Swett, railroad and education pioneers, while almost any adult or child has heard of the colorful Black Bart or Joaquin Murrieta. Although lamentable, this perverse human trait is at least understandable. When the colorful careers of hard-riding outlaws are compared to the important, but less exciting achievements of true pioneers, we tend to remember the colorful rather than the mundane.

Of course it would be more socially relevant to record the accomplishments of our worthier pioneers, but the renegades have seized my attention like they have so many others. Where did they come from? What made them tick and what forces shaped their misspent lives? In an effort to answer those questions I have tried, where possible, to explore a more personal side of the lives of five western desperadoes. These men didn't live in a vacuum. Road agents and renegades though they were, they had mothers and fathers, sisters, brothers, and sweethearts who felt the pain of their lawless existence and the horror of an often violent demise.

While the selected five are hardly known to a modern generation, in their day they were headline news throughout the country. They inspired dime novels and western fiction that stirred a nation eager to read of heroes, rugged individuals, and colorful characters.

But let's not kid ourselves. The world could have gotten along very nicely without these desperadoes. One and all, they were takers, not givers. They would destroy the West, not build it. They were dangerous men whose self-indulgent lives rivaled the wildest fiction. And, despite the waste of their existence, when we dig deep enough the more personal side of their story is often tragic and moving.

The subjects of this work span a century of time and though all were social outcasts, they were for the most part distinctly different from each other. It is difficult to imagine Charlie Mortimer taking on Abe Majors as a partner, or Procopio associating with anyone as inept as Harvey Lee.

Cherokee Bob Talbot walked a fine line between the law and the lawless during gold rush days. Although he once went to prison for horse theft, that was a crime of the moment. Bob was more likely to be convicted of assault or manslaughter than larceny as he shot and carved his way through the gold camps of the far West.

Throughout his lively life he was primarily a gambler—the stoic poker player of the mining camps and real-life model for the gambler of western fiction. Yet he was strangely unlike that popular image. Gamblers sought quiet anonymity. The last thing they wanted was trouble; it was bad for business. Bob, on the other hand, attracted trouble as a dog attracts fleas. He was always in a pinch. Whether that was because of racism and his Indian heritage, a death wish, or his constant efforts to prove something for dark reasons known only to himself, only he knew for sure. Like all such people, he eventually tangled with someone of the same temperament—and a faster trigger finger.

Charles Mortimer, more correctly Flinn, was a desperado of a different stripe. His autobiography, a psychologist's delight, is a bone-chilling portrayal of a nineteenth-century criminal whom we can follow in detail from cradle to grave. Mortimer! He was evil personified in 1860s California, yet his care for his mistress and concern for friends and family pose poignant questions concerning the tragic waste of his life.

Seldom do we get the opportunity to look into the mind of

a nineteenth-century criminal, and when we do we usually find a plethora of blame, excuses, and societal complaints. Mortimer's autobiography does not disappoint in that respect, but it is different. He complains long and loud about society's shunning ex-convicts, who returned to crime because of lack of opportunity and police harassment. Yet a few pages later he reports that most convicts spend their time in prison plotting escapes, the deaths of guards, and more crimes and violence when they are free.

Mortimer's complaints bore some truth, yet even at that early time there were always people ready to help sincere ex-convicts. Just examine petitions for parole in the California State Archives. They contain long signature lists of prominent lawyers, judges, public officials, and merchants—most of whom would have offered aid if asked. Also, a Prisoner's Aid Society was formed in San Francisco as early as 1865 for the express purpose of helping ex-convicts return to normal life. Mortimer, however, never had a thought of appealing to such people or agencies. Despite such contradictions, his story is both revealing and horrendous.

As a bandit shaped by ancestry, social conditions and environment, Procopio is an almost classical figure. While his criminal origins are certainly understandable, many others in the same circumstances never found it necessary to rob, kill, and pit themselves against society. Family informants recalled how Procopio's legendary uncle Joaquin Murrieta influenced him throughout his life, although he was a mere boy when the outlaw was killed. Procopio reportedly even posed as his uncle at times, as though he was a marionette directed by unseen hands. Handsome, dashing, and deadly, Procopio carried on the bandit traditions of his uncle and, in his own way, carved out a legend for himself.

Milton Harvey Lee is quite another story. His prison mug shot shows a plain man of ordinary ancestry who should have been a carpenter, raised a family, and lived out his years in quiet domesticity. Yet, he could not. Lee had a wild streak that he could not hide or resist. Frail by nature, he tempted fate all his life and found it impossible to lead an honest life. Still, he failed at every crime of which we have any record. His was a comic-opera career, and it is a toss-up whether to chuckle or cringe at his larcenous bungling. Never even a half-competent criminal, he spent most of his adult years proving the old maxim that crime does not pay. The triumph of his final years make his wasted life all the more sad.

Perhaps the strangest character of all was Abe Majors. Constantly at war with himself in his younger years, Abe fought a struggle between two worlds. He reportedly attributed his evil nature to an inheritance from the gallows, a legacy from his father. That was a ready excuse for a user and manipulator who caused untold grief for nearly everyone he met.

Yet there is much that is sad in his story. If a miserable stepfather hadn't deserted his family and plunged them into grinding poverty, who knows what Abe's future might have held. If only he had fulfilled his promises after his first prison term—but then Abe led a life of "ifs."

From all accounts Abe was bright and hard-working when it suited him, but he chose instead to follow a dark star, disappointing and betraying all those to whom he was most indebted. He lived a long, but empty life.

Although the personalities and careers of these men were quite different, they had one common denominator: all served time in state penitentiaries. In trying to give some indication of what prison life was like in that faraway time, a problem quickly surfaced. Despite a smattering of books on the subject, prison histories are few and far between, The inside story must be gleaned from the few available convict autobiographies, newspaper accounts, various official reports made to governors or state legislatures, and other obscure sources of information.

Perhaps the most interesting picture that emerges in early prison research is the evolution of such institutions. From dungeons of brutality and torture they became quasi-humane institutions that offered libraries, schools, and work programs as the institutions sought to give convicts a new set of values rather than merely punish them. Reading wardens' reports of those days reminds us that, then as now, asking legislatures for the means to improve the lot of criminals is ever an uphill battle.

Despite the inclination to hold these men up to social scrutiny and interpret their lives through charts and graphs (and with several the urge is almost overwhelming), that has not been my purpose. These are narrative histories of rough men, killers, and wanderers who lived on the edge. Analyze, if you will, but in the end it boils down to tales of restless boys abandoning everything they held dear to lead treacherous and misspent lives. Some became models for western fiction, while others were literal legends in their own time. Several are merely long-forgotten desperadoes. Although these subjects are fascinating historical figures, it is easy to conclude that they were all miserable failures as human beings.

William B. Secrest
Fresno, California

1 THE BULLET-RIDDLED BALLAD OF CHEROKEE BOB

1833–1863

Tradition, legend, and folklore have created an antebellum South often distorted in the public mind. The region indeed had large landowners who lived in stately, columned mansions and sipped mint juleps on shady verandas while watching fields of slaves harvest their crops. But they were a minority.

Most planters led a more humble life. They worked long, hard hours raising crops for market and to feed their family, employees, and slaves. Born about 1833, Henry J. Talbot grew up on such a farm and undoubtedly worked hard alongside his family in rural 1840s Georgia. His forebears had purchased 50,000 acres of land from Cherokee Indians in the late-eighteenth century and Talbots had worked the Wilkes County land ever since. His ancestors and relatives were prominent as county officers and state legislators, and one became governor of the state. Henry's father was a local judge whose Cherokee wife lent a delicate shading to the complexion of their offspring. Slaves worked the Talbot lands while Henry and his brothers ran errands, kept the fences in repair, herded livestock and did all the chores that kept the slaves free to work in the fields.

Young Henry undoubtedly disliked the constant drudgery of farm life. It is easy to imagine him dodging into the woods or climbing a grassy hillock to survey the others sweating and toiling in the sun.

In the nearby village of Washington he had sometimes seen gamblers in the saloons and hotel barrooms and envied their expressionless faces and fine clothes. Constantly on the move, the gamblers never stayed in the area for long. They seemed to be always traveling west—always west, as though they were looking for something. That's the way to live, Henry mused. Gamblers knew how to enjoy life, they weren't controlled by it.

In late 1848 talk spread of gold discoveries in distant California. The rumors were verified during the winter of 1849 and people from all over the world started a rush for the new territory. In Philadelphia, Boston, New York, and New Jersey emigrants formed into companies for the trip west. Closer to home, Henry heard of groups assembling in Virginia, Alabama, and Georgia. That was the chance he had yearned for, and he waited anxiously for an opportunity to leave for the storied land of gold.

We have no details of Henry's departure. He was still a teenager, and whether he left with or without his parents' blessing is not known. He probably made his way to the coast and acquired passage at either Savannah, Georgia, or Charleston, South Carolina. To young Henry, who knew little of the world outside Wilkes County, it must have been exhilarating indeed to watch the land recede as his ship put out to sea for his great adventure. We can assume he brought along his playing cards and sharpened his pasteboard skills considerably during the long voyage.

Disembarking at San Francisco, Henry found a noisy boom town full of shouting auctioneers, pounding hammers, rasping saws, braying mules, and foreign-speaking sailors and miners from around the world. Tents were scattered over the hills and construction was going on everywhere. Some 15,000 men had landed in town during the early months of 1849. The sight was thrilling.

As the boy wandered about town he quickly noticed the

gambling games in every hotel, saloon, and dance hall. The more prestigious games were conducted on the second floor of the Parker House on Portsmouth Square, while all of the popular places of entertainment had six or eight crowded tables. Gamblers used gold dust as well as the coin of many foreign lands. Young Talbot could not have been more delighted.

Henry quickly took up gambling and soon had a table in one of the saloons. He had a cadre of young friends who, like him, led wild, unrestrained lives and thoroughly enjoyed being away from home and other civilizing influences for the first time. In late January 1850 the *Alta California* chronicled what was probably one of Henry's first escapades:

> Police Court.—Five men were arrested early yesterday morning for riotous and disorderly conduct at a house in Kearny street. Their names were Robt. Benson, Alex. Speck, A. McGurley, Saml, Atkins and Henry Talbot. They were taken before the Alcalde who imposed a fine of $10 each on Talbot and McGurley, $25 on Atkins, and discharged Benson and Speck with a reprimand.

If this was young Henry, he may have decided it was time to move on. He had honed his gambling talents and was no doubt anxious to head inland to Sacramento, Marysville, and Stockton, the supply points for the mines. Any record of his travels is lacking, but gamblers kept on the move and he probably played in all these towns. He then headed for Tuolumne County, where rich mining camps attracted thousands of miners. The spring of 1851 found him in Sonora, gambling in the smoke-filled saloons of that booming village. By then he was fully initiated into his trade. Although still a boy, he was a gambler and delighted in acting the part. A contemporary description by writer Millicent Washburn Shinn may be forgiven a few dramatic touches perhaps added over the years:

> You'd look at him, and you'd want to keep looking at him, just as you'd look at a pretty woman. He never wore any beard. His mustache was jet black, too, and his face was just

as white as chalk—that is, it was dusky Indian color, you know, just the least coppery tinge, but pale and clear, and his eyebrows and mustache were so inky black they made his face look white.

He was very particular about his appearance. He always wore a long fine cloth overcoat, trimmed with beaver fur. Price never cut any figure in his purchase—the best we had in the store was none too good for him. Always wore gloves on the street...was extravagant about his boots and always had them made to order.

Henry was already acquiring a colorful reputation, and in keeping with the custom of the day he was given a nickname. His dark eyes and hair, coupled with the subtle copper hue of his skin, spoke of his Indian heritage. Since he had referred to his Georgia origins and Cherokee mother, a name came readily to the mind of friends. Although sometimes referred to as "Bot," the final syllable of his last name, he became more generally known as "Cherokee Bob."

The name gave a certain distinction to one so young. He was pointed out at the gaming tables, and men frequently sought the colorfully named boy for a game of cards. From now on he was Cherokee Bob, or simply Bob.

In Los Angeles a few years later Bob was pointed out as "one who had killed six Chilenos in one fight, and although he had been riddled with bullets and ripped and sliced with knives, yet he had never failed to get his man when he went for him." This is undoubtedly an exaggerated reference to a celebrated occurrence in Sonora, California, in June 1851. When Bob made his way there early that year, he found a wild and rich mining village nestled in tall pine trees and surrounded by lofty mountains. Miners from all over the world were there, along with opportunists of every description. "Gamblers," wrote merchant William Perkins, "are as 'thick as leaves in shades of Valambrosa.' Some decent fellows among them, most are infernal scoundrels. Wherever there are plenty of Mexicans, these bloodsuckers are sure to reap a good harvest." And as Mexicans had founded the camp, Bob and his cohorts found plenty to keep them busy.

When a quarrel began in a Mexican dance hall at the nearby small mining camp of Melones, an American and a Mexican pulled their knives and a general brawl erupted. The Mexicans quickly snatched five pistols from the belts of the Anglos and drove the Americans from the hall in a haze of gunsmoke, wounding several. Gathering reinforcements, the Americans counterattacked and retook the hall, killing three of the Mexicans and wounding others. Order was finally secured when large parties of Americans arrived from surrounding camps.

That was probably the fight referred to, although accounts don't mention Bob by name. Bill Owen and others of the American crowd were seen in Sonora later with "three, four and five bullet holes in their clothes," according to a witness. The brawl was just the type Bob delighted in.

Keeping on the move as most gamblers did, Bob toured the towns and mining camps of central California. Several shooting and cutting affrays kept the youthful gamester on the move. An incident Bob once recalled to a *California Courier* newspaperman indicated his increasing trend towards violence:

> When in the mines on one occasion he went into an eating house and called for meat without gravy. The waiter brought a plate dripping with grease. Bob refused to take it. The waiter said he should not have anything else. Bob threw plate, grease and all, at his server. The waiter started for a club and Bob drew and cocked his pistol. His hand had been covered with grease in throwing the plate, and in holding his pistol down by his leg, the treacherous grease allowed his finger to slip upon the hair-trigger, and the bullet cut a passage through his calf. He wiped his hand on the seat of his breeches, and cocked his pistol again and waited for the waiter, who did not wait for anything more, but disappeared at the top of his speed.

A brother was shilling for Bob now, but whether they had come west together or joined forces later is not known. Using the name William Ewing, he and Bob were running a game in

Jamestown, near Sonora, in early 1854 when a serious incident occurred. They had been gambling and drinking all night with a man named Rucker. At five in the morning on February 15, the three were making so much noise that a neighboring hotel keeper named Thomas Brown pounded on the door, insisting they quiet down. In the resulting shouting match, someone fired a shot and Brown staggered with a mortal wound in the stomach. He died nine days later.

Although Ewing was identified as the gunman, Bob's Navy Colt had apparently fired the fatal ball. Ewing fled the area, but was recognized and arrested at Big Oak Flat. He managed to escape, but was wounded by his captor and headed for Oregon. Brown's inquest established that either Rucker or Bob had handed Ewing the pistol which he used, but neither were held.

Bob lost no time heading south. Later that February he picked up a Mexican gambling partner named Velasquez, and the two worked a table in a Hornitos deadfall in Mariposa County. Apparently unable to stay out of trouble for long, Bob was party to an arrangement between his partner and a disgruntled Chilean. The two agreed to fight a pistol duel in a room with Bob as one second and an Indian assisting the Chilean. When the shooting began, Velasquez emptied his pistol with no results, while his antagonist scored two minor hits. Then the two men clinched. Bob decided his man was coming off second best and jumped in with his bowie knife. Bob told the *Courier* reporter he gave the Chilean a vicious "dig in the side," and when the Indian rushed into the fray, Bob slashed him also.

Shaking the dust of old Hornitos from his boots was suddenly very high on Bob's priority list. It did not seem like a good idea to wait around until one or both of the victims died. He hid out with two gambler friends, Sam White and Tom Mitchner. Apparently Bob and one of his pals were lacking a mount, having lost their animals in a race or card game. In any case, the three gamblers galloped south after stealing a gray mare from one John Kellett and a mule from a Chinese miner.

The theft was stupid. Being mixed up in a gambling brawl

was one thing, but horse theft was quite another. Kellett and a man named Martin quickly went in pursuit, catching up with the thieves at the village of Millerton on the San Joaquin River. A fight may have ensued, but Bob's pistol was broken and he and White were captured and returned to face the music. Apparently Mitchner wasn't arrested.

Attorney E. Burke accompanied the two horse thieves at their March 13 arraignment at the county seat of Mariposa. They pleaded not guilty and when Burke's plea for a continuance was refused a trial date was set for March 15.

Much has been made of the poor quality of jurors in those days, of how all the bums and loafers hanging about the saloons and courthouses were invariably selected as a matter of course. Apparently Mariposa County Sheriff John Boling didn't operate that way. Miner Horace Snow, writing home from Mariposa in April 1854, described his attempts to avoid jury duty:

> The miners are determined not to go if they can possibly help it, as they get nothing for pay. As soon as they see an officer coming, the shovels drop very quick and such running and skulking would beat the Indians. You see there were four of us in a store when the Sheriff rode up and we all made for the back door, but he was right after us. I got within about four feet of a large hole when he saw me and screams, "Your name, Sir, the man with the red shirt," and kept right on after the others, but he only caught two of us.

Bob and White were tried for grand larceny in the Fifth Judicial District Court as scheduled. The trial was a brief affair, and after testimony by Kellett and one José Valencia the jury retired and quickly returned with a guilty verdict. Judge Charles M. Creaner remanded the prisoners to jail "and from thence to be taken to the States Prison and there imprisoned for the said term of ten years in accordance with said verdict, and that they be kept at hard labor during the said term of years."

The sentence was tough. Bob must have complained loudly

to his attorney, who no doubt growled that he was lucky a posse of ranchers had not strung him up. Throughout his hearing and trial, Bob had refused to give any name other than his sobriquet of "Cherokee Bob." He was apparently terrified that someone would discover his identity and relay the news to his family in Georgia. He was even more disturbed because he had written home recently and given the Mariposa post office as his address. The day after the trial Bob and his partner began the trip north, as the *California Chronicle* of March 30, 1854, noted:

> DISTINGUISHED DEPARTURE.—Mook Chow, Cowal, John S. Steel, Samuel White and "Cherokee Bob," on the 16th inst., took their departure, under protection of Sheriff Boling, on a visit to the State Prison.... The last, a really noted pair, will go for ten years on the score of horse-stealing.

The state prison originally had been the abandoned brig *Wabau*, whose crew had deserted during the gold rush. In 1852 the ship was towed from San Francisco Bay to a southern peninsula of Marin County, just north of San Francisco, where the state had purchased twenty acres as the site of a state prison. Some of the convicts were put to work in nearby quarries, while others began preparing the clay-tinged soil of Point San Quentin for construction of the initial prison building.

The first prison cells were in a stone structure 180-feet-long by twenty-four-feet wide. It contained forty-eight cells in the upper story and a dormitory and turnkey's office below. Designed to hold two men to a cell, by the time the "Stones" was completed in January 1854, about 250 convicts were in the filthy *Wabau* quarters and a few shacks on shore. Only the guns they carried distinguished the poorly paid guards from the ragged convicts.

Young Talbot must have been discouraged indeed when he disembarked from a small sloop and saw the bleak stone prison building in the near distance. With the other prisoners he was herded up to the turnkey's office and logged into the

Sheriff John Boling, who hosted young Talbot in the Mariposa jail, also escorted him to San Quentin.

Author's Collection

California State Library

A contemporary drawing of San Quentin in 1859. The wharf where the bloody 1854 escape attempt took place is at the lower left.

prison register. Again he refused to give his real name, and the register read, "No. 354 Cherokee Bob: nativity—Georgia; crime—grand larceny; received—March 21, 1854; sentence—10 years; county rec'd from—Mariposa; age—21; gambler, 5' 9", dark complexion, black hair and eyes."

The prison issued Bob two blankets and a straw-filled mattress. At night he slept on a cot in a windowless stone cell with a bucket in which to relieve himself. The only air came through a small opening in the heavy iron door.

The days were long. Blacksmiths, carpenters, and other craftsmen could always be put to work at their trades, but most of the prisoners labored in the stone quarries or the adjacent brickyard sunup to sundown, seven days a week. Convicts with marine backgrounds handled the various prison sloops carrying brick and stone to the San Francisco markets. Others loaded and unloaded the heavy cargo. A daily parade of woodchoppers went into the nearby forests to cut fuel to feed the brick kilns.

Bob went to work in the brickyard and soon got used to the routine, but he must have been horrified at the situation in which he found himself. Day after day he was thrown into the company of robbers, rapists, killers, and criminals of every description from all over the world—and he had only stolen a horse! He was not like his cell mates. He looked about desperately for a way out of the hellhole and determined to escape at the first opportunity.

With no wall around the cell block, escape attempts were frequent. On foggy days guards often kept prisoners locked up because the fog could conceal an escape. In his 1854 annual report J.M. Estell, the lessee of the prison, complained of the lack of funds to finish the prison and make it safer. He said, "The California State Prison is an isolated building, standing in the centre of twenty acres of land without guard rooms, officer's quarters, infirmary or hospital rooms, and without even a kitchen. The cells are here for holding the prisoners and they are very safe. But the prisoners have to be marched three or four hundred yards for the purpose of obtaining their meals, and for the performance of their labor. Thus, an opportunity for a revolt is offered three times each day, whilst the whole of the prisoners (nearly three hundred) are embodied."

Estell was very properly concerned about the situation and there had already been casualties during escape attempts. One convict was missed at meal time and a search was made. He was suspected of hiding in the chimney of the steam boiler and when a fire was built he was promptly smoked out. Another fellow buried himself in a brick kiln and was only discovered when he was starved out. One hardy soul hid within an empty barrel in the water near the wharf. When the ploy was suspected he was told to come out, but kept quiet. A pistol ball through the upper part of the barrel caused him to quickly abandon his position.

Despite such comic attempts, Estell's worst fears soon bore fruit when prisoners decided to take control of a prison sloop preparing for a trip across the bay. Just how many convicts were initially involved is not known, but undoubtedly others joined during the confusion.

Cherokee Bob was apparently an escape leader—at least he was part of the group that took over the sloop. They were loading the vessel on December 27, 1854, when Bob seized Captain B.F. Pullen on the wharf and wrestled him onto the sloop. Pullen's rifle was turned on the other guards, and the convicts obtained several additional weapons as they sought shelter on the sloop from the increasing gunfire of rallying guards. Meanwhile, prisoners at the brickyard saw the fight at the wharf and scattered into the surrounding areas, either trying to escape or perhaps acting as decoys. At least fifty convicts were in active revolt.

With the fire of the guards forcing the convicts under cover, they had difficulty casting off. Several guards were still on the boat and Bob clasped Pullen in front of him, hoping to force the guards to ease their fire. When Pullen tried to seek shelter again, Bob pulled him up and later recalled crying out, "Stand up and die like a man for we all have to die together."

Several convicts were lying about the wharf, badly wounded, as the prisoners desperately tried to cast off in the pall of gunsmoke. Convict John Thompson, serving a seven-year term, was killed as he frantically tried to adjust the rigging at the top of the mast. Somehow in the shouts, smoke, and confusion the prisoners managed to cast off and maneuver into the bay.

The convicts steered the sloop across the water towards Contra Costa County, but the trip was dreadful. Everyone on the boat was wounded and blood was everywhere. Captain Pullen was groaning, shot in the hands and arms, while more than a dozen convicts lay sprawled on the deck, groaning in pain and trying to stop their bleeding. Bob nursed a wound caused when a bullet ripped through his lung and lodged in his side. When the sloop cruised onto the beach across the bay, the convicts fell and crawled over the sides and disappeared into the woods and brush. Even as they ran they could see their pursuers close behind in the other prison boats.

Newspapers were full of accounts of the great escape and Estell wrote a long letter to the San Francisco *Alta*. Published December 29, it listed twenty-two convicts who had escaped, all of them wounded. Five others were badly wounded during the fight around the sloop and were in custody. Estell said:

> Cherokee Bob was found whilst the pursuit was being carried on so lively on the hills in Contra Costa. He says Watkins was shot in the arm and another ball had passed through his lungs. He was spitting blood when they separated and was thought to be dangerously wounded. Colin Douglass was slightly wounded, Michael Hines was brought back badly shot. He was found in the mountains unable to keep up with the fugitives. William Powers was badly wounded in the leg. James Smith was also found by the road unable to proceed further in his wounded condition...
>
> Sidney Brown, alias Bryant, was shot through the body, and was in company with Cherokee Bob when Bob fell exhausted....Cherokee Bob was sinking rapidly this evening and could give but little additional information.

Dispatches conflict over the number of escapees and the number recaptured, but most of the prisoners were apparently returned to the prison. In early January nine of the convicts were retaken at San Jose and found themselves promptly back at San Quentin.

Despite the dire predictions of his death, Bob recovered and was soon back working in the brickyard. His wound healed, but the bullet remained near his backbone.

The desperate and bloody escape horrified the state. Some reports said the escaping convicts had plundered every habitation in their path and new escapes were expected daily. Finally, in mid-May 1855, news of a new break spread like wildfire. First reports appeared in the *San Francisco Herald* and announced that all the guards at the prison had been massacred. The steamer *Urilda* reported passing several sloops on the bay filled with escaping prisoners. Rumors persisted that boatloads of escaping convicts were landing near towns and were preparing to pillage the area.

The *Herald* of May 13 published a letter from Estell denying there had been any escapes but indicating that he and the guards feared an outbreak at any time. He wrote, "No prisoners have escaped, yet a determined resistance seems to manifest itself amongst the convicts, which may lead to the destruction of the entire guard, and consequently, to the escape of the whole of the convicts....Not a day passes without some manifestation of insubordination. Two revolts have been planned during this week, which have both been discovered in time to save the guard."

When the reports had been sorted out they were found to be only rumors; the boatloads of escaping prisoners were nothing more than workers returning from Mare Island. The rumors had some basis, however. At noon on the same day Estell wrote his letter, four prisoners escaped while on a wood chopping detail. On May 14 the *Alta* printed a long article exposing all the groundless rumors but also relating the real escape. Lieutenant John M. Gray had taken Cherokee Bob, Asa Carrico, Bill White, and James Stewart out to chop wood in an area some 300 yards from the prison grounds. According to the *Alta*, when Stewart rushed up to Gray yelling that the prisoners were escaping, the guard opened fire, killing White. The other three prisoners, however, got away.

The *Alta* account was accurate, except that even more prisoners were involved and White was not killed. Several years later, when White was recaptured, he revealed the escape was a plot to get rid of some of the troublesome convicts for various reasons. White was told he would be taken out with others on a wood-cutting detail and that when the first tree was felled they were to make their escape. Only blanks would be fired at them. Lieutenant Gray apparently did fire blanks—certainly he did not kill White as reported. Later, Gray was dismissed for that and numerous other infractions, although he was probably acting on orders from higher officials.

Whether Bob was part of the plot or just involved by chance is not known. One of the escaping convicts whom the *Alta* did not mention was Thomas Hodges, soon to become the notorious highwayman Tom Bell, who later took Bill White into his gang.

Bob split off from his convict partners at the first opportunity and made his way south. His shaved head (the sign of a troublesome convict) would be easily recognized. He could get by with his hat pulled down to his ears, but it was important that he secure a wig as soon as possible, probably in San Francisco. His hair would take several months to grow out again.

On the coast, Bob found work cutting hay at the Carmel mission. When the job gave out he went to San Jose and from there to the Pulgas Rancho on the southern part of San Francisco Bay. For a time he made shingles at Redwood City, but he gambled at every opportunity. He stayed at the Angelo House and was friendly with owner Frank Schell and several others who lived there, including former governor John McDougal. Bob was using his real name by then and apparently felt secure because he had only been listed by his nickname at the prison. He gambled constantly, playing poker and crack-a-loo and engaging in horse races. On occasion he indulged in shooting matches with McDougal and others. He managed to stay out of trouble, knowing that he must not call any attention to himself.

Still, Bob was uneasy. San Francisco was only twenty-five miles away, and the prison just across the bay. He watched carefully for strangers—anyone who might recognize him as an escaped convict. In November of 1855 he decided to move on. He would be much safer in Mexico.

Traveling alone, the safest route seemed to be the old mission road, which led from the bay through the Salinas Valley to San Miguel. From there the trail led south to San Luis Obispo, Santa Barbara, and across the mountains to San Gabriel, near Los Angeles. He had little money for the trip, but in the south he could gamble and raise a stake for the final journey to old Mexico. He left Schell's about November 15, his few belongings tied behind his saddle and his pony a poor one. Perhaps one of his reasons for leaving was a recent run of bad luck at cards.

Bob's own story of his trip is most interesting:

> Leaving in the morning I fell in with a Frenchman who had passed the house with two little mules. He said he was from San Francisco, and was going down the country to help some friends drive up cattle. Telling him that we could be a mutual protection in any difficulty, he said, 'Very well—he would be glad of my company.' We came to the Mission of Soledad about three o'clock in the afternoon, bought some bread and grapes and barley for our animals. The Frenchman said he had very little money; I told him I was in the same fix. As there was poor grass at Soledad, we went on into the night, some three or four leagues farther, until about nine or ten o'clock. This Frenchman appeared to have been a drover on this route, and to know it pretty well. He complained that it was a bad country we were in, a great many robberies had been committed on that road and it would not be a bad bet to bet that we would be attacked that night. I replied that I had nothing to be robbed of, and if we were attacked we would have to run or fight.

Traveling near La Poza on a bright, moonlit night, the two travelers saw horsemen coming up behind them at a fast gait. It seemed obvious they would be attacked unless they could hide or outrun their pursuers. Leaving the trail, Bob and his companion rode into an arroyo and stopped, only to see the other riders also leave the road and ride in their direction.

The Frenchman panicked and wanted to escape over a hill, but Bob refused.

> "No," I said, "I have run twice and far enough. I will not run any farther." By this time they had come pretty close and the Frenchman was evidently frightened, making some exclamation. I told him...we had the advantage as they could not see us, but we could see them....
> They passed within about ten yards and I rode out behind them and saluted them. They returned the salute and proved to be an old man carrying a little boy on his horse, a Mexican Indian and an Indian boy of this country. The last said he was going to San Diego. I told the old man that as we had come together so mysteriously—each taking the other for a robber—it should tend to make us better friends and we would all journey on in company. He seemed to have a kind heart and we conversed much on the political affairs of Mexico at this time.

Arriving at San Gabriel, Bob adopted the alias of Flemming and looked around the small village scattered about the old mission. The Headquarters Saloon, run by Roy Bean, was in the mission building, and Bob was soon in a poker game there with A.S. Beard, the local justice of the peace. Beard wound up owing Bob five dollars. The two had a dispute over the money, but Bob had to be careful not to call attention to himself.

Although Bob didn't know it, he was already in serious trouble. Several gamblers he had known in the north were in San Gabriel and recognized him. Lafayette Cotton and W.H. Burgess reviewed old times in the mines with Bob, but he asked them to keep quiet about his identity. "I have done all I am going to do in California," he stated, "and am now about to leave it." Burgess agreed to go to Los Angeles and get some money for Bob, with which he could buy supplies for his trip. Staying at the Noyes Hotel, Bob gambled for the next few days keeping a wary eye out for anyone who might recognize him. He kept his pistol with him constantly.

Two weeks before Bob had left the bay area, a double murder had occurred on the road near Monterey. A bloody feud

The village of San Gabriel, near Los Angeles, was a collection of adobes clustered around the old mission building where Roy Bean tended bar in his Headquarters Saloon.

over the Sanchez estate had resulted in much bitterness and several deaths, and no one knew when the next outbreak would come. William Roach had been appointed guardian of the wealthy estate, but after being removed from office he had gone into hiding with the Sanchez treasure. Lewis Belcher, the new administrator of the estate, surrounded himself with gunmen, as did Roach, and the feud resulted in some ten or twelve deaths over the years.

Isaac Wall, a popular young politician and constable, and Thomas Williamson left Monterey on November 5 with a pack mule. Rumor had it they were carrying money to Roach, who was still in hiding. Later they were found dead on the road, their belongings scattered. The scene offered no clues to the killer or killers. Investigators later established that the murderer was probably Anastacio Garcia, a notorious badman of the area.

Unfortunately for Cherokee Bob, however, someone had seen him riding along the old Mission road sometime after the murders. He was rightfully considered a suspicious character worth investigating.

A man named Parkinson and one T.A. Mayes had noticed Bob at Santa Barbara and followed his party south. At San Gabriel they voiced their suspicions to a local resident named Carter who agreed to keep an eye on the suspect. After several days, Carter and a friend named Smith Turner decided to confront Bob and see if he could establish his innocence.

Bob was startled at the accusation. He denied he would kill any man, especially a southern man, unless in self-defense. Carter had heard rumors that he was the noted Cherokee Bob and now asked if that was true. Bob admitted to going by that name and further related that he had been persecuted in the north, had killed a man, and been sent to the state prison and escaped.

When they seemed to believe his story, Bob was relieved, but the men told him he must stay around town for a time. He was closely watched, but Bob insisted he wanted to stay and clear his name.

"When I understood I was suspected of this murder," Bob

explained later, "I thought to myself, 'I will let them rip on and probably they will find out better; I would rather stay here and have my suspicion removed and prove myself innocent, than go away and let it be said I was the murderer of such a man as Isaac B. Wall is said to have been."

Still, he reacted in character when his worst fears came true a few days later. The December 22, 1855, *Los Angeles Star* related the story. "IMPORTANT ARREST.—Yesterday morning Mr. Peterson and Captain Heninger, upon information received of Mr. Parkinson of Santa Barbara, arrested at the Mission of San Gabriel, a man known and identified as 'Cherokee Bob,' and who is believed to be the murderer of Messrs. Wall and Williamson of Monterey. The prisoner answers the description of the murderer, and he will be examined on Monday next."

When first confronted Bob attempted to draw his pistol, but the arresting officers were too quick for him. He quietly admitted his identity as an escaped convict. Some false whiskers found in his effects were probably a disguise used after his escape. Despite his denials, a valuable ring, which he had lost in a game at the mission, was thought to be the former property of Isaac Wall. A hearing before Judge Benjamin Hayes was begun the day after his arrest.

The hearing took several days and many witnesses were interviewed. Several of Bob's friends did what they could to confuse their testimony and shield him from his reputation, and no evidence was elicited that connected him to the murders. Bob easily explained the suspected ring, although he tarnished any reputation he might have had as an honest gambler.

"The ring shown in evidence I took off the finger of a brother of F.M. Schell at the hotel, three or four days before I left," Bob said. "I am sure that Mr. Wall would never own such a ring as that and if he did, that he would never put it to the use I had it for—for it was a trick ring that I used in gambling."

Judge Hayes found little in the evidence and testimony to indicate Bob's complicity in the murders. He was an escaped convict, however, and Hayes ruled that he would be returned to Monterey for authorities there to deal with. Under the heading, "Cherokee Bob," the *Monterey Sentinel* commented, "This noted individual was examined before Judge Benjamin Hayes...on the charge of being concerned in the murder of Messrs. Wall and Williamson on the 9th of November last, in this county....The result of the examination...shows so far that nothing could be fastened upon him as a guilty party in the murders committed here.

"He was brought up as an escaped convict in the *Sea Bird*, which arrived at this port on Wednesday afternoon last."

On January 11, 1856, Bob again entered prison at San Quentin. He must have been relieved that the Monterey authorities were satisfied he was innocent of the murder charge, but he dreaded returning to the degradation of prison life. He had no recourse but to finish his term and hope for a pardon. In any case, escape seemed more difficult than ever now. Since he had been gone, an imposing stone and brick wall had been erected around the solitary cell block.

Bob once again settled into the routine of prison life. In March he made a favorable impression on a San Francisco newspaper reporter who interviewed him. The man wrote, "Bob is a lively, slender, active, young fellow, or was once; but brick-making, bullets and State Prison fare do not agree with him.... Bob is not a bad man naturally. His conversation and his face are frank and straightforward, and good humored."

As days turned into years, Bob determined to make a plea to the governor. He had nothing to lose and must have feared becoming involved in another escape attempt, one which he might not survive. Whether Bob actually wrote, or dictated, the letter is unknown, but it is a most interesting and eloquent plea:

Point San Quentin, 3 March, 1858
To his Excellency J.B. Weller,
Governor of the State of California

Excellency

Your humble servant, undersigned, most respectfully request [sic] your attention on the following statement of the circumstances of his present confinement in the Penitentiary of the State.

Convicted in 1854 for the crime of accessory in horse stealing, he was sentenced to serve ten years in the State Prison. It is not his province or wish to review or criticise the different testimonies by which he was convicted, but he would only say that at that time the law in California was striking indifferently the innocent as well as the guilty.

Your humble servant has been already confined four years, and, by his uniformly good behavior, has succeeded in enlisting in his behalf the sympathies of several officers of this institution.

Your Excellency has, doubtless before now, been acquainted with all the sufferings of an inmate of this gloomy prison and will, therefore, have compassion of a friendless prisoner, who has suffered already so long....

My motives in appealing to your clemency are of such a nature that I feel assured of your Excellency's approval in doing such a step.

I have been far from home since 1849, leaving my old father when I was only fifteen years old. I was twenty years old when I was convicted and ever since, shameful of my situation. I never wrote to my father. I could not be the bearer of such tidings; for my poor father could not have survived the disgrace, the shame of his unfortunate son. I could not and would not be the murderer of my genitor. For this principal motive, I have kept silent and, by so doing, refused, denied me the only help I could hope for. I have even concealed my name, for fear that my inquisitive and anxious father should, through his own exertions, be made cognisant of my condition. A confinement of ten years is the dear price of my silence, and I have undergone four years of my long sentence.

Clemency is, and has always been, the most beautiful perogative [sic] of men at power. I implore your mercy, Excellency, in the name of my old father, longing for his unfortunate son. Four years in this place of infamy have been more than sufficient to expiate the crime I was convicted for.

I am desirous to enjoy again my long-lost liberty, to enter again in the path of life, with renewed energies, and prove by my exertions that I am worthy of the clemency bestowed on me.

> I am most respectfully, of your Excellency the most obedient and humble servant.
>
> Cherokee Bob

Bob can be forgiven for neglecting to mention his escape and seven months of freedom in his letter. After all, if he included it he might as well forget any hopes of clemency. Perhaps he was aware of the faulty record-keeping at the prison and hoped a different governor didn't keep up with such matters. Just what happened is not clear, but Governor Weller was one step ahead of Bob. Prison records indicate that Bob was pardoned, but not until nearly twenty months later, on October 14, 1859, and he wasn't discharged until May 15, 1860. Whenever he was released, Cherokee Bob had paid dearly for the horse-stealing incident of so long ago.

The free air smelled good. We can only imagine Bob's movements after he caught the boat for San Francisco. Gambling was illegal in the bay city, but he could always find a game and soon had enough of a stake to buy an appropriate wardrobe. Perhaps he took a riverboat to Stockton or Sacramento, always looking for a horse race or a poker game. While in prison he had yearned to see the gold rush towns and mining camps again, but now they seemed somehow different. The flush times were over. Picket fences and cottages were scattered everywhere with accompanying women, children, and families.

A silver strike in early 1859 had caused a general rush to Utah Territory, and Bob was anxious to cross the Sierra to see Virginia City and the Washoe country. The excitement was almost like the days of '49 in California. The previous year stagecoaches only went part way over the Sierra before travelers had to take a wagon, horse, or start walking at Strawberry Flat. Wrecked vehicles and carts littered the road. By the time Bob made the trip in the spring of 1861, the situation had changed considerably—as the *Placerville Mountain Democrat* noted: "The stages to and from Nevada Territory are daily crowded with passengers, business is represented to be in a flourishing condition and improvements are rapidly being made in every section of the mines."

The trip was beautiful, edging along mighty gorges and luxurious forests, then skirting past magnificent Lake Bigler (now Lake Tahoe). The whole way a steady stream of travelers and pack trains traversed the dust-choked trail. Miners rode mules, merchants drove supply wagons, and gamblers rode spirited thoroughbreds. But most of the men walked, many with packs on their backs, some leading an animal or two.

After three days the walkers finally started downhill, out of the tall pines and into barren hills. A visitor in Carson Valley the previous year described the area as "a desolate, comfortless, miserable region," but still the miners streamed across the mountains.

Aside from the silver boom at Virginia City and other camps, a territorial government was forming and Carson City was filled with hopeful office-seekers, politicians, and lawyers. "The country," wrote young Mark Twain, who arrived in mid-August 1861, "is fabulously rich in gold, silver, copper, lead, coal, iron...thieves, murderers, desperadoes, ladies, children, lawyers...gamblers, sharpers...and jackass rabbits." He described the town itself as "four or five blocks of little white frame stores which were too high to sit down on, but not too high for various other purposes...in the middle of town, opposite the stores, was the 'plaza'...a large, unfenced, level vacancy, with a liberty pole in it."

Cherokee Bob found Carson City to be full of entertainment-seeking politicians and wealthy miners going to and from San Francisco. He was in his element. He could play cards all night and find a good horse race the next day. The place resembled the boom days of California. As soon as Bob picked up a few good poker pots he planned to head north to join his brother.

In Carson, Bob met a young Missouri gambler named William H. Mayfield. A few years younger than Bob, Mayfield had a stocky frame, cold, gray eyes, and thin lips set in a slightly pock-marked face. They immediately became pals. Besides being Southerners and gamblers, both had volatile tempers—which soon got them into serious trouble.

On the afternoon of August 6, 1861, Mayfield became involved in a dispute with William Gardner, a constable at nearby Genoa. The nature of the trouble is not known, but it developed into a wild knife fight with Cherokee Bob joining in. A press dispatch reported, "On Tuesday afternoon, an affray occurred at Carson City between Billy Gardner and Bill Mayfield and Henry J. Talbot. Gardner was severely cut about the head and groin, and is in a critical condition. Sheriff [John L.] Blackburn arrested the parties."

The sheriff took Bob and Mayfield before Justice of the Peace E.C. Dixson that same day. The prisoners posted bonds of $500 each and were released pending action by the grand jury.

Blackburn was also a deputy United States marshal who had once killed a man in a saloon shooting. He was now sheriff of Carson County as well as night watchman for the town. Historian Hubert Howe Bancroft refers to him as an excellent officer, but others remark on his heavy drinking, belligerent manner, and nasty temper. He did not coddle his prisoners, and while Cherokee Bob and Mayfield awaited their bondsmen, Blackburn put them in irons in the town's rough log jail. Bob was furious.

Although he apparently avoided the city officers for some time, one night in late September Bob found himself in the St. Nicholas saloon with both Sheriff Blackburn and his jailer, George Downey. Bob couldn't resist complaining to Downey that Blackburn had no cause to put him in irons after the Gardner brawl. When Downey objected to Bob's complaints, shouting ensued and the jailer jumped behind the bar to get his pistol.

"In coming from behind the bar," noted a newspaper account, "Downey's pistol was discharged, the ball striking the floor near a bystander's foot. Talbot immediately fired three shots in quick succession, one ball striking Downey in the chin, one in the hip and one in the breast. Downey bled profusely."

In a cloud of pistol smoke, Bob bolted out the back door

and disappeared. When he learned his victim's wounds were serious, but not dangerous, he turned himself in and again found himself in irons. Mayfield probably took care of his friend's bail and Bob quickly decided it was time to move on. He was in a good deal of trouble and had no intention of serving another prison term.

Throwing together his few belongings, Bob urged his pal to join him, but Mayfield shook his head. He had a girl in Carson and couldn't leave. They shook hands and Bob told him he was going to join his brother in Lewiston, Washington Territory. With a wave, Bob headed south, past Genoa and into the barren hills leading into the Sierra. The mountain air had a chill in it, and he soon rode down into the oak and manzanita-strewn foothills of California once again.

Bob learned of new gold strikes in the Idaho country, rich new diggings said to surpass even California in its prime. He could visit his brother and get in on the new gold rush at the same time.

In 1861, the Civil War engulfed the country and drew seasoned troops from the West to the East. In September 1861, the Fourth California Volunteer Infantry began organizing at Sacramento, Placerville, and Auburn. Herman Reinhart, a northwestern pioneer, recalled that Cherokee Bob had gotten into a gambling brawl and taken refuge with some army pals who were volunteers from Shasta County. Reinhart remembered that Bob headed north with a group of volunteers sent to staff army posts in Oregon and Washington.

On his return from Nevada, Bob apparently had become acquainted with some of the volunteers during poker games at the local army camps. He stayed among them in case someone from Carson City might be looking for him.

When five companies received orders to take ship for the north in early October, they marched to San Francisco and camped at the Presidio. Bob went along, as he was heading north to see his brother anyway. The city had a holiday atmosphere as the troops indulged in their final night on the town. Some of the boys took the good spirits of the town a little too literally, as the October 16 *Evening Bulletin* reported:

VOLUNTEERS OVER-LIVELY.—A company of California Volunteers, in view of their departure for the North tomorrow, took rather more liberties last evening than was consistent with the good order and excellent reputation of our town. They visited a drinking saloon on the corner of Jackson and Dupont streets, and the keeper thereof says that they insisted on having drinks all around, with no pay to show for them. A good deal of a muss resulted...when outside one of their number threw a brickbat through the window...then the police, whose instructions were to be lenient unless some violence were committed, sailed in and arrested the man who threw the brickbat. His companions loudly demurred...but officer Chappelle and his two aids [sic] assured them that they were armed and that a rescue could not possibly occur—so the captive was taken to the station house.

Several of the soldiers attempted a rescue at the police station and were heaved into the same cell as their buddy. The brawl was just the kind Cherokee Bob delighted in and he might well have been in the thick of things.

On October 17 the soldiers staged a grand military parade, and various presentations were made to the different military units. Major James F. Curtis, commanding the regiment, was presented with a magnificent sword after reviewing his troops on the plaza. Companies A, B, C, D, and E were then marched to the wharf, where they boarded the steamship *Pacific*. Bob joined some of his pals at the rail as a tug took the ship out into the Golden Gate.

The trip was uneventful for the troops and civilian passengers aboard ship. The first night out a baby was born as the ship plowed through a dense fog. The fog held for some forty-eight hours, but by the time the Columbia River came into view the weather was clear and beautiful. After discharging some freight and taking on a river pilot at Astoria, the *Pacific* continued upriver to Portland, docking at seven o'clock on the evening of October 21, 1861. While some of the troops proceeded to Fort Vancouver in Washington Territory, Bob prepared to continue his journey upriver.

In Portland people were excited over the gold country opening up to the east. The *Portland Oregonian* contained almost daily dispatches from the Salmon River and a mining camp called Florence in the Idaho country. A principal supply point for the mines was The Dalles, one hundred miles upriver. High prices gave clear evidence of mining excitement. Steamer freight rates from Portland to Lewiston, in the Idaho country, were $120 per ton, while a single passenger fare was sixty dollars plus a dollar each for meals and a bed. The high prices included a portage around the Cascades, where another steamer took passengers on the next leg of their trip. Bob probably decided to take a look at The Dalles before moving on to the mining country, so he booked passage on the steamer *Julia* to head upriver.

At The Dalles, Bob found a booming trade center full of teamsters, miners, soldiers, and packers. Late in the year, he probably headquartered at Fielding Brown's Mount Hood Saloon. Walking into the noisy, smoke-filled barroom, he would pick out the most prosperous looking fellow and invite him to take a drink. That usually resulted in a game. Bob often targeted teamsters, their pockets stuffed with the proceeds of freighting into the mountains.

Bob apparently got on a winning streak and stayed around town a little too long, and one of the bitterest winters on record trapped him there. By January 1 the Columbia River was frozen, bank to bank, and it stayed that way for some six weeks. Late that month Tracy & Company's Express got through from the mines after a hard trip. They brought 300 pounds of treasure and news that three miners had perished while traveling between Walla Walla and The Dalles. The expressmen pushed on; using snowshoes overland and walking on the river ice they finally reached Portland. Bob probably didn't mind the weather as long as he could find a game. Generally he did quite well, but like all gamblers he lived on credit while on a losing streak.

According to one story, a California friend of Bob's kept a general store at The Dalles. One day a disreputable soldier and an upcountry rancher came in, the latter giving the storekeeper a watch to send to Portland for repair. Some weeks later, when the watch was expressed back, the soldier came in and paid for it, remarking that the rancher had sent him for it. After signing a receipt, the storekeeper gave him the watch and thought no more about it.

Soon the rancher showed up and asked for his watch. After the store owner told him what had happened, the rancher shook his head. "I don't know anything about that," he grumbled, "I just want my watch."

The fellow was pretty drunk and even after seeing the receipt he insisted on having the watch or the money. He started to talk rough, and the storekeeper told him he would see his lawyer. If he said to pay, he would. Otherwise, the rancher would get nothing.

When the rancher kept up his threatening manner, the storekeeper pulled his revolver from a drawer. "If you say another word I'll blow your infernal head right off. I don't propose to take anything of the sort. If you keep civil you can wait here in the store; if you don't, out you go."

After his lawyer advised him to pay for the watch, the storekeeper angrily shelled out to the rancher, growling he knew full well he and the soldier were in cahoots and now had both the money and the watch.

"That soldier was dead broke when he came in here before, and he couldn't have got the money anywhere else in that time. You gave it to him to come get the watch and rob me. Now you get out of here," the storekeeper said.

Cherokee Bob was sitting in the store at the time, watching the proceedings. Bob and the storekeeper were quite friendly, the businessman having allowed the gambler credit when he was down on his luck.

"You were a fool to pay that money without getting even," Bob remarked. "I'm going upriver tomorrow and I'll keep my eye on that other fellow. He is a deserter—I know him. If I find anything that I can put you onto, I'll let you know."

When he returned, Bob dropped by his friend's store for a drink. He had interesting news. "If you've got the sand, you

The Dalles, Oregon, in the early 1860s. The Columbia River is in the foreground, with Fort Dalles on the hill behind town.

Carleton Watkins photograph, California State Library

can get your money back. That fellow that robbed you has just come in from the country and he's in Jack Oliver's saloon. He's been sitting up all night gambling and drinking and is as ugly as you ever saw in your life."

Bob agreed to go along and help his friend either get his money or get even. "I'll see you through," he mused.

The two walked down to Oliver's and found the owner alone behind the bar. When they explained what they were going to do, Oliver jumped over the counter and made himself scarce. The plan was for the storekeeper to throw open the door while Bob leveled his pistol at the soldier over the storekeeper's shoulder. The soldier was facing the door with his pistol on the table; the storekeeper was to rush over and throw the weapon out the window. He later described what followed:

> "All right," says I. I opened the door and he looked up, but Cherokee Bob had his bead drawn over my shoulder, and he sings out to him in his quiet voice, "Don't you move, or you're a dead man."
>
> I jumped at the table, you know, and caught his revolver and slashed it right through the window, and grabbed his arms as he reached down for his knife, and twisted them right up behind him. Bob walked straight forward, with his little gun right on him, and pulled a big silk handkerchief out of his pocket, and we soon had him tied. The other man dropped right down on the floor....Oh my, the man did cuss us for all there was in it! But we handed him over to the sheriff. And I got my suit against him, and we killed two birds with one stone, you know, for the military authorities took him down to Vancouver, and he was tried as a deserter and convicted. He'd sworn right up and down that he'd kill anybody that undertook to take him. My wife didn't know anything about that for a long time.

Bob must have been restless by the time the river ice began breaking up in early March 1862. By the fourteenth the steamer *Tenino* had made it to the Cascades, and river traffic to Portland was again established. The steamers *Colonel Wright* and *Tenino* left for Wallula every Tuesday, the first leg of the trip to Walla Walla, Washington Territory. Bidding good-bye to his friends at The Dalles, Bob took a steamer upriver, then caught the stage or hitched a ride the thirty miles up the Walla Walla River to the new town. A local resident described Bob's destination:

> Our town is filled with a variety of characters. Almost all grades and professions are represented. I think the Pacific Coast must be well near purged of this class of persons; at least there appears, when congregated here, more than a fair proportion of the sports. All kinds of devices are resorted to to entice persons to "buck" at their games.
> The recently acquitted slayer of Captain Staples is here, dealing out red-eye to his brother Confederates. A large proportion of the sports and patrons of such institutions are secesh, in principles; and the ballads and music furnished at the saloons are exceedingly "Dixie."...There are many hard cases here from California.

Walla Walla was just the place Bob had been seeking. The Civil War was raging in the East, and lines were drawn throughout the West. Bob hadn't realized the pride he took in his southern heritage and how much he had missed his family surroundings. Playing cards in the smoky saloons of the town with his new southern friends, he felt completely at home for the first time in many years.

Bob was surprised to find some of his California volunteer friends stationed at nearby Fort Walla Walla. Companies A and C of the Fourth Infantry were doing garrison duty at the post. Although Bob probably renewed his acquaintance with several of the soldiers, he noticed the glares of hatred from his southern gambler pals. Clearly he had to make a choice. Abruptly severing relations with the troopers, from then on Bob joined other Southerners in belittling the troops. Local merchant Herman Reinhart recalled, "When the soldiers from the fort came to town and got to drinking, they were slurred as 'Lincoln's hirelings' to kill southern people and drove them away from saloon bars and would not allow them to drink, and sometimes would make a soldier or volunteer drink to the health of Jeff Davis or Beauregard, and if he refused, kick him or knock him down. Most of the large gambling houses were kept by Rebs."

The soldiers, as evidenced by their San Francisco escapade, could raise hell themselves when drinking, and frequent clashes with rebels erupted on the streets and in the saloons. "Either the soldiers down at the post are the wildest boys that ever did soldier," complained the local newspaper editor, "or else the whiskey they get about town here is the meanest stuff that ever did duty as whiskey."

Tradition insists Bob once bragged that with a shotgun in hand and a black man following him with a basket full of pistols, he could whip the whole Yankee army. Whether he said it or not, there is little doubt of the friction between the local Southerners and the troops at Fort Walla Walla. A serious confrontation seemed inevitable, and it happened on the evening of April 10, 1862.

The town held a benefit for its fire company at the new local theater. The audience was large and a rowdy crowd of drunken soldiers insisted on constantly interrupting the performance. After several men and women left in protest, Sheriff James Buckley and City Marshal George Porter, both ardent Southerners, called on the soldiers either to behave or leave. When the interruptions continued, Porter shouted for Cherokee Bob and several others to help forcibly remove the troopers. A general fight broke out, with Bob and two pals pulling their pistols and bowie knives.

As the audience stampeded for the exits, a volley of shots exploded. In a few moments bodies were scattered in the aisle under a pall of gunsmoke. Sergeant John B. Lantzenhiser was dead; Private Ansil Hubbard ran out the door mortally wounded. Three civilians, including Marshal Porter, were down with serious wounds. Others had been nicked by bullets.

Various accounts of the fracas allude to a conspiracy between Bob, Porter, and several other secessionists to pick a fight and murder some soldiers, but they seem to be prejudiced exaggerations of the truth. A careful reading of contemporary reports indicates that while the trouble was undoubted-

Portland Oregonian, Autust 9, 1899

Mayor Elias Whitman was in the middle of the Walla Walla squabble with the military over Cherokee Bob's theater shootout.

Northwest and Whitman College Archives

Walla Walla was a new town filled with teamsters, miners, soldiers, farmers, and southern gamblers. Cherokee Bob was right at home.

ly rooted in the sectional animosity of the two groups, the fight resulted when drunken soldiers refused to behave after civil officers cautioned them to do so. From all accounts, however, Bob needed little encouragement to jump into the fray when called.

The local *Washington Statesman* put full blame for the incident on the soldiers, saying, "On the part of the citizens who were engaged in the affray, notwithstanding the fact that officers of the law had been suffered to be stricken down and their authority condemned and boldly set at defiance, we are satisfied they cherished no disposition to aggravate the difficulty either by word or deed. Remaining within the limits of the city, they have peaceably and quietly pursued their accustomed business. Not so with the soldiers."

The *Statesman* was referring to an incident that occurred two days after the theater riot. A large group of soldiers, blaming the trouble on Southerners supported by city officials, paraded through the streets of Walla Walla looking for Cherokee Bob and the officers involved in the fight. They had Sheriff James Buckley in custody when Mayor Elias Whitman intercepted them on the street. Whitman, a native of Boston who had been elected the city's first mayor only a few weeks previously, was infuriated by the volunteers' actions. Speaking sternly, the mayor persuaded the soldiers to release the sheriff and return to their post. He then quickly penned an outraged note to the fort's commanding officer, Lieutenant Colonel Henry Lee:

City Council Chamber
Walla Walla, April 13, 1862

Col. Henry Lee
Commanding Post Walla Walla

Sir—A number of citizens of this city have formally called my attention to the proceedings of an armed body of soldiers under your command to the following effect. That at an early hour this morning a company of some seventy-five or one hundred soldiers, purporting to act under instructions from the Commanding Officer, did appear in the streets of this city arresting the sheriff and otherwise obtruding upon the rights of sundry citizens, making threats and demonstrations manifestly of a belligerent character.

I cannot think for a moment that the proceeding has your countenance or authority, and would hasten to appraise you of the event that you may take such measures as shall relieve our citizens of any apprehensions.

The mayor's strongly worded complaint resulted in a surprising response from Colonel Lee the same day. Although insisting he was unaware of his trooper's actions, Lee put the blame for the incident squarely on the city officials of Walla Walla:

You are probably aware of the wanton, and most likely premeditated murder of one, and the probable mortally wounding of another, of the most peaceable soldiers in my command. It is but reasonable to expect some excitement on the part of soldiers when such action is allowed to pass without the proper attempt to ascertain the guilty parties and bring them to punishment.

From what I conceive to be reliable evidence, I have no doubt but that my men were shot by one of the most noted offenders who has for the past five years figured in the criminal annals of California under the sobriquet of "Cherokee Bob."

I cannot but express my surprise that the citizens of your city did not take interest enough in this matter to have this notorious criminal arrested.

The startled mayor hastily penned another letter further explaining the situation, but the two sides remained adamantly opposed. The incident was not resolved, but it is perhaps pertinent that Lee, who was certainly not in control of his men, was soon transferred.

Cherokee Bob, meanwhile, had seen the handwriting on the wall. He did not relish being lynched by a gang of soldiers some dark night, or being tried for manslaughter should it come to that. He still hadn't seen his brother, who reportedly lived in Lewiston, and it seemed like an opportune time to visit him. Most accounts say he stole a horse and headed east for the gold country. "Some dragoons followed on to catch Bob Talbot," recalled Herman Reinhart, "but he got past Lapwai Fort and Indian Agency before they got there, and they did not have permission to follow further."

Lewiston, just over the line in the Idaho country, was the jumping-off point for the Salmon River mines. The new town was on the Clearwater River and had been deserted most of the winter, but with the advent of spring was again in the midst of a boom. A miner wrote that by late May 1862 "every road leading out of Oregon into Washington Territory is one solid, moving mass of human beings and animals...as many as 600 to 1000 daily passing between Lewiston and Florence."

In Lewiston, Bob had a reunion with his brother and later opened his game at the Nicaragua saloon, a noisy, smoke-filled emporium that epitomized all the boom-town gambling halls in which he had played. Word of his Walla Walla exploit no doubt preceded him, and as a celebrity of sorts he was invited to join all the big games. He played with judges, officials, and men whispered to be outlaws preying on the lonely mountain trails. Henry Plummer, a mysterious former lawman and fugitive from California, gambled and drank at the Nicaragua. Bob remembered Plummer from San Quentin, where they had served time together.

In the Nicaragua one day, Bob was surprised to meet his old pal Bill Mayfield. He had heard that Mayfield had killed the overbearing Sheriff Blackburn in Carson City, Nevada, but was anxious to hear Mayfield's story of the affair. The sheriff had accused the gambler of hiding Henry Plummer when the latter had fled a murder charge in California. In a confrontation at the St. Nicholas Saloon, Blackburn had insisted he could arrest Mayfield on suspicion of hiding Plummer. Mayfield laughed, taunting the lawman by saying he couldn't be arrested without a warrant. After a brief shouting match, Blackburn went for his pistol, but friends restrained him. As he struggled, Mayfield rushed at the lawman and mortally stabbed him, then fled in the confusion.

Showing little evidence of its colorful past, this is how Florence, Idaho, appeared in 1896. Bob's saloon is the large center building in the background with the sign over the door.

Idaho Historical Society

Friends hid Mayfield for a time, but a $3,000 reward proved to be too much of a temptation. He was soon ironed and again looking through the barred windows of the city jail.

The murderous gambler was indicted in January 1862 by the new territory's first grand jury. Bob asked if he, too, had been indicted, but since he was known to have fled, his name was not on the list. Bob also asked about the stories that not a single Southerner or Democrat had been on Mayfield's jury. No, he really couldn't complain about the jury, commented Mayfield. His lawyer had gone through some 137 names to get the twelve men both the defense and prosecution agreed upon.

Tried in the Second Judicial District Court, Mayfield was convicted and sentenced to hang on February 28, 1862. He was housed in the improvised state prison on the outskirts of town, and he quickly formulated an escape plan with the aid of friends. Obtaining a file, he rid himself of his chains one night, then watched for his chance. Abe Curry, the warden, usually left Mayfield's cell door open until evening lock-up time. This particular night Abe was thoroughly absorbed in a poker game as Mayfield watched from the shadows. When Abe drew a king full to his opponent's queen full, Bill quietly eased out the front door.

"I came to the conclusion," Mayfield later commented, "that if I couldn't go out on that hand I never could, and so I went."

When he made his appearance in Lewiston, Mayfield had a woman with him, but whether she was his sweetheart from Carson is anyone's guess. Bob's storekeeper friend at The Dalles erroneously said she was the wife of a popular carpenter of that town who had skipped out with Cherokee Bob when he had left. Another tale reports her working at Lewiston's Luna House hotel, the divorced wife of saloon owner Jacob Williams. Barney Owsley, who was in Lewiston at the time, was very definite as to her origins. He said, "Bill had a lady friend named Cynthia. 'Red-headed Cynth,' we called her. Later, when people began getting romantic about Bob and Cynth they said she was the wife of a prominent Lewiston citizen and that she'd wandered off the straight and narrow. Hell, I knew who Cynth was back in Missouri. We came from the same town and if she'd ever been the wife of a prominent citizen anywhere it sure wasn't in Lewiston. Or in Missouri, either." Whatever the woman's background, Bob, Mayfield, and Cynthia became inseparable and joined the rush to the Salmon River country that spring of 1862.

Idaho was still part of Washington Territory at the time. The recent gold discoveries had seen hordes of miners flooding into the area and the establishment of the mining camps of Pierce City, Orofino, Elk City, Florence, and Warrens. When weather permitted, pack trains loaded with goods streamed into the rugged mountains, followed by long lines of plodding prospectors on foot and horseback, all headed for the mining camps that boomed one day and thinned out the next as new discoveries were made elsewhere.

Bob and his two companions made their way to Florence, although that high mountain camp was already showing signs of decline. Writing to the *Washington Statesman* from Lewiston, a Florence miner gave a good idea of just how rough and raw the area was. "Whatever may be the condition of that camp next season, it was dull enough when I left. People were leaving it fast and trains of merchandise and provisions were pouring in, as the merchants expect great markets from Warren's Diggings next season. There was some talk of the Indians being hostile in that region and along the Salmon.... But on the whole, the white ruffians that infest the diggings are a great deal worse than the Indians. Robbery after robbery is being committed with impunity, and no wonder when murder is allowed to go free of punishment."

The town consisted of a scattered bunch of stores, saloons, cabins, and tents lining a narrow and curving street in a forested mountaintop setting. Bob had seen a hundred such camps, or at least so it seemed. They were always the same—wild and free before law and order, rules and regulations arrived. He and Mayfield found a vacant cabin and moved in with Cynthia.

The town had several saloons, one of them run by an ex-convict, Cyrus Skinner, whom Bob remembered from San Quentin. Skinner was bad. He had belonged to Tom Bell's gang in California and spent most of the 1850s in and out of prison. Bob also recognized some of the thugs in Skinner's saloon and knew he was probably tipping them off to potential victims. Jacob Williams, formerly of Lewiston, operated another saloon in town.

Most accounts agree that Bob was now looking beyond just gambling for a living and had determined to open a drinking emporium. Barney Owsley recalled that a man named Will Pitman died and left his partner sole proprietor of their Florence saloon. The man was polishing his bar one morning when Bob and Mayfield walked in and accosted him. Bob insisted he had loaned Pitman the money to start the saloon, and now he wanted his investment back. The startled man offered to pay up with liberal interest, but Bob just shook his head. No, he was there to take over the saloon.

The barkeeper protested briefly, but when Bob stepped back and touched his pistol grip, the man gave in. After he had packed his personal effects, Bob gave him the contents of the cash drawer and wished him well. After that it was drinks on the house.

Meanwhile, there was trouble in paradise. For some time Mayfield had been noticing Cynthia's coolness toward him while she was smiling and talking to Bob at every opportunity. What was happening seemed clear, and one day he could stand it no more. Historian Nathaniel Langford obviously invented the following conversation, but it gives the gist of what happened next in the vernacular of the time.

"Bob, you know me," Mayfield stated one day.

"Yes," replied Bob, "and Bill, you know me."

"Well, now Bob, the question is whether we shall make fools of ourselves or not. If that woman loves you more than me, take her. I don't want her. But if she thinks the most of me, no person ought to come between us. I call that on the square."

"Well," answered Bob, "I do think considerable of Cynthia, and you are not married to her, you know."

The two men realized they were getting nowhere and finally asked Cynthia to resolve their dilemma.

"Well, William, Robert is settled in business now, and don't you think he is better able to take care of me than you are?"

The surprised Mayfield shrugged his shoulders. He could say nothing, agreed to leave, and admonished Bob to take good care of Cynthia. As they parted, Cherokee Bob insisted his friend take a generous sack of dust with him. They would never see each other again.

As 1862 ended, people in Florence made plans for a New Year's ball. Everyone was excited as there was so little entertainment in the high mountain placer camp.

Although Cynthia looked forward to attending the ball, Bob was hesitant. His reasons are not clear, but he was possibly too awkward on the dance floor, or perhaps expected some big games in his saloon that night and was obligated to remain. When Cynthia grew adamant, Bob prevailed on a friend, Bill Willoughby, to escort her, and she seemed satisfied.

On the night of the big dance Willoughby and Cynthia made their entrance, but quickly noticed glances of disapproval from many couples in the hall. Cynthia's social status was well known, and it wasn't long before Jacob Williams and Orlando "Rube" Robbins, the dance floor managers, approached and took them aside. Many of the women objected to their presence and threatened to return home if Willoughby and Cynthia did not leave. The encounter must have been awkward for Williams if he were indeed Cynthia's divorced husband. Startled, the couple looked around at the glowering crowd surrounding them. The situation took them completely by surprise, and they had no choice but to make an embarrassed exit.

Bob was furious when he learned what had happened. He was doubly upset because "Jakey" Williams ran a competitive saloon in town and the two had not been on good terms for some time.

Both Williams and Robbins were leading citizens of the camp. They represented the social organizations, schools, and civil government that pushed back the frontier where men such as Cherokee Bob flourished. Even though any antisocial feelings were perhaps subconscious, Bob undoubtedly saw Williams as someone trying to rub his half-blood nose in an emerging new civilization where there was no room for a rootless, gambling gunman the likes of Cherokee Bob Talbot.

Early on the morning of January 2, 1863, Bob and Willoughby armed themselves and stepped out onto the snow-crusted street of Florence. The gang of toughs and bar-polishers who lounged about his saloon would never let him live down Cynthia's disgrace. Neither would his own sense of pride. The snow crunched and crackled under their boots as they headed toward Jakey's saloon.

Details of what happened next are not clear, but Williams and Robbins were expecting trouble and quickly confronted Bob and Willoughby in the street. Was it a quick draw contest? Probably not. Men expecting shooting trouble in those days kept their pistol in their hand and under their coat. Besides, the cold weather argued against a quick draw while bundled up in several layers of clothes.

When the showdown came, Williams and Robbins reportedly had several friends as backup. They had no intention of taking any chances with two reported killers, and any shootout would be no more fair than common sense dictated.

The shooting commenced immediately. Seeing they were outgunned, Bob and Willoughby began a hasty retreat as they fired. Yelling for his attackers to stop shooting, Willoughby went down mortally wounded as Bob dodged behind the corner of a building. He probably did not even feel his several wounds as he pulled his other pistol and stepped into the street again. A fusillade quickly downed him also as the thick powder smoke drifted across the street. The Williams group held their ground for a moment to make sure there was no hostile movement, then slowly walked over and looked at their victims.

Cynthia must have been horrified when Bob was carried into her cabin. He was still alive, but badly wounded in five places. She was told Willoughby was dead from fourteen wounds. A doctor began working on Bob, but after stripping off his bloodied clothes, he could only shake his head.

Cherokee Bob lingered for several days, with whiskey helping numb the pain. As he drifted in and out of consciousness,

Bob reportedly once discoursed on his opponents in the fatal gunfight. "They are both brave men, but with this difference; Jakey always steps aside to get clear of the smoke of his revolver, while Rube pushes through it and keeps on coming, getting nearer his adversary with each shot."

Toward the end, when he knew he was dying, Bob insisted Cynthia join Mayfield at Boise as soon as possible. He mistakenly thought he had killed Williams in the shootout and as his eyes glazed his last words were, "Tell my brother I have killed my man and gone on a long hunt."

On January 6, 1863, a hearing was held before Justice of the Peace Jasper Rand. Attorney J.S. Gray represented Williams and Robbins and eleven witnesses testified, including the county sheriff. A plea of self-defense was easily sustained and the defendants were dismissed. Cherokee Bob and Willoughby had meanwhile been buried in a hillside cemetery.

The last shootout had its sidelights. Barney Owsley, for example, claimed Bob, not Willoughby, had taken Cynthia to that fatal New Year's ball. He said no one snubbed Cynthia for the simple reason that loose women were the only kind in town at that time. Bob had quarreled with Williams during the affair and that started the trouble.

Owsley also said that later, knowing there would be trouble, Cynthia had removed the caps from Bob's pistol to keep him from killing anyone. That hardly makes sense, except perhaps to a hysterical woman in love. Also, Bob certainly would have checked his guns before looking for trouble. In those days of cap-and-ball weapons men had to be very careful with their pistols, particularly in winter. Gunmen had to be sure the powder charge was dry and the small channel in the cylinder between the cap and powder charge was clear so there would be no misfire. Still, if Owsley were right, Bob had no chance in that shootout, and the lack of casualties on the Williams team makes more sense.

When it was over, such details of the gunfight made little difference. Cherokee Bob was dead.

It is unknown if Bob's family ever heard of his death, but his brother probably relayed the news. Although well-known during his lifetime, Bob quickly faded from public notice after his lonely interment on the hill above Florence. Thomas Dimsdale resurrected Bob's name with a brief notice in *The Vigilantes of Montana*, published in 1865. Nathaniel P. Langford's *Vigilante Days and Ways*, published in 1890, devotes several chapters to Bob's career in the Northwest and did more to perpetuate his story than any other published work before or since. But neither of those authors knew anything of Bob's California career, and later writers even say he went to the Northwest from Georgia to avoid service in the Civil War.

Anton Roman did much to establish an atmosphere in which California's literary traditions could blossom and flourish. As a bookseller and publisher, Roman cultivated San Francisco's writers and poets, anthologizing, encouraging, and employing them. Perhaps more than any other man he brought talented Californians before a nation anxious for news of the emerging culture of the far western frontier.

Roman named Bret Harte as editor of his new *Overland Monthly* magazine, which he established in 1868. Both Harte and Roman had a wide acquaintance among the literary lights of the Pacific Coast and talent flocked to the new journal, which featured poetry, fiction, and nonfiction about life in the far West. The magazine was an immediate success.

A sidelight of the *Overland* was the authors and old-timers who gathered there to proofread, swap stories, and recall their halcyon days in the mining camps. Prentice Mulford, John Cremony, Dr. Henry de Groot, and many others entertained Harte and each other with their tales.

Just as entertaining were the Protestant ministers whose newspaper, *The Pacific,* which presented their views for members of their congregations, was printed at the *Overland* office. The ministers, whom Dr. Joseph Benton exemplified, were "the greatest set of fellows to tell stories you ever saw" according to Millicent Washburn Shinn, an early contributor and editor. Harte, Shinn would later recall, sat among these various groups and filled in the gaps of his own, limited mining camp experience. There he absorbed the color, atmosphere, and

Cherokee Bob's grave in the old Florence cemetery, about 1926. Did Cynthia fence the lonely site, or did some later custodian?

Idaho Historical Society

characters that would later bring him prominence, fame, and fortune.

Gamblers particularly interested Harte, and he made them the principal characters in a number of his tales. John Oakhurst, the gentlemanly gamester of Harte's *The Outcasts of Poker Flat*, comes to mind, but Harte only featured him in that one story. A refinement of the Oakhurst character was Harte's gambler Jack Hamlin, who first appeared in the 1870 short story, *Brown of Calaveras*. In Hamlin, Harte shaped and conformed his gambler into an unmistakable pastiche of a very real person whom he had heard described many times in his office story-telling sessions. Harte's model was Cherokee Bob.

While Hamlin's character is very much traditional, the physical description and suggestion of a maternal Indian ancestor conform to the real man. If there is any doubt of the model, however, the name leaves no doubt. The number of syllables in "Bob Talbot" and "Jack Hamlin" are the same. And Hamlin's nickname of "Comanche Jack" mirrors Talbot's cognomen of "Cherokee Bob" almost exactly, syllables and all.

In a curious postscript to history, a nearly forgotten frontier gambler, convict, gunfighter, and brawler is immortalized in the work of one of America's most popular and well-loved nineteenth-century writers. Few fictional western characters, however, are as colorful as the very real frontier gambler, Cherokee Bob Talbot.

2 A BAD SEED: THE DEADLY CHARLES MORTIMER

1834–1873

In the tree-shrouded Pine Grove Cemetery at Lynn, Massachusetts, timeworn tombstones stand like sentinels of the past. Darkened and obliterated by the sediments and elements of a century, the crusted monuments tell stories of another age—tales of life and death, of love and war, of friends and family.

The Flinn family plot looks like many others in the cemetery, yet it is a haunted place that speaks of violence and murder in faraway places. Here, too, is a story of devotion and familial bonds so great that even death held no fear.

In September 1864, *San Francisco Call* reporter Sam Clemens wrote, "[Charles] Mortimer is one of the worst men known to the police." Although still learning his trade at the time, the future Mark Twain knew whereof he spoke. As a booming financial and trade center of the West Coast, San Francisco was filled with badmen—Australian convicts, political thugs, and highwaymen of every description. Horse thieves from the interior mingled with eastern con men and burglars fleeing from the law, or perhaps seeking greener fields. Police Captain Isaiah Lees and his detectives fought a constant, uphill battle against crime.

Born in Vermont in 1834, Charles J. Flinn (later Mortimer) moved to Massachusetts at an early age, living with his family at Boston and Worcester. While growing up in the shadow of the Bunker Hill Monument, young Charlie often skipped school. His sister, Mary, and brothers Frank, William, Thomas, and Edward, lived normal lives, but Charlie always roved about the woods or adjacent towns looking for any activity other than attending school.

He was a teenager when a pretty young girl named Ada attracted his attention. Rides and excursions impressed Ada, but Charlie quickly discovered he was spending more money than he could earn at odd jobs. When Ada announced she was looking forward to attending a local picnic with him, Charlie panicked. He had no money. He also did not have the nerve to tell her he was broke. A friend named Dick told Charlie there was a way to get the money if he had the nerve; Dick proposed a robbery.

Charlie had just renounced his truant and rebellious nature and pledged to resume a normal life. When he could not borrow money for the picnic, however, he abandoned his resolve. He and Dick were soon making their plans. One night they broke into a store and stole some money. Dick was ignorant, and when dividing the loot Charlie made sure he got the lion's share. He had begun a lifetime of crime.

Enjoying life as big spenders, Charlie and Dick made other raids, arousing the suspicions of a local watchman. When he harassed the boys, they determined to get even and later destroyed some property under his care. For that they were caught.

Charlie refused to "peach" on his pal and was sent to the state reform school at Westboro. When released, he thought he was reformed, but it required little effort to quickly resume his old ways. Although visiting his parents from time to time, he traveled about the Northeast, becoming mired ever deeper in crime and high living. Despite his explanations, Charlie's mother, Louisa, knew something was wrong and suspected the worst. He later wrote, "I continued plundering for some weeks, accumulating watches, chains, jewelry, etc. I then went to

Christian de Guigné Collection

Charles Mortimer. This San Francisco Police mug book portrait was apparently taken after his arrest for the Pfister robbery.

Boston and turned them into money. I then went to Salem to my home, where I always managed to give a pretty good account of myself. My good mother was a deep-thinker and I know she suspected all was not right from the way she would talk to me."

In Greenfield, Massachusetts, Charlie fell in with an old criminal pal and they did a number of "tricks" together. They were attempting to ship two trunks of loot to Boston when officers arrested them. Although the young burglars had arranged alibis involving other people, they had not planned to get caught with the stolen goods in their possession. Deciding to plead guilty, the boys received one-year sentences in the state prison at Charlestown.

Charlie later claimed that upon his release he vowed to change his ways and sought out a village where no one knew him. "I soon discovered," he wrote, "that I was talked of, was known as a discharged convict, and strange glances and avoidance constantly met me. I could not endure this, and resolved to leave the country at the first opportunity."

Attempting to call on his parents, Charlie found they had left for the West. He went to New York and signed up for a five-year hitch in the United States Navy. In a few weeks he was on his way to Rio de Janeiro aboard a United States gunboat. But old ways die hard. Charlie jumped ship and sailed between Panama and South America for some time, at one point actually rejoining the navy aboard a steam warship. In Panama he deserted again and was soon heavily involved in local burglaries. A petty officer from his ship tried to arrest him once but, as Charlie said, "a box in the ear and trip of the legs piled him up," and Charlie made his escape.

When one of his thieving cohorts tried to club and rob him, Charlie thought it was time to move on. He signed aboard a Pacific Mail steamship and worked his way to San Francisco, where he landed in early May 1858.

In his memoirs Charlie made no comment concerning his first reaction to the sprawling Bay City. He was looking for opportunity and, after all, it was just another big city. He must have been somewhat surprised, however, at the magnificent stone and brick buildings along Montgomery street, the gas-lit avenues, and the structures clinging to the hills throughout the town. Chinatown and the dance halls and saloons of the Barbary Coast were just emerging. San Francisco was no longer a rough frontier town.

Anxious to look over the country, he moved on to Sacramento and found employment on a ranch near Stockton. While working at various jobs he engaged in several highway robberies and developed a drinking problem. "I tried hard to stop drinking," he later wrote, "but never fully succeeded, nor from keeping away from old associates."

In early 1862 Charlie received news of his father's death. He determined to go home but, as usual, "business" interfered with his plans. He returned to San Francisco and was waiting for a steamer when he visited a Kearny street saloon the night of February 5. He saw two Germans give a sack to the bartender for safekeeping. After striking up a conversation with the Germans, one Conrad Pfister and a friend, Charlie noticed two other men eyeing the transaction and suspected they had the same idea he had. When the Germans left, Charlie discussed the matter with the two men who told him the sack in question contained $1,000. The three thugs joined forces.

When Pfister and his friend returned for their sack, Charlie left the saloon with them, walking along Kearny Street toward Broadway. His two new pals followed some ten feet behind them. At the corner one of the Germans left, and Charlie continued his stroll with Pfister. From then on it was a typical heist, as Charlie described it. "When half way in the block I slipped the roll. It was six or seven inches long, wrapped around with a white cloth, and hence I pretended at the same time to trip and jostled against him. Had I been alone I should have boxed him over into the gutter, and before he could have given the alarm should have run off. As it was I intended to leave him at the corner quietly. But he missed the weight and caught hold of me and cried out, 'Give me that; give me my money.'"

The two confederates came up and Charlie called out, "Gentlemen, this drunken wretch has been trying to rob me.

Hold him while I call an officer."

"No," wailed the German, "he has my money." As his pals turned and ran, Charlie used Pfister's sack like a blackjack and beat him severely. The German slid to the ground as the beating continued, all the time screaming he was being robbed. By then a crowd was running up, and the battered Pfister began gasping out his story.

Officers James Bovee and Ben Bohen took both men to the station house, where Charlie was charged with robbing Pfister of $980. He gave his name as Charles J. Mortimer and was surprised to have his two accomplices testify against him at his hearing. He was quickly convicted and sentenced to a year in the state prison at Point San Quentin. Mark Twain later commented, "Our lenient court...as usual, only gave him a year in the State Prison. For the same offense, in the interior of the State, he would have got ten years at least."

A newspaper correspondent for the *Red Bluff Beacon* described the prison just a month before Mortimer arrived there. He wrote:

> The location, as you are probably aware, is on the mainland bordering on the bay and about fourteen miles from San Francisco, on the route to Petaluma. A more eligible or beautiful location could not be found in the state. As we sailed up toward the prison, the walls loomed up like a frowning fortress, differing in this respect only; the walls were built to resist an assault from the inside rather than the outside.
>
> In the rear of the prison beautiful hills rear their heads forming a splendid background to the scene and also for the accurate aim of the guards in case their skill requires to be tested on the escaping convict. The approach to, or rather from the gates, are guarded by several brass bulldogs who belch from their capacious mouths grape and cannister, when occasion requires.

Mortimer was admitted to the prison on March 7, 1862, as prisoner number 2323. The entrance to San Quentin was through a brick-paved courtyard, with the offices of the warden, clerk, and captain of the guard lining each side. The clerk took Mortimer's personal belongings, but Mortimer retained his clothes as the prison had no uniforms for the inmates. Cells designed to hold four men often held more. Mortimer was assigned cell number three in "The Stones," as the first cell block was called. His room was a mere ten and one-half feet by six feet, with only a small slit in the three-eighths-inch boilerplate door for ventilation. Next to The Stones were two other cell blocks. The last cells were completed in 1859 but were already leaky and dilapidated; they housed nearly 600 prisoners. Mortimer was put to work in the tailor shop.

San Quentin housed a number of noted criminals at the time, including a notorious Sacramento hack driver named Mike Brannigan, serving a ten-year sentence for raping a popular actress named Ellen Mitchell. The prison was a college of corruption where anyone who desired it could obtain a degree in any form of crime. Mortimer wrote:

> At this time prisoners could go where they pleased inside the walls, and knots of two, three, four and even eight or ten could be seen talking together. Thus they would talk over their past life and future hopes and plans. Very few made good resolves. The young and old in crime alike looked to the future only as a period to commit fresh crimes in. They would coolly discuss plans of escape and calculate how many lives would be sacrificed in contemplated breaks....What I did not already know of criminal life I could easily learn here. There were some ten or fifteen of the most notorious highwaymen on the coast, all in consultation.

Adolph "Dolph" Newton, who had robbed the Trinity Express while a member of Rattlesnake Dick's outlaw gang in 1856, was at San Quentin along with Jim Smith and Ike McCullum, both noted stage robbers. McCullum was one of Mortimer's cell mates; they must have swapped many a crusty tale.

Private contractors operated several industries inside the prison, including a blacksmith shop, a farming implement manufacturer, a cooper's shop, and a wagon maker. Only the brick-making yards were outside the walls. The tailor shop, where Mortimer worked, operated sixty-five sewing machines, assembling sacking and army uniforms. Nearly a hundred convicts, many of them Chinese, worked there.

Charles Harmon, a snitch who had betrayed several of Mortimer's friends a few years earlier, was foreman of the tailor shop. Harmon knew what Mortimer thought of him. Mike Brannigan also worked there. Mortimer despised him not only for the rape he had committed, but because he bragged about it.

Apparently Harmon and Brannigan determined to let Mortimer know just who was in charge and framed him for stealing burlap. Burlap sacks made at the prison were in big demand for wartime use in the East. Having himself been severely punished once for selling prison cloth, Harmon decided Mortimer should get a dose of the same medicine. He planted the material under Mortimer's workbench; then Brannigan testified he had seen Mortimer hiding it there. "I got twenty lashes," Mortimer later recalled, "with a four foot rawhide in the hands of a powerful man, [Captain Edward] Vanderlip, who seemed to delight in seeing how deep he could sink the lash into a man's quivering flesh. Every blow laid open my flesh from six to fifteen inches."

On July 22, 1862, about 130 convicts assigned to the brickyard filed out the front gate on their way back to work after lunch. After being counted, ten of the crew ducked along the wall and quickly made their way to Warden John Chellis' office. Seizing the warden, the convicts rushed to the gate and held him as a shield while a general break was signaled. Pandemonium reigned as alarms sounded and both convicts and guards dashed to strategic locations.

Convicts rushed Chellis to the West Gate, where prisoners were beating guard Con Murphy for refusing to give up his keys. Convicts finally took them from him as they broke down the inner gate. When the outer gate was open shouting convicts, carrying whatever they could grab as weapons, streamed from all the shops and flooded through the exit shouting,

"Liberty!" Mortimer later recalled, "I saw the whole thing from a front window. I did not join in the escapade because I was a 'short-termer'; besides, in going from the store to the gate I would have been a fair mark for half a dozen guards. Some short-termers joined in, it is true, and I can give no reason for it."

Pushing the portly Chellis in front of them, the yelling convicts headed for guard post five, which overlooked the brickyard and blocked their way to the hills. Behind them, guards on the walls were shooting into the mass of 200 to 300 convicts. As guards trained the cannon on them, Chellis screamed, "For God's sake, don't shoot!" Recognizing the warden in the nick of time, the guards fired the cannon off to one side, then spiked it to keep it out of the convicts' hands. As terrified guards abandoned other posts, the convicts prodded Chellis ahead of them into the hills.

With the bodies of convicts scattered around the prison yard, Vanderlip organized a pursuit of foot and horse guards and rounded up some fifty stragglers. A guard on horseback galloped to nearby San Rafael and spread the alarm among the terrified residents. After putting their families in secure positions, a small local posse quickly formed and caught the escaping convicts in a pincers movement.

As Vanderlip's posse nipped at the escapees' heels, the convicts forced Chellis across a slough at Ross Landing, then told him to get up over a high wall on the other side. Dripping wet in the hot afternoon sun, panting and exhausted from his ordeal, the overweight warden refused to climb. When several convicts tried to hoist him over and were nearly crushed for their trouble, they left Chellis where he collapsed. The prisoners pushed on without their hostage.

With Chellis safe, Vanderlip and the San Rafael posse opened fire as the convicts scattered like quail into the surrounding marshlands and woods skirting Mount Tamalpais. Gradually most of the escapees were rounded up and by eight o'clock that night a line of forty-seven convicts was being herded back towards the prison. Thirty-three inmates were still unaccounted for when the muster roll was called in the San Quentin yard. By the end of the month most had been recaptured. Four convicts had been killed outright, while three others died later. Thirty-two had been wounded. "For the next two weeks," Mortimer wrote, "the groans and cries of the wounded and dying could be heard day and night."

Released exactly one year after entering San Quentin, Mortimer was given some extra clothes and $2.50. The ferry to San Francisco cost one dollar, and the ex-convict found himself nearly broke as he wandered the streets of the Bay City. His fortunes took an upswing, however, when he struck up a conversation with a tipsy pedestrian. After several rounds of drinks for his new friend, the drunk made the mistake of allowing Mortimer to escort him to his room. "I took him to a lodging house," Mortimer later wrote. "I undressed him, but in this act of kindness my hands slipped into his pocket and a few half dollars stuck to my fingers. In putting him to bed I gave him a good searching and found seventy-two dollars."

After working for some months in San Jose, Mortimer moved on to Nevada's boom town, Virginia City. He was broke again, but it was a lively town and he met many ex-convict pals. He quickly took a walk with a likely prospect and put a knife to his throat on a dark street. His purse well-filled again, Mortimer laid low for a few days, then he changed his appearance and again went to work.

For a time he worked with a man named Pete Goodwin, then paired up with Tom Mitchell in nearby Gold Hill. They boarded up the entrance to an old mining tunnel and camped there, going out evenings to find "good injuns" to pluck. One night Tom brought back John "Black Jack" Bowen and two pals named Cockey Wright and French Frank, who all took up lodgings in the cave. In a few days a thief named Three-fingered Robinson also joined them.

Mortimer related a typical foray:

> Going by the Illinois lodging house one night with "Black Jack," I took a notion to go in. I walked boldly in as if I belonged there. I went into a long room with bunks on either side, like steamer berths, and all full of lodgers. Some of them woke up and I spoke to them. I talked with one and

San Francisco Police Department

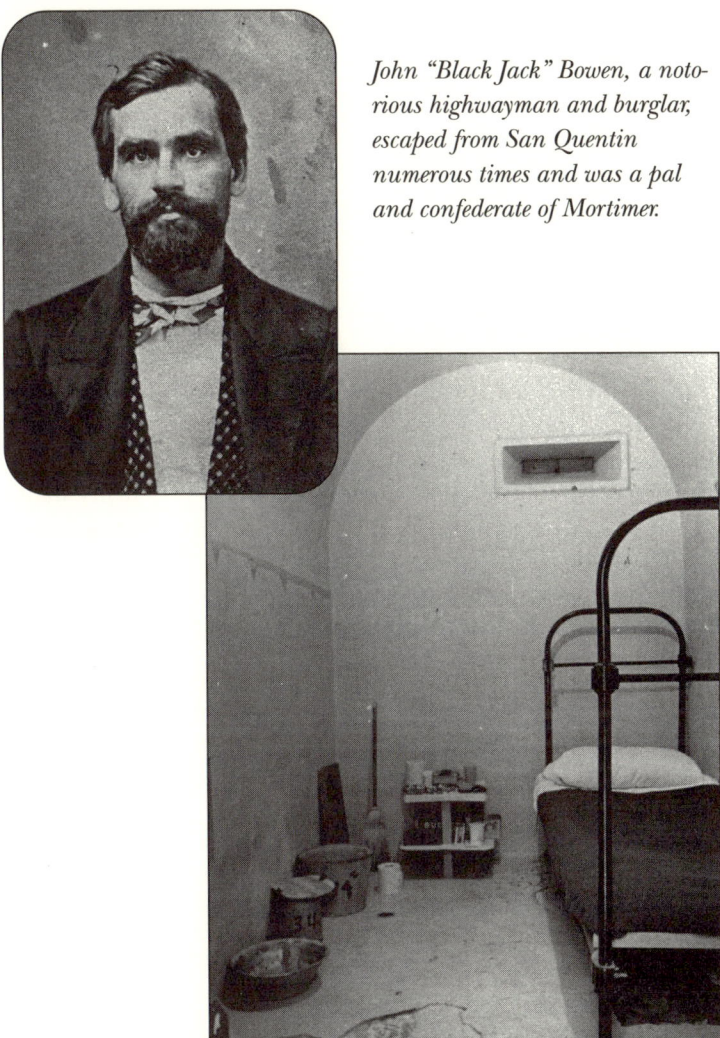

John "Black Jack" Bowen, a notorious highwayman and burglar, escaped from San Quentin numerous times and was a pal and confederate of Mortimer.

San Quentin Museum Association

This old San Quentin cell from Mortimer's day often housed as many as four convicts.

another on all kinds of topics, and all the time kept my fingers doing duty. Presently I went out and met Black Jack, when this conversation followed:

"Where have you been?"

"In there."

"Why, there was some one talking in there."

"Yes, I and the lodgers."

"You! Why, what on earth did you talk about?"

"Oh, about politics, mines, religion and one thing and another"—showing what I got.

"Well," said Jack, "you've got a hell of a lot of cheek."

Mortimer broke from his gang after a squabble and soon was nearly caught following a stick-up. Later he made a nice haul from a pedestrian on the trail between Virginia City and Gold Hill but fled when two men approached and his victim gave the alarm. He jumped into a prospect hole and heard an impromptu posse run past him. After crouching in the hole for two hours, he returned to his camp for several days.

On the street one day, Mortimer had to run for his life after someone, perhaps one of his victims, pointed him out to an officer. As he dodged into a group of buildings, three bullets buzzed by him and a few hours later he was on his way to Sacramento. Nevada was becoming a mite uncomfortable.

Back in California Mortimer picked a few pockets at the state fairgrounds in Sacramento, but generally laid low. One night three local police officers entered and searched his hotel room while Mortimer and a girlfriend stood by and watched. Officer Fred Chamberlain soon announced Mortimer and his friend were under arrest, although admittedly they could not find any stolen goods. Mortimer later growled that he had been arrested merely because he was an ex-convict and wouldn't be used as a stool pigeon. The judge gave him three months on a vagrancy rap.

Upon his release, Mortimer quickly left town. He went to Folsom with Ike McCullum, but soon felt the tug of the big city and returned to the coast. He made his headquarters in Belmont, about twenty-five miles south of San Francisco, and operated in the surrounding area. Whenever one place got too warm for him, he switched his operations to another location.

One night Mortimer was standing on a San Francisco street corner when he heard several shots, followed by a rush of people from a basement saloon. Running down into the place, Mortimer saw a soldier in the middle of the floor with a smoking pistol in his hand. When a man jumped from behind the bar and ran out, the soldier fired and missed.

"Where'd that son of a bitch go?" he yelled.

"Didn't you see him run out?" Mortimer asked.

The soldier said he was looking for someone else, then walked over to the bar. "I've found him!" he shouted, and fired at someone behind the bar. When he walked over to the Kearny Street door, Mortimer told him he had better give himself up to the provost marshal, and he said he would. As the gunman stepped out the door, Mortimer rushed behind the bar and cleaned out the till. The victim was sitting on a sack of oysters with a bullet through his forehead. By then some cautious patrons and an officer began entering the saloon and Mortimer calmly walked out.

After a variety of muggings ("garrotings" in the parlance of the day) in the bay city, Mortimer tackled the wrong man one night. He was badly cut up but managed to escape and hid in Belmont for several weeks. Returning to San Francisco in early September 1864, he went for a walk with what he termed a "friendly" police detective, and the two had a drink in a saloon. The lawman pointed out several young men with money who were out on the town and remarked that if Mortimer would stick with them he would probably find a "good injun." As the officer left, Mortimer eased up to the group. He was soon talking and drinking amicably with young Charley Wiggins and his pals until dawn.

Mortimer walked Wiggins to the front of his home that early morning, left him there, and started downtown for breakfast and a shave. Wiggins, clerk to Mayor Henry Coon, was independently wealthy and ripe to be plucked. Mortimer already had his plan worked out. By seven that morning he was back at Wiggins' home and knocking on the door. When a maid answered, he told her he had an appointment and was aware

Mr. Wiggins had been home only a short time. Admitted to Wiggins' upstairs room, Charlie found him sleeping soundly. After hanging his handkerchief over the keyhole, he swiftly cleaned out the room of all jewelry and money. At the foot of the stairs he again encountered the maid.

"How does Mr. Wiggins feel this morning?" she asked.

"I find him very much as I expected. He has a severe headache and is going to try and sleep it off. Good morning."

Mortimer next called on his detective friend and gave him some of his loot. He then caught the train for Belmont.

The previous month a particularly violent pawnshop robbery had occurred in which a clerk named Henry Myers had been nearly beaten to death. The police were having little success investigating it and various other crimes, and the Wiggins robbery set them scurrying. Police Chief Martin Burke ordered all local thieves and stool pigeons rounded up, but to no avail.

Special Detective George Rose picked up George Sibley, a naval deserter from the *Saranac*. "Special" officers were under the command of the department, but paid by residents of a particular neighborhood instead of the city. Rose knew Sibley was down on his luck and had recently pawned his clothes. After a grilling, Sibley suggested Rose search Mortimer's house in Belmont for evidence of the robberies. Discussing the matter with Chief Burke and Detective Captain Isaiah Lees, Rose went to see what he could turn up. He was on the next train south.

At Mortimer's house, an unidentified old man admitted Rose and a stage driver and told them Mortimer was not at home. Rose prowled through the place and turned up several pieces of suspicious jewelry. At that point Mortimer stepped out of a hiding place and confronted the officer. "He pretended he wanted to arrest me," Mortimer later recalled, "but when the stage driver's back was turned he told me it was only for a blind. He denied having found the jewelry, but finally owned up to it and said if I'd own up it would be better for me, and so tried to laugh the matter off. I knew he intended to arrest me, and so put my wits to work to prevent his return to San

Francisco, as he intended, on the afternoon train."

Mortimer was desperate as San Quentin again loomed before him. Rose had a list of items taken in the Myers robbery, and he was already mentally spending the reward when he found a watch and chain fitting the description. Mortimer told him his loot was buried near Santa Clara, about twenty-five miles away, and the two men headed south.

Mortimer led Rose to a site one and a half miles from town. By then it was 9:00 P.M. and the spot was quite secluded. Rose was careful, and Mortimer noticed his hand was always on his revolver. Pretending to have trouble lighting a match, Mortimer let the detective try to light it, and Rose's hand left his pistol. Mortimer had the moment he had been waiting for. He said:

> The moment his match blazed, I garroted him. I gave him a good squeeze so he should see I was in earnest. He tried to reach his pistol. I gave him another hug and cautioned him not to go after it again, but as I eased up he went for it, and I gave him another hug and took out my penknife, opened it with my teeth, and told him I did not want to hurt him, but I was master of the situation, and should disarm him and take what property he had of mine and let him go. His pistol was well behind and his coat buttoned up so I did not need to be very rough with him. He said:
> "For God's sake, think of my poor mother."
> I replied, "I think most of my own mother, but I don't want to hurt you."
> I then tried to get his pistol, but he made a quick dive for it. I gave him a very severe hug and shoved the blade into his neck. The back of the blade must have turned towards me, hence the apology for not taking his head entirely off.

Flinging Rose to the ground, Mortimer began to search him. As Mortimer rolled him over to get at his back pocket, Rose made a desperate grab for his weapon, but a furious Mortimer snatched it from him. After brutally beating the officer with the pistol, Mortimer left him for dead, dug up his loot, and fled the scene.

Battered and bleeding, the desperately wounded Rose later came to his senses and crawled to a nearby farmhouse. The sleeping family heard his feeble cries and knocking, and quickly administered first aid. Two days later the family put him on the train for San Francisco.

Rose miraculously survived to give his version of events. He maintained Mortimer had left the scene at one point, then quietly returned. As Rose lay bleeding on the ground, Mortimer stood behind him, disguised his voice and asked if he could help him. When the detective feebly responded, Mortimer said, "Oh, so you're not dead yet!" He then began the brutal beating with the pistol. Rose told a harrowing tale of swallowing his blood when it threatened to choke him as he feigned death. On September 16 reporter Clemens wrote, "Detective Officer Rose, who a few days ago was beaten and stabbed near Santa Clara by a prisoner named Mortimer...is now entirely out of danger and will be about the streets again shortly. We are glad it is so, for while rascality is so plenty hereabouts, the city could ill afford to lose so accomplished a detective."

At first news of the attack, Captain Lees and a posse of officers hurried to Belmont and fanned out over the country searching for Mortimer. Although he was spotted several times and had some close calls, Mortimer managed to elude the lawmen and disappear.

After foolishly walking to San Francisco and spending a week there, Mortimer was relieved to hear that Rose would recover. He promptly headed north. At Napa he fell in with Black Jack Bowen again, and a man named Shanks. After holing up in Napa for two weeks, Mortimer and Shanks left on horseback for the upper country. They traveled through Woodland, Knight's Landing, Marysville, and up through Shasta and Yreka. According to Mortimer they were "doing highway robbery along the entire line."

At Yreka Tom Boulton, who had recently escaped from the Nevada penitentiary at Carson City, joined the two highwaymen. Boulton had a previous police record in town, and when he and

Shanks went on a drunk police picked up the ex-convict. The *Yreka Semi-Weekly Union* said on November 16, "On the 21st of October last, Tom Bolton [sic] made his appearance in this City and the same night was arrested for disorderly conduct and sent to jail....He stated that on the night he got drunk and was arrested it was his intention to steal a horse and leave, that he had stolen a saddle for that purpose."

Meanwhile, Mortimer traveled to nearby Scott's Valley where he joined a new partner named Bob Ferry. By then it was late 1864 and traveling was hard in the snow-covered Siskiyou Mountains. Mortimer and Ferry took on another partner named Bill Richardson, who had recently escaped from an Oregon jail. Besides committing highway robbery, the trio burglarized homes, stores, saloons, and inns.

Making camp on a mountain overlooking the notorious road house of Cherokee Mary near Yreka, the outlaws went to steal provisions one night from the storehouse of one Dutch Charley, who operated a nearby saloon and hotel. Stepping through the door, Mortimer heard a cap snap and immediately dropped to the floor. In a moment he struck a light and saw a trap had been set with the door knob tied to the trigger of a rifle. Luckily, the damp powder didn't explode. Taking all they could carry, the men destroyed everything else and disappeared into the snow-shrouded darkness.

Moving on, the outlaws came upon a store on McAdams Creek at about 8:00 P.M. Eight or ten men were in the place, and it looked like easy money. The three robbers burst in and, holding the occupants at gunpoint, took nearly $1,000 in money and property. They then headed north down the Klamath River.

At Scott Bar, a village comprised of hotels, stores, and many saloons, the outlaws lost most of their money at the gambling tables. Hoping to disguise their appearance, they purchased new clothes, then continued their journey. High mountains formed a deep gorge on both sides of the river, and the scenery was spectacular. The outlaws guided their horses over the rock-strewn trail close to the river, then up over spurs and ridges of the canyon.

But their plundering had not gone unnoticed. A posse under James M. Luttrell, constable of nearby Fort Jones, was promptly on the trail. After questioning some of the locals at Scott Bar, Luttrell was confident their quarry had preceded them, and the posse pressed on. Some miles downriver at a Chinese ferry they captured Richardson. They lashed him to his horse and rode on.

Mortimer and Bob Ferry had gone ahead and stopped at the Sciad Creek ranch of a New Yorker named Reeves. The outlaws had been traveling fast for several days and decided to rest and wait for Richardson to catch up. Mortimer and Ferry were still waiting when Luttrell and his posse surprised them. Resistance seemed hopeless and they surrendered without a fight. The posse tied Mortimer and Ferry to their horses and proceeded with the three prisoners to Fort Jones on the first leg of their journey to the county seat at Yreka.

Mortimer must have cursed bitterly as he thought of another term in San Quentin. He did not feel any better when Richardson managed to untie himself and disappear during the trip. The journey was bitterly cold and the prisoners were at least grateful for a hot meal and warm cell in the Yreka jail.

The two outlaws did not appear for trial for nearly three months. Then, before Judge Alexander Roseborough and using the name "George Foster," Mortimer pleaded guilty on February 10, 1865. He received a three-year sentence; Ferry got two years.

Mortimer had been thinking of escape for some time, and on the evening of February 11 he put his plan in motion. About 7:30 P.M. that Saturday evening he removed a lock-picking device from the lining of his coat. The five cells were fronted by an enclosed corridor that opened into the main room of the small, wooden structure. The jail was crowded at the time and an army deserter, George Maguire, alias Keefer, was sleeping in the corridor. Letting himself out of his cell, Mortimer released murderer Tom King and Ferry, and the three induced Maguire to call the deputy for water. When Jailer E.A. McCullough opened the door to pass through the water bucket, Mortimer was waiting in the shadows. He later recalled, "I slipped out and up to Mr. Jailor and garroted him and brought him into the hall where he was tied and gagged. We took his weapons, put him in a cell and left."

Leaving was no easy matter, though, as Mortimer, Ferry, and King were shackled about the ankles. They took what food they could find, along with knives, blankets, and the jailer's weapons. The night was bitter cold, and the escapees knew they must get their irons off or the escape was doomed. Mortimer had already weakened his twenty-five pound irons before the break, but it still took him an hour to get them off. King dodged into a thick patch of chaparral, where he spent the night trying to file off his irons with a table knife. Weak from long confinement, he did not even get a mile from town before possemen recaptured him. Ferry got separated from the others and posses caught him about daylight, his shackles making him easy to track.

Mortimer and Maguire fared better. Maguire had no leg irons, but Mortimer's broken links made clear tracks through the snow. They made their way across the Greenhorn range of mountains, apparently heading for Scott's Valley. Soaked to the skin and exhausted, they stayed near the Forest House on Sunday night. Unable to find food, they hid until the next night, then headed for Cherokee Mary's Ten Mile House about nine miles from Yreka.

Siskiyou County Sheriff A.D. Crooks and a six-man posse had reached Cherokee Mary's early Monday, anticipating the escaping prisoners' route. Sheriff Crooks sent several men to the nearby roadhouse of Dutch Charley. Crooks, Jesse Sherman, a Dr. Longley, and A.V. Burns stayed at Mary's and made it plain she had better not try to signal the prisoners if they arrived. The lawmen were bone-weary; they had had only a few hours sleep after being out in the mountains for two days and nights in rain, snow, and bitter cold.

The Yreka stage had just left Mary's at 4:00 A.M. when Mortimer and Maguire tramped through the snow and up to the house. The possemen immediately spotted the outlaws and cautioned Mary to get them into the house. Mortimer later recalled what happened:

> I knocked and she came to the door and gave my hand a squeeze, but I was so hungry and worn out I did not understand it and so stepped in, when a gun was at my head in an instant. I sprang back, pulled the door to and ran up the road. Three shots were fired, one of which hit me in the back of the neck and down I came. Three men ran up, covered me and made me throw up my hands. The ball had grazed my jugular, broken my right lower jaw and lodged in my cheek.

Maguire dashed in another direction, but the posse soon caught him also. Returned to the Yreka jail, Mortimer was promptly re-ironed while waiting for the doctor. He was given a bottle of brandy also, and was suitably giddy as a Dr. Ream probed for the shotgun slug in his cheek. Apparently Mortimer's jaw was not broken, as he claimed, for a newspaper account noted "the wound is slight and will soon be well." Full of brandy and good food, Mortimer was soon his old self despite the pain in his cheek. The *Yreka Weekly Union* reported, "Foster [Mortimer's alias] is quite jolly over the affair, takes it as a matter of course and has no fault to find with any one."

With their heads newly shaved, the two outlaws again went before Judge Roseborough, who sentenced Mortimer to seven years and increased Ferry's term. Early the following month Sheriff Crooks escorted Mortimer, Ferry, and two Chinese prisoners south toward San Quentin. They caught the Sacramento steamer at Red Bluff and landed at San Francisco on March 14, 1865. Mortimer must have been nervous. They were to stay overnight at the City Hall prison before the final leg of the trip to San Quentin in the morning. His neck was still bandaged and he hoped his hat and heavy clothes would help hide his identity. He was still using the alias "Foster" and no one in Yreka had ever learned his real name.

When the prisoners were escorted down to the basement jail, all hell broke loose. According to the *Alta California*,

> As the procession entered the Calaboose through the outer office, [Detective George] Rose was standing by the doorway conversing with Captain Baker and chanced to look up as the prisoners with clanking chains filed past him. Foster had

his head completely muffled up on account of his wound, and hid his face as he passed to avoid recognition, but the quick eye of the detective recognized him at a glance by the outline of his figure, and with the exclamation "that's Mortimer, by God!" Rose was by his side in an instant. The officers who stood around with difficulty restrained Rose from some act of violence...and hurried him away.

Mortimer claimed to have grabbed Sheriff Crooks, "who was shaking like an aspen leaf," and used him as a shield. Rose had actually drawn his revolver a moment before Captain William Douglass and an Officer Brown could hustle him away. In a life of danger and violence, that was probably Mortimer's closest call.

The police were delighted to have Rose's assailant in their custody, but they could not hold him. They had to be content with the option of grabbing him again once his sentence was up and prosecuting him then.

In the morning the prisoners left for San Quentin. "My arrival created a great excitement," Mortimer said, "and thousands assembled to see me depart....At the coach as I passed out stood Rose; brave man, why didn't he shoot me then....

"At the boat another crowd met me, bigger than the first. I was in thirty-two pound irons with riveted wristlets, and leg irons with a heavy bar between."

Even though San Quentin officials now knew his identity, they admitted Mortimer on March 15, 1865, under the name "George Foster." After the clerk registered him, it took two blacksmiths half an hour to knock off his chains. As number 2915, Mortimer was assigned cell eighteen in "The Stones," where three others already bunked. The ventilation was as bad as ever and the smell of excrement still hung in the air, but Mortimer noticed various changes. The convicts were soon to wear uniforms. A San Francisco woolen mill was manufacturing a black-and-gray striped material that inmates would assemble in the prison tailor shop where Mortimer had been assigned.

More importantly, the previous year Governor Frederick F. Low had signed the "Goodwin bill" allowing "good time" or "copper" credits for convicts who behaved themselves. Five days could be subtracted from every month of trouble-free time served. In addition convicts were now being granted full pardons on completion of their terms.

Despite other changes, the place was still very much a prison. "With the exception of the convicts being better fed, better clothed, and the officers showing a more humane feeling towards the prisoners," Mortimer later wrote, "matters were much the same as when I was there the first time."

Prison routine varied little. The wake-up bell rang about 6:30 A.M. After dressing, the convicts made up their bunks, then stood by the door with their night buckets. After trusties had opened the doors, the men filed out into the corridors and lined up at the cistern known as the "Rose Bowl," where they dumped their buckets of urine and feces. Next they washed their hands and faces in cold water and marched off to breakfast.

Although many of the prisoners ate in the mess hall, the various factories had their own eating halls where the contractors often provided slightly more or better food. In the main hall the convicts sat at long, foot-wide tables and began and finished eating when a guard banged his mallet.

Convicts not working in the factories stayed busy on the grounds doing maintenance work. Others tended gardens, did grading work, or loaded and unloaded wagons and ships. Up to one hundred convicts often broke rocks in the time-honored fashion. Those without work had the freedom of the yard as long as they behaved.

At 11:20 A.M. the dinner bell sounded and again the inmates filed to their mess tables for fifteen minutes, then they went back to work. At 3:30 P.M. another ring signaled the end of the work day and the men returned to the mess halls for the evening supper of bread and black coffee. When the mallet descended they were marched off to their cells for the night and counted.

Mortimer was again assigned to the tailor shop and was there eating his supper during a big escape attempt on January 13, 1866. The escape was known as the "mush break" because the prisoners objected to that particular menu item and used it as an excuse to plan a break during the evening meal.

Some 600 convicts had filed into the main dining room and were standing by their tables as the officer in charge, James Fitzpatrick, stepped through the doors. Several cons seized him, hoping to hold him as a hostage. As Fitzpatrick struggled and yelled for help, a trusty ran to his aid from the kitchen wielding a large butcher knife. The action startled the convicts, allowing the guard to break away and get back out the door. His savior dashed out on his heels, but not quick enough to avoid a blow from a club-wielding prisoner. Although staggering, he managed to keep his feet and just barely made it through the door.

J.J. Green was in charge of the commissary and began an immediate dialogue with the break leaders. With much patience he cautioned the guards not to shoot and counseled the prisoners to return to their cells quietly. The situation was tense as dark clouds swept in and a heavy rain commenced.

Some of the other prisoners eating in the tailor shop ran for their cells when the alarms sounded. Mortimer recalled the scene:

> When the alarm bell rung for all to go to their cells these others were for going. I told them I'd not take the chances of being shot by those crazy guards, as we did not know how things stood and we might be turned loose upon by the guards at any moment. Just then two shots were fired and that fixed them not to leave the shop. Three shots were fired by a guard over the lower gate. He blazed away into the dining room windows, but fortunately did not hurt anyone. Our reasons for not going to our cells were considered sufficient and we were excused.

Mortimer also recalled that about a dozen men at work outside the walls headed for the yard, returning to their cells at the sound of the alarm. As they waited for the gate to open, a guard panicked and fired a load of canister into their midst, killing several and wounding others severely.

At the dining hall Green's patience finally paid off as the convicts began moving to their cells. Soon, all were back under lock and key. According to Mortimer the plan had been to hold the guard until dark, then run for the walls under cover of night and the rainstorm. It would have been a blood-soaked affair.

"The convicts who were engaged in the attempt," noted the *Alta California* "were all secured and ironed, but on Sunday night three who were not implicated in the rising dug under the wall of the new addition to the prison and made their escape. They have not yet been recaptured."

An investigation quickly isolated the break's ringleaders, who received fifty lashes. The lesson was a bitter one the convicts did not easily forget. "Some of those men's backs and sides," Mortimer later wrote, "were masses of corruption for months after, and some did not leave the hospital till they went feet foremost to the graveyard....George Wingate...after being struck fifty [times]...was cross ironed and put into the dungeon and was kept there several weeks. He was then removed to the hospital, at which time his back was alive with maggots, and was horribly offensive. Others were nearly as bad."

Mortimer managed to keep his nose clean and, with his "coppers," was discharged on January 20, 1871. Immediate freedom was to elude him, however. Some years earlier he had been indicted for the Wiggins robbery, and now he was released into the custody of San Francisco police detective James Towle. Catching the ferry, the officer soon had his prisoner lodged in the San Francisco city prison. "Mortimer is about 36 years of age," commented the *Alta California*, "and from his looks the climate of San Quentin agreed with him very well."

George Rose had disappeared some time prior to Mortimer's release from prison. Considered an excellent detective who, according to Mark Twain, "could follow footprints on pavement," Rose lost his place on the force when he hired another to look after his duties. Later he was reportedly involved in some trouble in Salt Lake City, and his local friends and acquaintances wondered what had gone wrong. When a

San Jose reporter interviewed him, Mortimer finally blew the whistle. The reporter wrote:

> Mortimer...said Rose, was for years his partner, and many were the "jobs" they put up successfully together. He said the robbery of C.L. Wiggins was planned by Rose, and when it was discovered that Mortimer was the robber, Rose, to screen himself, asked and was granted the work of capturing the accused. Mortimer says he met Rose at Belmont...and...suspecting that Rose desired to dissolve their co-partnership...made up his mind to come out ahead, and to that end he lured Rose to a lonely spot on the Stockton Rancho...and there, as he thought, finished Rose. Mortimer says that it was through a dread that he would blow on Rose that prevented the latter from afterwards prosecuting him.

Although the reporter commented that "among the thief-takers Mortimer is regarded as the very prince of liars," there seemed little reason to doubt his accusation. When Rose was later arrested as a suspect in a Utah train robbery, the charge gained more substance. In any case, with the chief prosecution witness gone, George Tyler, Mortimer's lawyer, was able to get him released on his own recognizance and a $1,000 bond. The Wiggins case was later dismissed.

Free again on the streets of San Francisco, Mortimer contended that he tried to find a job, but his past always got in the way. He claimed he was too weak from long confinement to do hard work, although obviously he had been working throughout his prison term. He was picked up once for having some stolen clothes in his room but was able to prove he was merely holding them for a friend.

After failing several "dipping," or pickpocket jobs, Mortimer finally got back his "touch" and soon was again knee-deep in crime. On the night of April 29, 1871, he stepped into Kate Dunn's Kearny Street saloon looking for whiskey and a woman. As midnight approached, he joined friends for a few drinks. When the bar closed everyone adjourned to a rear room, and the carousing continued.

Mortimer noticed a new girl who appeared to be tired and sick. In the back room he sat next to her and, after calling for drinks, learned her name was Carrie Spencer. She had recently arrived from Napa with a man who robbed and deserted her. She had only been working at Kate's for three days.

Mortimer took an interest in the girl, who was only twenty-two years old. Whoring was a bad business, he told her, and she was working in one of the worst dives in town. When he learned she had a baby, he reiterated his warning, advising her to find a place with a family in the country.

"Think of the life you are going to lead before your child," he said.

When she asked what he did for a living, Mortimer had to admit he was no better than she and had just been released from prison. "I'm a 'cross-man' and live by my wits and felony."

"Do you have a woman?" she asked.

"No," he shook his head.

"Would you take me for your woman?"

Mortimer replied that he would see, but in any case he would help her all he could. Although she had a room, Carrie asked to spend the night with him. He demurred. He had work to do, but he would call on her in the morning.

Returning at dawn from a burglary, Mortimer discovered Carrie had left her baby alone and spent the night with an ex-con who lived in Mortimer's lodging house. At breakfast he learned more about his new friend, including her infection with several venereal diseases—one in its worst form.

Carrie was desperate, sick, and broke, with few clothes and even less hope. She begged, "Charlie, help me—pity me! I don't know what to do or where to go. Help me, and I will devote the balance of my life to your happiness. You may find women better educated, but you will not find one who will be more true to you than I will be."

Mortimer wrote that the girl's plea touched him. Perhaps it did. He had been in the same boat, and knew what it was like to need a friend. He felt even more pity for the child. He agreed to take care of them both and nurse the woman back to health. After she had recovered, and if she felt the same way, they could go on from there. The fateful liaison was sealed.

True to his word, Mortimer put the baby in a boarding home while he nursed his new companion and consulted with several physicians. When he took her south to Santa Cruz for several months, she became ill again, but soon recovered under his steady attention, and they returned to San Francisco.

When they stopped to visit Carrie's baby they learned he had been lost for several weeks. Mortimer conducted a search and finally located the child at the police station. He said,

> I appealed to Chief Crowley, but when he learned that the child's mother was living with me, he would give neither Carrie nor me any satisfaction. He and others connected with the police department had sworn to "settle" me on some old scores. Crowley knew that by keeping the child out of our reach, that no matter where we went, we would be more or less likely to return to San Francisco in search of it. He was correct, for if we (more properly speaking I, for I truly believe I felt a warmer and more earnest desire to find the child than its mother did—he was a pretty boy two years old) had recovered the boy, I should have left the state that Fall and never returned to it.

Mortimer found a job for himself and his paramour on a farm outside Sacramento. Meanwhile, Carrie had stolen some money from a local hotel, and Mortimer was only able to resolve the situation by borrowing money from his employer to make restitution.

Mortimer and Carrie skipped out one night and made their way to the gold rush country. They stayed at a roadside inn in Calaveras County, but again Carrie robbed the house and caused more trouble. Finally the couple returned to Sacramento, where Carrie once more stole some money at a hotel. Mortimer could not get her to return the loot, and they barely made it aboard a riverboat before again being discovered.

"She will do most anything," Mortimer later lamented. "She has the nerve, but she has very little forethought—her caution is small."

When Mortimer took Carrie to visit her family at Healdsburg, they received a cool reception. Moving on, they stayed at several towns where Mortimer obtained work at various odd jobs. But it was always the same. While Mortimer was at work, Carrie was romping with boarders at the hotel. Time after time they were asked to leave. Mortimer finally gave up and started drinking. After a three-day drunk they returned to San Francisco in early January 1872.

Back in the bay city, Mortimer eagerly went to work. He sent Carrie to Nevada to look into a "speculation," while he investigated a "job" in Santa Cruz. Meanwhile, he needed money and went out into the streets and saloons "on the dip." He would strike up an acquaintance and, while walking on the street, would mysteriously acquire the man's watch and chain. He described a typical expedition:

> In a saloon I met a gent who had been indulging. I walked out with him....I showed him the rear of a house and told him it was my residence and invited him over. We went into the yard by the rear way, when he fell. I lifted him up very indignant, and told him I could never take a man before my family in that condition. I helped him up, but in doing so my hand accidentally slipped into his pocket and his purse stuck to my fingers. I could not shake it off till I put my hand into my own pocket. I sat him up against a wall, but in the act his watch and chain got tangled in my fingers, too. My friend took a nap and I took a walk.

By the time Carrie returned from Nevada, Mortimer had a nice nest egg set aside and they took a room on Montgomery Street. His other project was now set up. Mortimer met his partner, a man who used the alias of Folensbee, in Santa Cruz on January 31, 1872. The job they planned was a particularly daring one.

For some time Mortimer and Folensbee had been scheming to rob the Santa Cruz public treasury in the court house. A third party had been involved, but when he ducked out at the last minute the two thieves knew they must do the job that night lest their late partner "peach" on them. The men knew that county treasurer S.W. Blakely, who may have been involved in the crime, would be working late for several nights. Watching as others came and went, Mortimer and his ally were sure Blakely was alone when the treasurer prepared to leave around 10:00 P.M.

Blakely unlocked the front door, then turned back to extinguish the gas lights. Wearing masks, Mortimer and Folensbee quickly followed him in. In a moment Folensbee had grabbed the official's arms, while Mortimer pressed a pistol to his head and cocked it. "I wished Blakely to hear the 'music' of the click of the pistol," Mortimer later said, "to convince him we meant business."

They forced Blakely to open the vault door and, as Mortimer kept watch, his partner packed up all the gold they could carry. Working quickly, the robbers securely tied Blakely and locked him in the vault, then left the building and made their way to the outskirts of town. Quickly, they "whacked up" (divided) and buried much of their loot. Their haul reportedly totaled over $16,000.

Mortimer had noticed lately that Carrie was becoming increasingly possessive and there seemed to be little he could do to assuage her jealousy. When he returned to San Francisco she gave him a grilling, insisting he should have returned home sooner.

"If it was only an hour or so you could have come home if you care for me," she wailed. "I understand you perfectly. Well, you have some woman, but you will find no truer one than I am to you."

"It is a very bad habit of yours," shrugged Mortimer, "to be dreaming while you are awake. Please give us a rest." He went to sleep with Carrie still complaining in his ear.

Although Mortimer would often use Carrie as a lure for potential victims and as a diversion during pickpocket excursions in crowds, he always believed she was temperamentally unqualified for the actual "dipping." After helping Mortimer and some friends work the crowds at the cornerstone-laying ceremony of the new city hall on February 22, 1872, Carrie was impatient to go out on her own.

She had ventured out alone several days prior to the ceremony, with near disastrous results. She picked up a man called "Yank" and managed to steal his watch when they went for a stroll. When she showed the watch to Mortimer, he lectured her sternly. "Carrie, you are not qualified for this work. Suppose Yank had followed you home and obtained an officer. He would have found the watch and taken you to the station house. I would have been taken down too, instead of remaining free to help you. Under no circumstances bring any property that's not honestly got into the house we are living in."

Carrie was defiant. "Why don't you say what you think. You think I am 'green,' and that I have not got nerve."

Mortimer shook his head. He reproved her and told her how to behave and what to say in case she was ever caught. But Carrie was sure she had all the answers. An old-time thief called Uncle Bill was living with them at the time, and while Mortimer was away on a trip, Carrie asked him a favor. "Uncle Bill, whenever you go out on the 'dip' I do wish you would take me along with you. I want to see if I can't learn to do that kind of business."

"Very well," the old man responded, "if Charlie don't object and the 'push' [crowd] is a proper one for a woman to be in."

"We will keep Charlie in ignorance of our little arrangement," she smiled, "until such time as I shall become an expert...then we will give him a surprise."

But Uncle Bill could see what was happening. "Carrie, you must at all times look to Charlie for advice. When you commence pulling the opposite way from him, he will become dissatisfied and everything is sure to go wrong. You should bear in mind that what he knows it took him years to learn and for some of his knowledge he paid dearly."

Carrie pouted. "Yes, I know all this, but sometimes when Charlie gets a little angry with me, he tells me I am dull and stupid and I want to convince him to the contrary."

"Very well, the quickest and most sure way for you to accomplish that is to listen to his advice."

Soon Carrie insisted on accompanying Uncle Bill on a "dipping" expedition at a funeral. Yank spotted her on a street cor-

California State Library

Mortimer and his friends were actively picking pockets during the cornerstone-laying celebration for the new San Francisco City Hall in 1872.

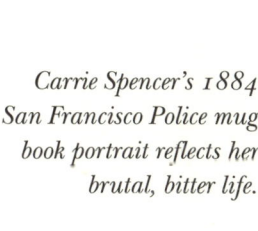

Carrie Spencer's 1884 San Francisco Police mug book portrait reflects her brutal, bitter life.

Special Collections, Henry Madden Library, California State University, Fresno

ner and tried to make a citizen's arrest. Uncle Bill drove him off, threatening to cane him, but they noticed he followed them on the opposite side of the street.

Dodging up an alley, Uncle Bill ran and got Mortimer, who advised Carrie to get on the horse cars and ride as far as they would take her. Mortimer followed and watched Yank accost them at the end of the line, showing a warrant for Carrie's arrest. Running up, Mortimer asked what was going on. As Mortimer read the warrant, Yank insisted he help in the arrest, but Mortimer had other ideas.

"Yes, I will assist you," said Mortimer. "It's my opinion you are an impostor, a pimp, and want to kidnap this lady. I think these papers are like yourself—frauds."

When Yank grabbed Carrie's arm, Mortimer hit him hard and knocked him down. As Yank sprinted off, the three thieves took a roundabout route to their rooms and hoped they had seen the last of him. Mortimer tried to get Carrie to return the watch as a means of smoothing out a bad situation, but she stubbornly refused.

Some weeks later Mortimer became worried when Carrie was not home by late evening. He went down to city hall and called through the sidewalk gratings that opened into the police cells below. Carrie answered. Yank had caught her on Dupont Street and had her arrested. After coaching her on what to do and say, Mortimer told her he would send a lawyer in the morning.

When Yank's case didn't hold up in police court, Carrie was released to ponder the validity of her lover's sage advice. She was soon off to prove herself again, however, and managed to steal the watch of a local street inspector named Uhrig.

One day in May 1872 Mortimer left Carrie in a Pinckney Alley deadfall while he attended to some business. Later he was returning by way of Dupont Street and stopped for a drink in Owen Gafney's saloon. A tipsy French woman came in and sat down near him. Gafney introduced her as Caroline Prenel, and after talking with her for a time Mortimer became convinced she had money. She asked him to accompany her home, where they had more to drink. By the time they slipped into bed, Caroline was so plastered she quickly passed out.

Easing himself out of bed, Mortimer quickly searched the rooms, but could find no cash. He dressed and returned to pick up Carrie and told her where he had been, neglecting to mention going to bed with the woman. Carrie was immediately jealous and accused him of being unfaithful. Trying to pacify her, he said Caroline was about her size and they might be able to find some dresses there she would like. They went directly to Caroline Prenel's house, slipped inside, and locked the door behind them.

When Mortimer showed Carrie the sleeping woman, she suddenly turned on him. "Charlie, you lie if you say you have not been with that bitch."

Mortimer tried to calm her down, but she began talking louder and louder. Afraid someone would hear them, Mortimer attempted to leave, but Carrie took the key from the door. When Mortimer poured himself a drink, the frenzied woman went over to the bed.

"You bitch! You whore!" she shouted.

That roused Caroline, but being on the edge of the mattress she fell off head first, her legs remaining on the bed. The furious Carrie put her foot on the woman's neck with all her weight behind it. Mortimer said he thought someone was at the back door and a few moments later someone tried the front door.

Alarmed, Carrie now wanted to leave. She unlocked the door and looked outside. Mortimer went over to lift Caroline back into bed, but Carrie snarled, "Let the bitch lay!" A moment later the two quickly left the house and walked up Washington Street.

They strolled along Kearny Street beside the plaza, and Mortimer noticed several police detectives talking in front of city hall. Thinking they might need an alibi in case someone else walked into the unlocked Prenel house and looted the place, Mortimer and Carrie walked across the street and talked for a few minutes to detectives John Coffee, Billy Jones, and several others. When they continued their walk, Carrie insisted on returning to Prenel's to see what she could find for herself.

A heavy fog swirled through the streets. Dawn would break in just a few hours. Mortimer was furious and tired, and after an argument he sat down on a door stoop and tried to talk some sense into his paramour. When she insisted on having her way, he told her to go ahead herself and took a big drink from his whiskey flask. Carrie went down the street, but she quickly returned to find Mortimer fast asleep where he sat.

He woke up at daybreak. Fog still filled the streets as they walked to their rooms and fixed breakfast. Later in the day, Mortimer was reading the paper when Carrie asked, "What do you think of my jewelry?"

Mortimer looked up. "What jewelry?"

"Where are your eyes—look at my ears."

"Where did you get them?" he returned, his eyes narrowing. "Yes, I know, damned if you didn't take that woman's rings from her ears."

"Yes, and the ring off her finger. You call me dull and stupid, but I take notice and have an eye for business."

That evening Mortimer went to a grocer's for some beer and bought a paper. He was startled to see an account of Caroline Prenel's death, and he hurried home to beg Carrie to dispose of her jewelry. She refused.

On the first of June Mortimer took Carrie to an evening performance of the circus. Tired of sitting, he got up and went for a stroll. As usual his "fingers became entangled in a man's watch chain." Mortimer had made a bad move and he should have been more observant. The man was standing amid a group of friends who all worked at a local woolen mill. When the victim reached for his watch it was gone, and Mortimer was the only stranger in the group. An officer quickly had him in tow.

At the police station he pleaded guilty hoping nothing more serious would be brought up against him. When Carrie visited he noticed two detectives following her, and he was sure she was in trouble over one of her personal expeditions. Talking to Billy Jones later, Mortimer learned that street inspector Uhrig was after Carrie for the watch she stole.

Mortimer and his woman both wound up in jail, Carrie on

the Uhrig charge. She had dreaded being locked up. "You should have thought of that," observed Mortimer, "when you was taking the watch. You begin to see it is a dangerous business."

Henri Bec, a boyfriend of Caroline Prenel, had been arrested for her murder, and to Carrie's horror she now found herself jailed in the cell next to him. Talking to Carrie later, Mortimer found her quite distraught.

"Charlie, that man Bec is in the cell next to me and I have been talking to him. He is almost crazy. He said that he felt sure that the guilty party would be found out some time. When he said that I thought I would drop—that I would faint."

Mortimer received a sentence of three months in the county jail, and Carrie was moved there to await action of the grand jury. When the grand jury failed to act against her, she was released. Mortimer pleaded with her to get a position with a family to avoid any contact with officers until he got out. He managed to obtain a position for her, probably as a maid, with a friend named Blackwine and hoped she could behave herself at least until he was released. He should have known better. Before long he had the whole story.

Carrie remained with Blackwine for only a brief period, then she obtained another position. When she moved she took with her various items belonging to her former employer. Blackwine began following her, and she lost her new job after her employer overheard them arguing. On her next visit with Mortimer, he begged her to stop her petty pilfering and return Blackwine's property before she was in jail again.

"Well, I'll go," she grumbled, "but I hate to give anything back after he cost me my job yesterday. If I could have remained there for two or three weeks I could have got the run of the house. I could have slipped into Mrs. Wetzler's bedroom some night and got his and her watch and chain, and all the money I could have found—and he keeps his purse well-filled."

"Then what would you have done?" asked Mortimer.

"I would have got up and left the house."

"Yes, and you would have been arrested before sundown

next day. As soon as the detectives got a description of the woman, don't you know they would suspect you? They would then take your photograph to the lady and she would recognize it. They would then put a watch on the jail knowing you would come to see me sooner or later. Then you would go to San Quentin....You don't look ahead—you have no caution or forethought."

When Carrie mumbled about hiding her loot, then opening some doors and windows and going back to bed, Mortimer shook his head. "In that case the detectives could tell whether the windows had been opened from the inside or outside. At a glance they would see that it was done from the inside. At the next glance they would recognize you—then you would be doomed. Now take my advice and stop such work. I am going to try and turn over a new leaf when I get out of jail."

Carrie promised to give back Blackwine's property, but when she didn't return to the jail for several days Mortimer became concerned. Then, while reading the *Chronicle* one day he saw a brief dispatch from Oakland stating that Carrie and several others had been convicted of stealing three boxes of cigars from a saloon. Mortimer could only shake his head.

When his sentence ended on September 5, 1872, Mortimer lost no time catching a boat for Oakland. After paying Carrie's fine they were a little short of cash, so Mortimer pawned some jewelry he had acquired. Carrie also gave him a ring of Caroline Prenel's to pawn. He was glad to get rid of it. He had thought she had disposed of the jewelry some time ago.

The couple took a room at a hotel on Broadway, but Carrie quickly lapsed into her old tricks and stole a box and watch from their landlord. When she wouldn't return it after Mortimer begged her to do so, they had no choice. They packed up and took the boat for Sacramento.

In the capital city Mortimer met police detective Len Harris on the street. He had known the lawman when he was turnkey at San Quentin. Later in the day, when he saw Harris point him out on the street to another officer, he became worried.

Back at their room, Mortimer told Carrie of the incident and said it would be safer to move on. The state fair was due to open in a few days, however, and Carrie insisted on staying. After an argument Mortimer walked out, slamming the door as he left.

Like most alcoholics Mortimer needed little excuse to go on a binge. He spent the day in Sacramento saloons and was quite drunk when he returned to his room that evening. As he lay down on the bed Carrie told him he was full of whiskey.

"I know I am....You see, I am willing to acknowledge my faults."

"Yes," fumed Carrie, "go off and leave me in this house alone all day—shut up like a prisoner. You don't care so long as you are with your friends drinking and enjoying yourself. Yes, and if the truth was known, I'll bet you've been down among those damned fancy women...maybe to that house they call the 'Palace.'"

"For God's sake don't talk to me about going around the 'free and easy' women," Mortimer said. "The last place of that kind I was at is enough to last me for the balance of my life. There is not a time that I pass one of their houses—particularly if it is a small brick [house]—but that affair flashes across my mind. It comes to me in all its horrors...but I can't help it. I make a dive into the first place where whiskey is sold and take a drink or more. Oh God, if I could..."

Carrie kept up her assault until Mortimer finally went outside. By then it was 4:00 P.M. and he was still unsteady on his feet. In a few minutes Carrie joined him. They decided to go for a walk, Mortimer offering to take her any place she wished. Standing with Carrie on the balcony of the Mechanics House, where they were staying, he had earlier pointed out the saloon and grocery of Mary Gibson near the river and waterworks. They had talked about the place as a possible source of plunder. As they walked in that direction Carrie suggested they stop in and see what it looked like. Mortimer agreed, but he said he would go in first and she should then follow. That way people would not know they were acquainted.

Mortimer entered Gibson's, a one-story frame house built on poles above a slough, and was enjoying a drink at the bar when Carrie walked in. He invited her to drink with him and commented that she looked good enough to kiss.

"Yes," agreed Mary Gibson, "give the man a kiss. If you don't, I will." As Gibson moved toward him, Carrie quickly threw her arms around his neck and kissed him. Mortimer noted the jealous fire in her eyes. The three of them had several beers and the women seemed to get along well. Soon Gibson suggested they retire to a back room where they could be alone and talk.

As the three talked in the back room, Gibson frequently had to leave to tend her bar. Carrie said the woman had told her of having an expensive wardrobe and a nice bank account. She had also seen some gold. Mortimer was dubious until Gibson bragged of her belongings to both of them. "I have a wardrobe as full of as fine silk dresses as any lady in the city has got," she insisted.

When Gibson again left to tend bar, Mortimer wanted to leave. "This is one of the meanest places in the city. And did you see how dirty she is? Even if she does have what she says, we are going about this wrong. I'm going back to the room to get some sleep. If you want to stay, size up the place and let me know about it later."

"No," Carrie snapped, "you won't give me credit for anything. You're always leaving me alone in the room and I'm going to see what is here."

Afraid she would throw a tantrum and give away the whole situation, Mortimer stayed. Drunk as he was, he suddenly realized Carrie had encouraged his drinking all evening so she could have her way. His plan now was to leave as soon as he could, knowing Carrie would probably follow shortly. "I don't want it to be understood," Mortimer later wrote, "that I had any objection to Carrie getting Mrs. Gibson's money and dresses if she had any—but I did object to her lack of caution."

About 6:30 P.M., Mortimer finally found an excuse to leave. Outside he met a friend and suggested they go down the street for a drink. When his acquaintance insisted on going into Gibson's, Mortimer reluctantly followed him and soon had rejoined Carrie and their hostess.

After his friend had left, Carrie told Mortimer that they

were to have supper with Mrs. Gibson and spend the night. The three of them went to the spare bedroom and talked and finished their drinks while sitting on the beds.

A single candle lit the dark room. Soon Mortimer gave Carrie the high sign and said he was going outside to relieve himself. He left the room, then walked to the front door which he opened and closed. Retracing his steps he walked quietly down the hallway and was opening Gibson's bedroom door with a skeleton key when he heard the proprietor's voice.

"What are you doing? So that's your game?"

A moment later he heard Carrie cry out, "Charlie!"

Rushing into the spare room, Mortimer found Mrs. Gibson holding Carrie by the hair with one hand as she held her hand with the other. "Well, you began quarreling soon enough," he said.

"The damned bitch had her hand in my pocket," Gibson said.

"Let her go," suggested Mortimer, "let's talk the matter over."

When Gibson refused, Mortimer tried to grab her in a headlock, but she was too quick for him. Releasing Carrie, she flew at Mortimer, who grabbed a beer mug and smashed it into her forehead. As the mug broke, the woman fell into Mortimer, clawing at his face. She had hold of his whiskers as he pushed her violently away, and she fell heavily on the bed next to Carrie.

As he clutched his bleeding face, Mortimer told Carrie to lock the front door, which she did. Returning, she picked up the broken mug and struck the groaning Gibson several times with it. As Mortimer sat down on the opposite bed, Carrie suddenly took out a pen knife and began cutting Gibson's throat. In a moment she looked up from her bloody work.

"Now Charlie, don't you think I got any nerve?" She then brutally stamped her foot on the dead woman's neck and Mortimer followed suit. Suddenly, it was very quiet.

After robbing the body of some coins, the two entered Gibson's bedroom and packed dresses and other goods into a trunk. Making sure no one was in view outside, the pair quietly moved into the street carrying the trunk between them.

A friend of Gibson's discovered her body in the morning after she didn't respond to knocks on the door. At first investigators thought some Indians who had been camped behind the building had committed the murder. They had left that same morning, but were later located and exonerated. One of the investigating officers later wrote, "When found Mrs. Gibson lay on her right side, her head pointing to the east, the floor under her neck being covered with the blood that had flown from a terrible gash in the left side of the neck. There were several severe wounds on her face, one over the left eye, another across the bridge of the nose and two or three on the sides of her head."

Police Chief Matt Karcher put all his officers on the case, but detectives Len Harris and Nick Dole immediately suspected Mortimer. They had been watching him for several days, and Harris described him as one of the "worst men in the state." They had last seen him at two o'clock that morning in a saloon with his face all scratched up. He said he had been in a fight in a K Street saloon. Although the officers remembered he had been pretty much broke the previous day, now he had a purse full of money.

Calling at the Mechanics House, several officers picked up Carrie and took her to the police station. They also confiscated jewelry, dresses, and other goods they found in the room. Dole and Harris quickly found Mortimer standing on the corner of J and Second streets. He was freshly shaved and cleaned up. Arrested and lodged in the city prison, Mortimer was unaware that Carrie was also in custody.

The following day the detectives took Mortimer to see Mary Gibson's body at the undertaking rooms. Len Harris asked Mortimer if he knew the victim, and Mortimer replied that he knew she was a woman who lived on Jibboom Street. After several other questions, Harris lifted up Gibson's hand which clutched some whiskers.

"This tells the story, Charlie," the detective said.

"What is that?"

"That's your whiskers."

Sacramento police detective Leonard Harris arrested Mortimer for the Gibson murder. Harris was a turnkey at San Quentin when the two men first met.

California State Library

This faded portrait of Mortimer was taken after his arrest for the Gibson murder. It bears little resemblance to the handsome man of his first mug shot taken some ten years earlier.

Sacramento City Archives

"Oh my God, Len," Mortimer cried out, "don't say that. That's not my whiskers. So help me God it ain't."

Back at police headquarters Detective Harris and three other police officers subjected Mortimer to a vigorous questioning. He stuck to his story of an evening of drinking in various saloons, but he realized his situation was serious.

Several days passed before Mortimer discovered Carrie was also in custody. Their cells were close enough that they managed to communicate late at night, and they correlated their stories as best they could. Mortimer thought he had disposed of most of Gibson's property, but he learned Carrie had retrieved it and police had found it in their room. That news upset Mortimer, but he was determined to save Carrie if he could. One of them must be on the outside to work for the other. He would say he bought all the property and somehow make the story work.

When they appeared before the grand jury, Mortimer saw his lover for the first time since their arrest. While Mortimer was indicted, the jury took no action with Carrie; it was apparent the officers were making her promises in an attempt to break her down. Later they allowed her to visit Mortimer's cell and talk to him. He was chained to the wall and she could barely see him through the small window in the door.

On Thanksgiving morning, November 28, 1872, Carrie was allowed to visit him again. She looked ill and sad, and Mortimer confided that he had feelings of foreboding. "The truth is," he told her, "I sometimes imagine you are doing or trying to do something against me. Then the next moment I attribute these notions to weakness." Carrie quickly reassured him that she would never do anything against him—she wouldn't dare!

Mortimer got a welcome break from the chains of his Sacramento cell in late January 1873, when he went to testify at the trial of S.W. Blakely, the Santa Cruz treasurer Mortimer had robbed the previous year. Detectives had cast doubts on Blakely's story of the robbery, which investigators generally thought to have been an inside job involving him and the thieves. Accompanied by several officers, Mortimer journeyed to Santa Cruz by train and stagecoach. He spent several days testifying that he and an accomplice had committed the robbery and that Blakely was not involved.

At one point in the proceedings, Prosecutor Campbell mentioned that witness Mortimer had been indicted in San Francisco for the murder of Caroline Prenel. Newspapers had carried items about Mortimer and Carrie's being tied to the Prenel murder, but Mortimer had hoped it was just newspaper talk. Now he was worried. At the first opportunity he sought out his old attorney, George Tyler, who had also been summoned to Santa Cruz as a witness.

"Mr. Tyler," he began, "I wish you would explain matters to me—let me hear what you have heard or know of the Prenel indictment. I begin to suspect some villainous treachery."

"Why, don't you know what Carrie has been doing?"

"I have heard something," Mortimer continued, "but don't believe it. I want to hear it from you."

"Carrie testified at the Bec trial that you gave her the finger and ear rings [sic] the morning after the murder; that you was out all night; that you had done the murder."

"It can't be possible she has done that," blurted Mortimer. He was furious and horrified that she could turn on him with these lies after all they had been through together.

After returning to Sacramento, Mortimer talked to Carrie, who vigorously denied the stories. She had only told the officers what they wanted to hear so as to get all she could out of them.

At his trial, she promised, she would recant and stick to her previous testimony. Mortimer wanted desperately to believe her. That had to be her game—she could not turn on him. She could not tell such lies when she was so deeply involved herself. Still, he was so tormented he made several half-hearted attempts at suicide.

When the Gibson murder trial began on March 12, 1873, the Sixth District Court was jammed with spectators, many overflowing into the hallway. One observer said Mortimer, whom Sheriff Mike Bryte led into the courtroom, was white as marble from frequent bloodletting—his suicide attempts—and his long confinement. "He was utterly undemonstrable," noted the *Sacramento Daily Bee*, "only nodding in answer to the few questions put to him."

The trial, a procession of damning witnesses and evidence, lasted four days. When Carrie was called, all eyes turned toward the door that would reveal the woman who had shared her life with the most desperate criminal in California. The *Bee* reported, "It opened and a tall woman, tastefully dressed in black throughout, with black hat and plume, entered. Her hair was held up with a crimson, red velvet band...and a string of pearls circled her neck. She had on a broad, blue neck tie and a short veil drooped over her face. Mortimer looked at her, but evinced no emotion."

After being seated, Carrie was led through an extended account of the events surrounding the murder. Mortimer was aghast when she reported he had confessed the killing to her and had brought all the loot up to their room the night of the murder. A number of notes Mortimer had smuggled to Carrie instructing her what to say were also introduced as evidence. Mortimer listened in mounting agitation as she pounded the final nails in his coffin.

"Mortimer watched her closely," reported one account, "never taking his eyes off her, using every effort to catch her eye, but failed. He appeared very nervous and greatly excited. His countenance became very blanched and haggard; his eyes and hands twitching nervously."

The jury retired at 10:30 P.M., Saturday, March 15. They returned a guilty verdict in just thirty-five minutes. Samuel C. Denson, Mortimer's attorney, assured him there would be an appeal as the prisoner heard Judge T.B. Reardan set March 29 for sentencing.

Despite the outcome, Mortimer was greatly relieved the trial was over. "On Saturday night," noted the *Bee*, "after Mortimer, who is an excellent singer and knows a great many songs, was taken down to his cell, he sang them all and was in the best of humor."

In the silence of his cell, however, the prisoner was very bitter. Carrie had betrayed him. He was surprised when several days later she came to his cell, crying. She begged him for some way to undo what she had done, but Mortimer knew she was only trying to salve her conscience. He shook his head. The only way she could help, he counseled, was to say she lied and tell the truth. "I don't know what to do," she sobbed.

Sheriff Bryte informed Mortimer one day that Carrie was being removed to Alameda on an old charge and had asked to see him. Surprisingly, Mortimer agreed, and Carrie was taken to his cell-door wicket. They looked at each other in silence for a moment. "I am going away," Carrie murmured. "I hear that you are telling everything you know against me."

"No," he said, "not everything, but before long I intend to. Oh, Carrie, how could you have the heart to perjure yourself against me? I must now have the true facts brought to light."

"Then what will become of me? I could not help swearing in that way. If I didn't there would be charges made against me and I would go to state prison."

"That's a poor excuse for you to help take the life of a true friend....The officers feel sure that if I am guilty, you are, too, and want me to assist them in arriving at the truth and this I am going to do."

Carrie collapsed in a flood of tears. "No, Charlie, don't... don't, they will hang me or send me to prison for life."

"I did not think you were so selfish," Mortimer said. Carrie pleaded for his help, and he reminded her that if she had listened to him they would both now be free.

Composing herself, Carrie realized she would never see him again and wiped away her tears. "I have to go now. I have some sugar and coffee if you will take it." She disappeared and came back in a few minutes dressed to travel. Handing him the sugar and coffee, the tears again welled up in her eyes.

"They say I must go. Oh, Charlie, good-bye." Mortimer reached out and took her hand, but she quickly pulled it away. She said she didn't want the officers to see she was not afraid of him.

"That's alright," Mortimer responded, "they know better than that." Later he heard she had tearfully told jailer Bill Shearer how sorry she felt for him. Selfish, foolish Carrie was gone.

On the appointed day, Judge Reardan sentenced Mortimer to hang on May 15, 1873. Mortimer had recently begun writing his memoirs, a detailed reminiscence of his life that he would present to Sam Denson in lieu of a fee for his services. Several newspaper writers had snickered when Mortimer pleaded poverty. They recalled the buried Santa Cruz loot and money from other jobs that Mortimer had deposited in his "sand banks."

Across the continent a New England family had read several California news dispatches with disquieting interest. The four Flinn brothers supported themselves and their widowed mother with several cleaning and tailoring establishments in Lynn, Massachusetts. They had read several articles about the west coast murderer, Charles Mortimer, and were startled to see a reference to a tattoo on his arm reading "Flinn." They didn't want to believe he was their long-lost brother, but they couldn't ignore certain similarities, and they had received no letters from him in many years.

Frank, William, Thomas, and Edward Flinn decided to keep the news from their sister and mother who had thought Charlie was dead. After all, they still were not sure. Even if it were he, what would they do? The murderer was not the Charlie they had known. From all accounts the California killer was a brutal and conscienceless murderer sentenced to die for a heinous crime.

One day an excited William Flinn sought out his brothers with a letter from the West Coast. The California killer had written and asked for his help. The men no longer doubted Mortimer really was their brother, but the situation seemed so hopeless.

At 1:20 A.M. April 16, 1873, the bell rang at the yard door of the Sacramento County jail. Deputy Sheriff Manuel Cross jumped from his cot and pulled on his trousers. He checked his revolver as he walked to the door, then opened the steel-grated gate. Inexplicably, the barred, wooden outside door was ajar, and Cross cautiously pushed it open with the barrel of his pistol. Stepping into the walled yard, he looked around, but

Author's Collection

An early newspaper sketch of a California hanging. Mortimer feigned insanity to the end, refusing to speak to a minister or even his brother.

could see no one. The night was cool, and as he walked further into the yard he had the uneasy feeling that someone was watching him. Still, he could see nothing.

Turning to retrace his steps, the jailer was startled to see a man standing near the door pointing a pistol at him. The figure was bareheaded and in his stocking feet. Quickly raising his revolver, the deputy fired, hitting the man in the chest and staggering him against the wall. As the man fell, his pistol discharged, but the shot went wild. Cross quickly fired again, the bullet crashing into the man's mouth and taking out several teeth.

In a haze of gunsmoke, the bloody figure lurched to his feet and plunged through the door with Cross in close pursuit. The man ran toward the cell block as the deputy again leveled his pistol, but the weapon only snapped without firing. Running through the cell block, grunting in his death agonies, the man finally sprawled face down in front of Mortimer's cell. With a few gasps, he was dead. Mortimer looked on in horror from the shadows of his cell. He did not know what was going on.

An examination of the body disclosed various personal effects, along with a slip of paper on which was written "W.F. Flinn." Investigators recalled Mortimer's tattoo and noticed the close resemblance between Mortimer and the dead intruder. Other personal items were discovered in a building adjoining the jail where the intruder had climbed over the wall. Lawmen found the man's hotel room, where a carpet bag contained an advertisement for the Flinn brothers' business in Massachusetts. The officers stared at each other incredulously. The dead man was undoubtedly William Flinn, Mortimer's brother!

During the day Mortimer was told what happened and that it was his brother who had been killed. Newspapers insisted Mortimer had been involved in his brother's plot to rescue him, but Mortimer sheds no light on it in his memoirs. Perhaps it was too painful to reveal he had instigated his brother's death. Taken to the morgue, Mortimer examined the corpse closely as the terrible truth slowly enveloped him. He later wrote, "I found the end of the finger to the first joint bent over just as it was eighteen years ago. There was no longer any doubt in my mind. There lay my dead brother cold in death. His devoted, brotherly affection had not cooled after an absence of sixteen years. He had sacrificed his life in trying to liberate me."

An investigation disclosed Flinn had been in town for over a week trying to find some way to aid his doomed brother. Using the assumed name of Williams, he had met with Mortimer's lawyers and offered to help in any way he could, but there was nothing he could do. With the execution date but a month off, the only means of eliminating the shame of his brother's situation was to take a terrible chance, and it had failed.

Mortimer was visibly affected after viewing his brother's corpse at the morgue. Perhaps he was finally realizing that he had not only ruined his own life, but his family's, also. He asked for a lock of hair, and when the body was photographed for identification, the condemned man begged for a print. Back at the jail he retreated to the recesses of his cell, where he finished the remaining pages of his memoir.

In Massachusetts, the Flinn family was horrified to receive news of William's death. After the shock had subsided, they realized no blame could be placed on the Sacramento officers and concentrated on doing what they could for Charlie. In a letter indicating Mortimer was now corresponding with his family, Thomas Flinn wrote to Sam Denson on April 27, 1873:

> Mr. Denson—Dear Sir:
> My brother speaks of you as a friend, so shall you be a friend of mine; not a friend today and enemy to-morrow, but a friend for life; and it shall be as a brother's friend, and as you have seen some of that friendship it will show to you whether it is true or not. Enclosed you will find some pictures of my mother, sister and myself, Please give them to my dear brother, Charles. I will write again. May God bless you. You will always have our prayers. I remain your friend till death.
>
> THOMAS H. FLINN,
> 193 Washington Street,
> Lynn, Massachusetts

Frank Flinn arrived in Sacramento on May 10. As he stepped off the overland train, the tragedy that had overwhelmed his family was evident in his haggard and drawn features. After obtaining a hotel room he immediately proceeded to the county jail, where he introduced himself and asked to see the doomed prisoner. Jailer Bill Shearer led him down the corridor to Mortimer's cell.

For some days Mortimer had been behaving strangely. In the past he had feigned insanity and now he seemed to be playing the same game. Opening the cell door, Shearer said, "Mortimer, here is your brother Frank who just arrived from home and wishes to speak with you."

Mortimer didn't look up. He was sitting on his bunk rocking back and forth while moaning. Before him, the photo of his dead brother was nestled on his folded coat in the midst of a bouquet of flowers. From time to time he seemed to be shooing imaginary flies from his makeshift shrine.

As Frank eagerly grabbed his brother's hand, Mortimer looked up with blank indifference.

"Charlie, I have come to see you. Don't you recognize me? I am your brother Frank."

Mortimer ignored him and went back to rocking and moaning. His brother, obviously very much affected by the meeting, broke down and threw himself across the bunk. Seizing the intruder, Mortimer hurled him against the cell door, then went back to his rocking motion. Picking himself up, Frank again approached the bunk, but Mortimer ignored him. Shock and disbelief showing on his haggard face, he left and returned to his hotel room.

That evening Governor Newton Booth visited Mortimer with Dr. Shurtleff, a physician from the state asylum at Stockton. During a previous examination it had been agreed he was putting on an act. The asylum physician was in accord. When Frank was asked if he thought Mortimer was insane, he shook his head.

"I would rather see the rope around his neck than have him attempt any such villainous trickery at this hour. I believe his mind has given way and if he is hopelessly insane it were better for all. I cannot believe he is playing idiocy."

If he was indeed feigning insanity, Mortimer played it to the end. Despite the pleadings of the officers, he refused to see his brother or speak to any of the ministers and others who attended him in his last minutes. At noon on May 15, 1873, he walked stoically up the gallows steps in the jail courtyard. As hundreds watched from the jailyard and surrounding buildings, he dropped silently through the trap into eternity. Sane, or insane, one of California's deadliest desperadoes had died as he had lived—violently.

Carrie's Alameda burglary charge was lessened to petty larceny, and she managed to evade any serious charges from Mortimer's revelations. She had saved her life but not her soul. For a time she operated a bordello in Sacramento, but by early 1874 she was back in San Francisco. She was before the police court in May for stealing from a patron in a Dupont Street whorehouse where she lived, but was acquitted for lack of evidence. In January 1876 she was arrested for drunkenness and the following June fined for vulgar language. "She got to be a regular street-walker," noted policeman Edward Byram in his journal. "May 1, 1877, with Mary Ann Carr [she] was arrested on the street for disorderly conduct and was sent to the county jail for 60 days." Her final fate is unknown.

Both Charles' and William Flinn's bodies were released to Frank Flinn, who returned with them to Massachusetts. The local press makes no mention of Frank's arrival with his tragic brothers. Nor does it note any funeral arrangements. The *Lynn Semi-Weekly Reporter* of April 30, 1873, reprinted much of the story, but the family apparently had quietly asked the other local newspapers not to mention their troubles. Although the family's avowed purpose was to inter the bodies in the Flinn plot at Lynn's Pine Grove Cemetery, they apparently had second thoughts. Cemetery records account for all of the Flinn family but Thomas and Charles. William is there, but no Charlie Mortimer. The disposition of his body is a mystery.

Author's Collection

This portrait of Procopio could be found in many California police mug books during the 1870s.

3 THE
NEPHEW OF JOAQUIN MURRIETA: PROCOPIO

1842–1892(?)

Many outlaws terrorized California in the nineteenth century. While Tiburcio Vasquez, Dick Fellows, Black Bart, and Joaquin Murrieta are legendary, others are lost to all but a few dedicated outlaw researchers. One such badman, a nephew of the notorious Murrieta, cut a trail of robbery and murder across southern California, only to die mysteriously in Mexico.

Tomás Procopio Bustamante was born about 1842 and raised near San Jose de Guadalupe in Sonora, Mexico. His mother, Vicenta, was an older sister of Joaquin Murrieta and had married at an early age. Procopio was only a few years old when Indians killed his father, Tomás Bustamante, while he was driving the stage between Ures and Hermosillo. Seeking safety from the marauding Indians, Vicenta took Procopio to Guadalupe, where they lived with Tomás's family.

Procopio's uncle, Joaquin Murrieta, left his native village in Sonora in 1849 and traveled north to California during the gold rush. His wife, Rosa, and other members of his family accompanied him on the trip. Besides mining and gambling for a time in the California foothills, Joaquin and a brother established a ranch in Niles Canyon, in Alameda County. He returned to Mexico in 1852 and gathered another group of friends and relatives. That party included his widowed sister, Vicenta, and her young son, Procopio. Leaving some of the group in Los Angeles, Joaquin returned to his Alameda ranch, where his sister and nephew took up residence with Rosa.

Earlier, Joaquin Murrieta and his wife had been assaulted in the mining country, and he had killed several of his American attackers. That was only a few years after the Mexican War, a time of much white prejudice against Mexicans and native Californians who arrived early in the gold rush, were good miners, and often appropriated the best claims. Contemporary newspapers are full of clashes between Americans and Hispaños, and no doubt Murrieta endured some cruel experiences.

Driven from the mines, Murrieta took up driving wild horses and rustled stock to Mexico. By early 1853 he had also evolved into a bandit with a well-organized gang that made bloody raids throughout central California. Responding to numerous calls for help in the mining country, the California legislature authorized a unit of California Rangers to track down Murrieta and break up his gang. Commanded by Captain Harry Love, the rangers finally located some of Murrieta's men camped on the west side of what is now Fresno County. On the morning of July 25, 1853, the rangers clashed with the outlaws at Cantua Creek, gunning down or capturing about six of them. The rangers killed a man identified as Murrieta, cut off his head, and took it back to the settlements. Rewards were paid and the Murrieta gang was history.

Evidence suggests that was indeed the fate of Murrieta and his gang. Although many people recognized the head as it was displayed over the years, doubters questioned Murrieta's death. Still, they could not answer one question: if Murrieta were alive, where was he? He had disappeared after the fight on Cantua Creek and was never heard from again. Doubters insisted he had simply returned to old Mexico, but they never offered any proof.

Over a century later, historian Frank Latta thought he found the answer. Beginning in the 1920s, he interviewed family members and survivors of the outlaw gang and pieced together a strange story. Joaquin had not been at the Cantua Creek fight—another member of his gang had been killed and beheaded instead. That theory was already well-worn, but Latta had more.

He claimed Joaquin had arrived following the fight and, after helping bury the dead, left to visit relatives in Monterey. Later, he began the long ride home with a companion. On the way a sheriff's posse mistook them for other outlaws, and Joaquin and his friend had to race for their lives. Murrieta was shot in the leg and his horse killed. Riding double with his companion, he lost a lot of blood. By the time they reached Niles Canyon, Joaquin was barely alive.

The bandit chieftain did not want the Americans to know they had killed him, and he made his family promise to bury him inside his home so there would be no outside grave. His family complied. Young Procopio held hands with his mother as his uncle was buried, the grave tamped down, and the furniture replaced in the room. Later Vicenta told her son of his outlaw uncle.

Latta's story has many holes, too many to detail here, but Procopio's family handed down the story of the burial in the Niles Canyon home, and it would seem that someone was buried there. Procopio was told, and apparently always believed, that his uncle was in that lonely, secret grave.

Sometime in early 1854, Vicenta married Francisco Valenzuela, a miner, packer, and sometime member of Murrieta's gang. The couple had two daughters, but the union was not a happy one. The Valenzuelas moved to Los Angeles where Procopio, by then a teenager, started running with a bad crowd. The family undoubtedly lived in Sonora Town, a cluster of old adobes where the Hispaños of the area gathered. Mexican culture and a communal, familial feeling existed there, but it was also a place of poverty, crime, and segregation. Although three-quarters of the Los Angeles population was Hispanic, most were poor or transient. Sonora Town early became the tough district where vice and saloons flourished.

Procopio did not get along with his stepfather, but whether that was a result of his Sonora Town companions or more personal conflicts is unknown. Eventually Valenzuela took the two girls and moved away. Vicenta apparently returned to her old home in Niles Canyon, where Procopio visited her when it was convenient.

Crime was rampant in southern California. The *Los Angeles Star* carried frequent articles complaining of bands of stolen animals being driven north through the mountain passes into the great San Joaquin Valley. Procopio was probably involved in such raids. Many Mexicans and Californios resented the Americans who had taken over California, invalidated many of the large Mexican land grants, and otherwise changed their status, culture, and ways. To a Mexican vaquero with little property who needed some cantina money, it was easy to justify taking some horses or cattle from the hated "gringos."

In early March 1862 Procopio was indicted in Los Angeles for grand larceny along with a pal named Antonio Rodriguez. The *Star* reported on March 15 that the Court of Sessions had convicted Rodriguez and sentenced him to ten years in prison, while Procopio's hearing had been continued until the next term. Apparently the young horse thief was released on bail and disappeared.

Before the year was out, however, Procopio had become a suspect in the murder of John Rains, proprietor of the large Cucamonga Ranch in San Bernardino County. On the morning of November 17, 1862, Rains hitched up his wagon and headed for Los Angeles to transact some business. When his horses returned home several days later and friends discovered he had not arrived at his destination, a search was quickly instituted. On November 29, the *Los Angeles Star* announced the news that everyone expected:

> Yesterday the body of Mr. Rains was discovered. It was lying about four hundred yards from the main road, in a cactus patch. The body gave evidence that the unfortunate gentleman had been lassoed, dragged from his wagon by the right arm which was torn from the socket, and the flesh mangled from the elbow to the wrist; he had been shot twice in the

back, also in the left breast and in the right side. His clothes were torn off him and he lost one boot in the struggle.

The brutal murder sent shock waves throughout southern California. Rains, a stockman, former Indian agent, vineyardist, and one-time candidate for sheriff and state senator, was quite popular and had married into the prominent Williams family of the Rancho del Chino. Although considered wealthy, Rains was heavily in debt and many people coveted the property he had acquired by marriage. Robert Carlisle, a brother-in-law of Rains, quickly offered a reward and took charge of rounding up suspects to aid the sheriff.

By early December investigators had isolated several suspects. In a letter to a friend in San Diego, Los Angeles Judge Benjamin Hayes gave some details of the manhunt:

> We are now on the track of [Manuel] Cerradel who is believed to be still near the old mission. The best information we can get of Procopio and [Tal] Juanito is that they are near the San Francisquito Canyon on the Tejon Road.
>
> Carlisle is now in this city. Tomorrow he goes to the Monte with a warrant for the arrest of John Moirel of the Mission Viejo. The warrant grows out of his conduct a few nights since when Officer Trafford attempted to arrest Cerradel at his home. Moirel is supposed to have been harboring these scoundrels.

By mid-February 1863 Manuel Cerradel had been arrested. The *Star* reported the suspect had smallpox and believed he would die. That and other threats prompted him to identify Rains's murderers, and parties went out to arrest them. When one Louis Sanchez was found in San Gabriel Canyon, he was taken before Cerradel, who identified him as one of the murderers. In a letter dated March 8, 1863, Bob Carlisle listed further developments, "Well, we have got some of the murderers of John Rains. Manuel Cerradel, one Tal Eugenio, and one who calls himself Louis Sanchez, or better known per el Molacho. The bal [balance] are Procopio Bustamente, Jesus Asteanes, and one 'Tal Juanito.' Cerradel, being the first caught says that Don Ramon Carrillo paid him $500 to do the deed. Cerradel denies being one of the party, but says Procopio told him all about it."

Cerradel's confession and other information indicate the perpetrators had carefully planned the assassination. An Indian boy stole Rains's pistols so that on the day of his fateful journey he was armed with only a derringer. The *Star* reported, "It appears Mr. Rains was met on the road by five men, whose names are given. One of them asked Rains where he was going, and he replied, 'to town,' to which the assassin replied, 'I think not. We have got you now.' Mr. Rains drew his derringer and fired, striking the assassin when stepping out of the wagon. He was fired on by the others. He was lassoed, being still able to make resistance, and finally the body was disposed of."

Of all the suspects, Cerradel was the only one convicted, and not for the murder of Rains, but for an assault on the officer who arrested him. On December 9, 1863, Cerradel was being taken aboard ship for the trip to San Quentin. While a tugboat was taking the sheriff and his prisoner to the steamer *Senator*, vigilantes surprised them, lynched Cerradel, weighted his body down with rocks, and heaved it overboard.

Although a principal suspect, Procopio was never apprehended for the Rains murder. Amid so much talk of lynching, he and his pals must have been terrified. With visions of their lynched *compañero* burned into their minds, Procopio and several companions headed north through the Soledad Canyon and on to the Mojave Desert. Alameda County Sheriff Harry Morse's later recollection that the outlaws took a herd of stolen horses with them might be true, for the *Star* frequently ran notices of stolen stock during that period.

Procopio must have been out of the area by the first of the year, making his way up through the San Joaquin Valley. Rains's killers were never brought to justice, but rumors insisted that white men—notably Bob Carlisle—were behind the plot. Carlisle died a few years later in a desperate saloon shootout with the King brothers, prominent Los Angeles lawyers and lawmen.

Procopio was riding the outlaw trail now and not looking back. He took up rustling, operating out of the Livermore Valley, a notorious outlaw hangout bordering his old home in Niles Canyon. Two of his associates were Chano, or "Chino," Ortega and Narcisso Bojorques, both tough characters with sordid pasts. Harry Morse, who knew all three well and years later wrote about them, described Bojorques as "a magnificent-looking Mexican, about nineteen years of age, five feet ten inches high, very light complexion, large, Roman nose [and] hair black as night." Morse merely referred to Ortega as "a great, swarthy-looking Mexican."

Originally from New York, Harry Morse went to the West Coast as a boy in gold rush days. After various business ventures, he was elected sheriff of Alameda County in 1863 and had numerous encounters with the many outlaws infesting the area. Procopio, he said, "was six feet tall, slim, a handsome face, brown-gray eyes, brown hair, and, in general appearance looked more like an American than a Mexican. A close observer, however, would soon detect the devilish look in the eyes of the Mexican desperado as he swaggered about among his fellows. Procopio...was cool, cunning and deceitful."

In 1863 Procopio became a suspect in another brutal murder. Aaron Golding lived on his ranch in Corral Hollow, some miles south of the Livermore Valley. On the evening of January 29, 1863, Golding, his wife, a young boy living with them, and their Mexican vaquero were murdered and their bodies burned when their ranch house was torched. The crime was fearful—even the barn and some animals were destroyed.

Various motives were ascribed to what the *Stockton Independent* called "one of the most horrible and barbarous outrages ever recorded in California's annals of crime." Money was never considered an incentive for the murders as most people knew Golding had little. Newspapers said, however, that Mrs. Golding, a Mexican woman, had formerly lived with a member of Joaquin Murrieta's old band in Tulare County, where Golding had met her. Also, many native Californios were still extremely bitter over the inroads of Americans into Mexican rights and property in California. Local Mexicans who had long trapped wild horses on the plains of the San Joaquin may well have resented Golding's horse trap corrals.

Procopio, Ortega, and Bojorques were principal suspects because Ortega was known to have quarreled with Golding over payment of some wages. Neighbors had also seen them in the area at the time. Officers who picked up Ortega at his ranch some thirty miles from the Golding property reported meeting several escaped convicts in the wild country they traversed. "There is a band of daredevils infesting that section of the country," they said, "that it will take at least twenty active and well-armed men to capture."

As if to underscore the officers' reports, two other murders occurred in the Livermore Valley a few days after the Golding slaughter. Also, a gang rape took place at a lonely ranch in the area, while an armed group of riders galloped into Mission San Jose and, according to one newspaper, "romped about the streets for a short time, and then rode off."

Despite Harry Morse's assertion that it was "morally certain that these three fiends were guilty," a preliminary examination disclosed little in the way of hard evidence against Procopio and his two pals, and they were released. Ortega disappeared and rumors said he went to Mexico. Procopio decided it was a good time to visit some friends to the south. A brief item telegraphed from Firebaugh's Ferry on April 5, 1863, to the San Francisco *Alta California* chronicled his visit: "Juanito, one of the men concerned in the murder of John Rains, near Los Angeles, was mortally wounded near this place yesterday evening. He was trying to steal a horse belonging to an Indian, and shot at the Indian, wounding another man named Nuenes. The Indian then shot Juanito three times, also cut him severely. Both Nuenes and Juanito are mortally wounded. Procopio, another of Rains' murderers, is in the vicinity."

When Procopio returned to the Livermore area, his rustling proclivities soon caught up with him. Along with Bojorques and a young native Californian, he ran off a herd of cattle belonging to an Alameda County rancher named Pope. After investigating the incident, Pope learned Procopio and several others had driven the stolen animals

Narcisso Bojorques was a cattle rustling pal of Procopio's in old Alameda County.

Top: Overland Monthly, *August 1888. Bottom: Los Angeles Public Library Collection*

Young Procopio was running in bad company in the early 1860s and was a principal suspect in the murder of rancher John Rains, shown here about the time of his death.

to Alvarado and were trying to sell them to a local butcher.

San Leandro Constable O.B. Wood obtained warrants for their arrests and rode to Alvarado on July 9, 1863. The butcher knew Procopio's character and agreed to let the officer hide in his shop. When the rustler appeared he stepped into a back room to be paid, and Wood got the drop on him. Feigning surprise and fear, Procopio threw up his hands and insisted he was unarmed. A newspaper reported what happened next as Wood fumbled for his handcuffs: "Wood put back his pistol when quick as thought Procopio drew and shot Wood through the arm and escaped in the excitement. He was followed by a posse of citizens and his further escape across the bridge was cut off. But he was equal to the emergency, and taking his pistol in his mouth he plunged into the river and swam across. He then ran for the salt marsh, closely followed by the citizens. Finding that they gained on him he turned at bay and fired at them, wounding a constable." One wonders about either the strength of Procopio's jaws, or the size of the pistol he carried in his mouth, but most accounts of the incident note this detail. Regardless, the posse apprehended Procopio.

Jailed along with Bojorques and their other confederate, Procopio used the alias of Tomas Rodundo and assumed all the blame for the crime. He was quickly convicted of grand larceny and sentenced to nine years in prison. He arrived at San Quentin on September 4, 1863. The prison register describes Procopio—Number 2603—as twenty-one years old, a laborer, five-feet, eleven-and-three-quarters inches tall, and dark complected with hazel eyes and brown hair.

San Quentin had changed a great deal since the mid-1850s. The wall surrounding the prison grounds needed constant repair because inferior bricks and sea water mortar had taken their toll. Besides The Stones, the prison had two other buildings housing cell blocks, a two-story brick office building, a tailor shop, mess hall, and kitchen. Next to those buildings were the blacksmith, cooper, and carpenter shops. The prison also had a separate jail with dark cells and dungeons, and a laundry.

The offices and sleeping quarters of the prison staff were in a brick building outside the walls, along with various other outbuildings. The prison had five small brick guard posts, three of which had artillery pieces. Seven convicts had died and some thirty-two had been wounded during a mass escape attempt the previous year, but for now things seemed quiet.

Procopio's Los Angeles pal, Antonio Rodriguez, had been pardoned in May, but he undoubtedly met other friends and acquaintances in prison. The prison population was about seventeen percent Hispanic then, with most of those prisoners in for rustling or other grand larceny charges.

Although most Mexicans and native Californians considered the criminal justice system unfair to them, Procopio found that in prison, everyone was at least equal. Flogging, confinement in dark cells or dungeons, and high-pressure hosing on naked and bound convicts were punishments common to all San Quentin inmates. Talking at the dinner table could get a man twelve lashes, while an escape attempt might net up to 150. Prisoners also sometimes wore cross-irons and heavy chains as punishment.

Another bloody escape attempt occurred in April 1864, but it was one of the last such mass efforts. The following year the famous gray-and-black-striped uniforms were introduced, and the prison had a more established routine. Most of the convicts labored inside now, contractors paying for their services on a bid basis—usually influenced by politics.

In 1867 Procopio became acquainted with an old San Quentin alumnus who had recently been readmitted. Tiburcio Vasquez was from a respectable Monterey family, but had turned to crime at an early age. He had successfully escaped from prison once and made several other attempts, and the older inmates respected him as a brave and desperate man. When Vasquez was discharged on June 4, 1870, he undoubtedly told Procopio to look him up when he was released. Vasquez had in mind assembling a gang of stage robbers.

Procopio's long confinement finally ended. With time off for good behavior he was released on March 1, 1871. As he stepped outside the prison and headed for the San Francisco boat, Procopio was no longer the boy who had entered the grim walls so long ago. San Quentin was little more than an institution of higher learning for criminals. He had heard all the stories and learned all the tricks of the trade. Far from being rehabilitated, he was ready for more prestigious projects now, and a newspaper colorfully stated that "he returned to his old practices as a dog to his vomit."

Returning to the Livermore Valley, Procopio heard that his old pal Narcisso Bojorques had been chased from the area by Sheriff Harry Morse, only to be killed later in the gold rush country. Undeterred by the news, Procopio promptly reverted to his old ways.

On March 31, 1871, Procopio and a *compañero* stole a cow from John Arnett's ranch in the Sunol Valley. Arnett and several officers quickly tracked them to the saloon of one Juan Camargo, a notorious fence. There they found the head and horns of the missing animal and arrested Camargo. That night a party of masked men tied up the constable and hauled Camargo out into the night. They jerked him up and down by his neck until he identified Procopio and his partner as the rustlers. The men released Camargo, and lawmen pursued the outlaws, but by then they had scattered and disappeared.

Tracking Procopio now becomes a game of educated guesses made by assembling scraps of information from newspapers. When Juan Soto and several other bandits killed a clerk and robbed his store in the Sunol Valley in January 1871, Procopio was still in prison. He is reported, however, to have been with Soto a short time before Sheriff Harry Morse tracked that desperado down and killed him in May. With Morse on the prowl, Procopio must have had strong feelings about a change in climate at that time, and he headed for Monterey.

On the coast Procopio looked up his prison acquaintance, Vasquez. With several others they formed a gang of highwaymen, committing various local robberies, notably one at a Salinas road house. On the morning of August 17, 1871, Vasquez, Procopio, and another outlaw stopped the Visalia stage at Soap Lake, near Gilroy. They had tied up a traveler named Moore and taken fifty-five dollars from him just before the stage arrived. Then they directed the coach into a field

California State Library

In the late 1860s, San Quentin had become a sprawling collection of cellblocks, offices, and factories. It was home to Procopio for many years.

Author's Collection

A street scene in Livermore, one of Procopio's favorite hangouts.

where they had deposited Moore, tying and robbing four male passengers while leaving a woman in the group unmolested. After securing about $500 and several gold watches, the robbers mounted and prepared to leave.

"Don't make a move till we get back," cautioned one of the outlaws, "or we'll murder every one of you." They then galloped down the road. In a few minutes they returned with a teamster, whom they also tied and robbed. They then left again after reiterating the same threat.

The outlaws next robbed an old man named Grewell, later allowing him to drive down the road. He secured the aid of a friend and chased the robbers, firing several shots at them as they disappeared into the mountains. When Vasquez and his men spotted other posses, they decided to lay low for a while. "We then directed our course along the mountain range to those hills lying immediately around Monterey," Vasquez later recalled. "I spent several days on a ranch, resting, amusing myself with dancing, etc., with the senoritas." Presumably Procopio was with him.

On August 28 the *San Francisco Bulletin* ran an article on Procopio, who was rapidly gaining stature among the outlaw fraternity. It reported, "Monterey County seems to be the headquarters of an organized band of robbers and cutthroats under the command of 'Red Dick,' alias Tomas Redondo, alias Procopio, alias Muriata; and we are able to give some particulars of the antecedents of this thoroughly heartless and unprincipled wretch and some of his unprincipled coadjutors. He is a nephew of the infamous Joaquin Muriata [sic], whose deeds of crime constitute so prominent and bloody a chapter in the history of California, being a son of Joaquin's sister."

On the alert for the outlaws, lawmen were notified late on the night of September 13, 1871, that several suspicious characters had been seen near Santa Cruz lounging around the house of Mattias Lorenzana. Undersheriff Charles Lincoln and several others investigated the area, but found no evidence of the strangers. When they noticed a boy talking near the barn, Lincoln entered and crawled under a stack of hay in the loft to see if anyone was hiding there. When the lawman grabbed a leg in the hay, a man jumped to his feet pulling a pistol. Having lost his own weapon while crawling through the haystack, Lincoln leapt through a window, calling for his men to shoot. The stranger jumped to the ground after Lincoln, and the officers killed him in an exchange of gunfire.

First reports of the shooting identified the dead man as Procopio, but he was later reported to be one Francisco "Sancho" Barcenas, a sometime member of the Vasquez gang. When Lorenzana was arrested, a gang of masked men visited the jail one night and took him from the jailer. They later returned him, unharmed. "The opinion prevails," reported the *Santa Cruz Sentinel*, "that all that was wanted with Lorenzana was a confession as to what he knew about the Mexican bandits, Procopio and others, now marauding in this vicinity, and that a little 'gentle' persuasion was applied for that purpose, but without the desired effect."

Vasquez and Procopio got the message of all this and hastily fled to Mexico. Their route is not known, but certainly the first leg of their journey was by steamer to lower California. Indications are they sojourned in the Hermosillo area, Procopio's old home, where he had relatives. Some of Frank Latta's informants told of Procopio's visits home and of his attempts to account for the many droves of horses his uncle had sent south so many years before. The horses were no longer an issue, of course, but their offspring and the money involved caused trouble and at least one man died. Possibly that is why Vasquez and Procopio were back in San Francisco after only three months' absence.

While enjoying the Bay City's Mexican saloons and fandango halls, the two outlaws reportedly had a falling out and Vasquez left town. An old newspaper account later noted, "Vasquez had a poor opinion of Procopio, while Procopio always sneered when Vasquez' name was mentioned and spoke of him as a little coward. A woman was the cause of the coolness between them."

Apparently Procopio had money enough to continue his vacation as a stranger in a big city. He could never relax completely, but at least no sheriff's posse would suddenly descend on him in San Francisco.

Nevertheless, someone spotted the fugitive. One of police Captain Isaiah Lees' detectives saw him in a Mexican bagnio on Morton Street and alerted his superiors. Sheriff Harry Morse was notified and was quickly on the scene with Deputy L.C. Morehouse. Captain Lees detailed detectives Ben Bohen and Appleton Stone to aid the sheriff and the lawmen put the desperado on a round-the-clock watch. The lawmen waited until he showed up again at the Morton Street house on February 11, 1872, then quickly laid their plans. The *San Francisco Bulletin* of February 12 reported, "The officers made entrances simultaneously by different doors. Procopio was sitting at a table, eating, and seeing the officers enter at the front door he jumped to draw his revolver, but before he could pull it Sheriff Morse, who had entered at the rear, had him pinioned by the throat and in a moment he was handcuffed and on his way to the...San Leandro jail."

So Procopio was caged again. How he must have cursed his luck at overstaying his vacation. He had been out of San Quentin just over seven months, and now he was facing yet another term in that hated place. After holding up stagecoaches and robbing stores, they were going to put him away now for merely stealing John Arnett's cow!

The trial began on the afternoon of April 25 at the Alameda County courthouse. Procopio's lawyer, W.C. Kennedy of San Jose, tried for a change of venue, claiming the press had prejudiced his client's case, but the judge disagreed. John Arnett and Juan Camargo testified for the prosecution and gave hard evidence of the defendant's guilt.

Harry Morse next detailed a conversation he had with the outlaw while transporting him to the Alameda jail. After Procopio asked Morse what Camargo had said, "I told him that Camargo had said he had stole the cow....[Procopio said,] 'By God, Morse, I did steal that cow, I wanted something to eat'; he asked how many cows he was charged with stealing. I told him one. He said that wasn't much. He admitted all the time that he had stole the cow, and I supposed that he intended to

John Boessenecker Collection

Sheriff Harry Morse's capture of Procopio was an exciting event in a life filled with dangerous encounters. This photo of the famous lawman was taken probably about the time of the arrest.

plead guilty until the lawyers got hold of him."

Procopio took the stand and of course denied all knowledge of the theft. "I am defendant. I did not tell Morse anything about stealing the cow. I was not at Camargo's house at all. I don't know anything about stealing the cow. I did not steal or take the cow, did not say that I did. I was at Livermore at Smith's dance house all of the day and night of March 31, 1871 and all of the nights of April 1st and 2nd. I slept there. I went to bed about 11 o'clock on the night of the 31. Met with Ignacio Morales and slept in her room with her until the next morning."

Miss Morales testified next. "I knew defendant. I saw him on the day and night of March 31, 1871. He slept with me that night and the next and the next. He was in the house all that day and night.... He slept in the same bed with me and didn't get up during the night....I remember it so well because that was the only time I was in Livermore."

Cross examining Morales, District Attorney A.A. Moore asked her if the dates might not have been February or April 30.

"It might," she replied.

Both the owner of Smith's dance hall and his wife testified that Procopio was there for three days, but both admitted they were not sure of the date. With that, the defense rested.

All the evidence was in by 6:00 P.M., and the jury was secluded just before 7:00 P.M. In fifteen minutes they returned with a guilty verdict.

The *San Francisco Bulletin* insisted the evidence fully sustained the verdict and commented on Procopio's appearance, noting, "The defendant is a fine-looking young man of about 32 years of age, rather tall. He had a well-built frame, with countenance that one would scarcely believe could belong to a man of such bad instincts." Procopio's attorney filed the usual appeal based on legal technicalities, but the state supreme court dismissed the case in October.

On May 4, 1872, Procopio returned to San Quentin under the name Tomas Rodundo. He had received a seven-year term, but apparently was resigned to keeping his nose clean and getting out as soon as possible. As Number 5247, the outlaw once again embarked on the regulated, hard life of a convict.

Nothing had changed within those twenty-foot high walls surrounding the six acres of San Quentin proper. The prison officers were all the same. The state's lieutenant governor acted as warden except when the legislature was in session. He presided over various clerks and officers, including a captain of the yard and captain of the guard, a turnkey, fifty-two guards, a physician, and assorted engineers and stewards.

Procopio's work assignment is not known, but most of the prisoners were kept busy. Stone and Hayden, a saddle and harness making firm, had a three-year contract at that time to employ 200 convicts, while Merriam & Cole, furniture manufacturers, were working just over 200 convicts. The boot and shoe manufacturing firm of A.W. Baldwin was working between fifty and one hundred prisoners. Convicts were also employed within the walls in the tailor shop and as coopers and cabinetmakers at various times.

Those numbers were never constant, but the firms accounted for 500 prisoners at most. The clay deposits were nearly exhausted, so few bricks were being made any longer, but there was always work to be done. Several prisoners did masonry work, repairing the walls and buildings, while others painted and did carpentry to improve the facilities. Always there was laundry and gardening to do and firewood to gather, and the ever present stone-breaking details still operated. Other convicts kept books, worked in the mess hall and kitchen, did locksmithing, kept the yards clean, or repaired equipment in the tin shop.

Despite complaints of harshness, prison life was constantly improving in large and small ways. Efforts, mostly from the outside, were always being made to do away with flogging and limit punishment to confinement in the dungeons and rations of bread and water, but even some of the prisoners thought bad inmates deserved tough punishment. Convicts were now allowed to read in their cells until 9:00 P.M. if they could buy their own candles. That led to the theft of candles and tallow, however, so authorities were considering giving free candles to all prisoners.

Probably the greatest advancement was the prison school conducted in the chapel after Sunday services. A majority of the convicts were illiterate and many took advantage of the school. A 3,000-volume library had been established, mainly from visitor donations and contributions from San Franciscans. Educated convicts conducted the classes under the supervision of the prison moral instructor, clergyman C.C. Cummings.

Just what Procopio thought of all that is not known. His personality would indicate that he kept quiet, minded his own business, and probably associated with Californio vaqueros he could identify with. Burglars, con men, and petty thieves didn't interest him. He was a man of the plains and mountains, a skilled vaquero who took what he needed and made his own laws.

Going about his assigned chores, Procopio watched, waited and bided his time. His lawyers worked at getting his sentence commuted, and finally the good word came. He was to be released on June 6, 1877.

When Procopio again walked through the San Quentin gates, he was anything but a reformed convict. He must have been bitter over his long sentence for the theft of just one cow. Criminals, then and now, tend to focus on what they consider injustices to themselves, but ignore crimes for which they escaped prosecution. With his previous prison record and probable involvement in numerous robberies with the Vasquez gang, Procopio was undoubtedly the recipient of the maximum sentence the judge could impose.

Bitter, unrepentant, and perhaps determined to make the gringo pay for those long prison years, Procopio likely headed for one of his old haunts at Livermore, San Jose, or Firebaugh. There he could rusticate for a few months, enjoying women and good Mexican food, while planning for the future.

Just when Procopio went back into "business" is not known, but he certainly had by late summer. An Alameda rancher named Dougherty lost eleven head of cattle and trailed them to Martinez, where they had been sold to several butchers. A man named Avelino Tesca received the payment at Vallejo, then returned to Martinez, where he reportedly divided the money with Procopio. Realizing he had overstayed his welcome in the area, Procopio and several associates then headed south, riding through the Livermore Valley and into the great San Joaquin. Tesca made the mistake of remaining in the area and was later arrested along with the two butchers.

At 9:00 P.M., November 12, 1877, the clerks of Brownstone's Store in Grangeville were getting ready to close up. The village was a cluster of frame buildings of the false-front variety situated on the vast plains of the valley. The store catered to the supply needs of the farmers and stockmen of the area southwest of Fresno.

As clerk Tommy Thompson was locking the front door, someone suddenly forced it open again and five masked men burst into the room. With a pistol in his ear and a knee in his back, the intruders tied Thompson's hands and shoved him under a counter. They treated Julian Toomstrap, the other clerk, in a similar fashion. Toomstrap had tried to yell "Robbers!" at the top of his lungs, but the cry came out a quiet croak.

Store manager Herman Nathan was sleeping in a back room when the commotion awoke him. He had just grabbed his pistol when the robbers burst into the room. Before he could get off a shot, one of the men slashed him with a knife, causing a ragged wound in his hand. The robbers quickly disarmed and tied him also.

The men seized a box containing about $250 in coin from Nathan's room, then looked around the store. They were not equipped to break into the store safe, so they decided to call it a night. Backing out of the building with their pistols at the ready, the five robbers dashed across the street and disappeared into some brush.

The clerks soon freed themselves and spread word of the robbery. All agreed that the masked men were Mexicans or native Californians, and local deputy sheriffs and constables were promptly in the saddle. Two suspects were promptly arrested from a group of newcomers who had lately been loafing about town.

The robbery, commented the *Visalia Weekly Delta*, "may well be called bold when it is considered that residents of the place within a hundred feet of where the robbery took place were all up; and at the hotel, only a short distance off, a party of men were in the saloon playing cards. So quietly was the thing done that not a word or sound was heard until it was all over, and the robbers had got away."

The bandits escaped. Lawmen noted the old Vasquez style of tying up the victims. But Vasquez had been dead for over two years, hanged in March 1875 for murdering three people in an 1873 raid in San Benito County, and his gang had dispersed. People generally thought Procopio was back in action.

On the evening of December 16, 1877, ten or twelve Mexican desperadoes invaded the small community of Caliente in the Tehachapi Mountains southeast of Bakersfield. Reining up in front of the express office, the bandits rushed inside and forced the agent to open the safe, but it was empty. They then proceeded to the hotel and several stores, where they obtained about $300 and a supply of clothing and other goods. Fortunately, express office workers had received warning of the raid, but they barely had time to hide the contents of the safe before the robbers appeared.

Townspeople also blamed the gang for various stock thefts and mischief in the area, and a posse promptly pursued them when they fled town. In the Tejon Mountains possemen captured six Mexicans whom they recognized as members of the gang. They took the prisoners to the county jail in Bakersfield on the evening of December 21. Lawmen suspected Procopio of leading the group, but if so, he had made a clean getaway. Chances are he and several others had taken charge of some stolen horses and left the area.

That night a vigilante mob took the six prisoners from jail and tried them in the county courthouse. The vigilantes quickly convicted all six and hanged them from a gallows rigged up while the trial was being conducted. A coroner's jury the following day found that the six men had died at the hands of persons unknown, although newspaper accounts said, "The lynchers made no attempt to conceal their identity and comprised some of the leading citizens." Curiously, only five of the victims were identified: Antonio Maron, Francisco Encinas, Miguel Elias, Fermin Eldeo, and Bessena Ruiz.

One of the victims, Miguel Elias, was apparently a young sheepherder who was on his way back to Mexico and had inadvertently stopped to have lunch with the outlaws. He had just been paid about $300, but neither the money nor his horse was recovered to send to his people in Mexico.

If Procopio did indeed escape the fate of his gang at Bakersfield, he lost no time in assembling another group of thieves and thugs. Indeed, it would have been easy enough to do so, for the nearby Mexican settlements always had men waiting for such an opportunity. They were vaqueros, sheep herders, and day laborers perfectly willing to take the outlaw trail when occasion demanded. Except for the leaders, few gang members were full-time bandits.

On the evening of December 26 Mexican bandits struck the store of Phillips and Weinshench at Hanford, another small farming community near Grangeville. Again the robbers tied up the clerks and looted the store of money, watches, and other valuables. The *Fresno Weekly Republican* reported, "The robbers succeeded in getting several watches and about three hundred dollars and making their escape, leaving the people in a wild state of excitement. But a few weeks ago the town of Grangeville was robbed in a like manner and it is supposed by these same highwaymen. This thing should be stopped. We hear it rumored that if they are caught their fate will be similar to those robbers who were hanged at Bakersfield last week."

A call for a posse brought only five men willing to pursue the robbers. None were professional lawmen and they were poorly armed. Rather than taking time to assemble a larger group, Jose Cunningham, Doc McPherson, Sol Gladden, Bill Dikes, and Jon Whitesides began tracking the bandits the day following the robbery. The weather was bitter cold and foggy, making the chase all the more difficult as the group headed west toward the foothills of the Coast Range.

That evening the posse arrived at a cabin where the two occupants agreed to let them spend the night. After a meal the

> Reward
>
> I, William Irwin, Governor, do hereby offer a reward of Five hundred Dollars, to be paid for the arrest and conviction of the murderer of Solomon P. Gladden, who was murdered on the 28th day of December 1877, in the County of ~~Ventura~~ Tulare.
>
> Witness my hand and the Great Seal of the State this the twenty ninth day of January AD 1878
>
> William Irwin
> Governor
>
> By the Governor
> Thomas Beck
> Secy of State
> By Wm A. Beck
> Deputy
>
> Increased by Gov.
> May 1879 to $1000

California State Archives

State reward proclamation issued for the capture of Sol Gladden's killer.

men gathered around the fireplace in which they were burning sagebrush and scraps of wood. When fuel ran low, Whitesides and Theodore Draper went outside to gather more. Returning with an armload of brush, the two men heard a noise behind them and turned to see a bulky figure walking toward them through the fog. The figure carried a saddle. In Spanish, he asked the way to La Libertad, a nearby Mexican settlement. Whitesides had apparently met Procopio previously, for he later recalled, "As soon as the man spoke, I recognized him as Procopio."

While Draper engaged the outlaw in conversation, Whitesides hurried inside to grab his weapon. As he did so another of the party stepped to the door and called out, causing Procopio to drop his saddle and start running. By then all the men were tumbling from the cabin, but the outlaw had disappeared in the fog.

Early the next morning the posse was again on the trail, following Procopio's tracks to Gus Kreyenhagen's store at the small Mexican settlement at Posa Chane. Kreyenhagen told them Procopio had been there an hour earlier, about 3:00 P.M., and purchased some crackers and sardines. He had then gone up Jacalitos Creek, probably to the home of the Yguerria brothers.

The posse quickly rode up to the Yguerrias' cabin, where Whitesides asked a Mexican sitting on the porch if a man had been there. He refused to answer. Whitesides later recalled what happened next:

> We all dismounted and tied our horses to a pole hitching rack which stood in front of the cabin. The cabin was of mud and brush construction with walls about six inches thick. There were two rooms with a sort of hallway between.
>
> We entered the large room and found four Mexicans seated about a table playing cards. They seemed somewhat alarmed at seeing us, but kept quiet. They almost immediately went outside.
>
> In the adjoining room we saw Procopio. He was lying on the bed with a large overcoat over him and appeared to be asleep. I covered the men with my revolver and told

McPherson to cover him with the rifle while I brought in some of the rest of the posse. I did not see what happened, but I do not believe that McPherson really covered him at all.

In answer to my call for help Sol Gladden appeared in the door. As I turned back toward the bed Procopio was raising himself to a sitting position. As he arose he grasped two six-shooters that were concealed under the blankets at his sides. Immediately Procopio began firing. Sol Gladden was shot through the mouth. As he fell backwards out of the door he was again shot, this time through the body from side to side.

By this time McPherson and I were outside. I jumped around the corner of the house and McPherson ran directly from the house about forty yards.

Procopio kept shooting. McPherson was the only member of the posse in a position to fire in at the door. He emptied the Winchester as rapidly as he could, but could not see inside the house because the smoke from Procopio's guns had filled the hallway. We later found that, with the exception of one, all of the bullets from the rifle had lodged in the wall of the house. The other bullet had killed my horse.

I took a position at the corner of the house. Procopio came to the door a couple of times and I emptied my five shot revolver without hitting him. By this time all our guns were emptied. The only loaded gun was the one dropped by Sol Gladden which was lying on the ground beside him.

Procopio sprang from the door, fired two shots at me, grabbed Gladden's gun as he passed and started toward the creek. Before anyone could reload he had crossed the creek bed and was attempting to climb the opposite bank which was about fifteen feet high and almost perpendicular.

The outlaw scrambled up the bank and disappeared, leaving the demoralized posse to lick its wounds and wonder what had gone wrong. They had a dead man and horse on their hands and didn't know what to do. Night had fallen and they could think of all kinds of excuses to wait until morning to resume the chase. At daybreak one of the possemen went back to Hanford with Gladden's body while the others took up

Procopio's trail. By all accounts it was a half-hearted pursuit by a discouraged posse.

Procopio had killed Gladden the way he had shot Constable Wood so long ago, by feigning resignation and compliance, then drawing and shooting when the officer dropped his guard. If anyone ever doubted the desperado was as deadly as a rattlesnake, the issue was clear now.

Fleeing the battered posse, Procopio circled to the south and forced a nearby Mexican family to give him their only horse. Reinforced posses from Lemoore and Hanford trailed him to Monterey County. They found a Mexican riding Procopio's horse and carrying a new suit of clothes to his hideout in the hills. Instead of following him they went into San Luis Obispo, where officials said if they had a warrant they could arrest the outlaw when he came to town.

After waiting for a day or so, the possemen decided to give up the chase since they were out of funds anyway. A disgusted editor of the *Visalia Delta* concluded, "It is news to me...that a noted criminal cannot be arrested without a warrant, wherever found....One thing is certain, however, about this whole affair; that, although a second time almost within gunshot of this noted bandit and murderer, they failed to secure him, which either speaks little for the pluck of the posse or for the zeal and intelligence of the San Luis officials."

Procopio's friends insisted he had been at Firebaugh during the Hanford robbery and the Gladden killing, but few people bought the alibi. The *Fresno Weekly Expositor* expressed the suspicions of many concerning the incident, stating, "The Mexican who killed Gladden was not an escapade [sic] from the Fresno county jail as stated by the Tulare county papers, but was a recent graduate from the San Quentin College of Arts. He is known by the name of Procopio, and is a nephew of the renowned bandit Joaquin Murietta [sic]. Posa Chine [sic], where the killing was done, is but a short distance from Joaquin's old headquarters. Procopio is supposed to have led the bandits that raided Caliente."

The state was horrified at the wanton murder of Gladden— a grim reminder of the days of Vasquez and his savage Tres

Pinos massacre. Despite local reward offers, Procopio vanished into the wild plains and mountains that he knew so well. In May 1879 Governor William Irwin offered an additional reward of $500, but still the desperado remained at large.

For the next few years rumors of the now phantom desperado abounded, but no one ever saw him. Every indication suggests he fled to Mexico and remained there for the rest of his life. He knew too well what happened to bandidos who didn't know when it was time to leave. His uncle, Joaquin, was the best example, but there were many others.

As he took up residence in the Hermosillo area, Procopio probably didn't realize the mythical status he had attained. The *National Police Gazette* carried an article about Procopio with an engraving of his mug shot, while Ned Buntline had done a dime novel treatment of his career, calling him "Red Dick, the Tiger of California." Still, he was undoubtedly aware of the rumors that surfaced from time to time which kept his name in the public memory and embellished his legend.

On August 3, 1882, the Arizona *Daily Star* published a startling story which raised eyebrows all along the border:

> On Monday last at four o'clock in the afternoon, Aurelio Cantabrana, an actor, was shot and killed by Procopio Murrieta in a house of ill-fame in Hermosillo. Cantabrana was a native of Yacatecas, State of Zacatecas, and has been a resident of this state for over four years following the profession of actor and was one of the stars of the Molla Company that are now playing in Hermosillo. He leaves a wife and several children. Murrieta is the nephew of the celebrated California outlaw, Joaquin Murrieta. He killed two men in Los Angeles, California, a few years ago, and then made his escape from prison to New York, where he was for some crime incarcerated, but succeeded in making his escape with a Chinaman and an Irishman, taking with them a policeman for hostage. He had been employed on the police force in Hermosillo up to the time of his killing Cantabrana and at ten o'clock in the evening of the same day he was shot by an order of the governor. He had a brother killed about a year ago at the feast of Cumoripa.

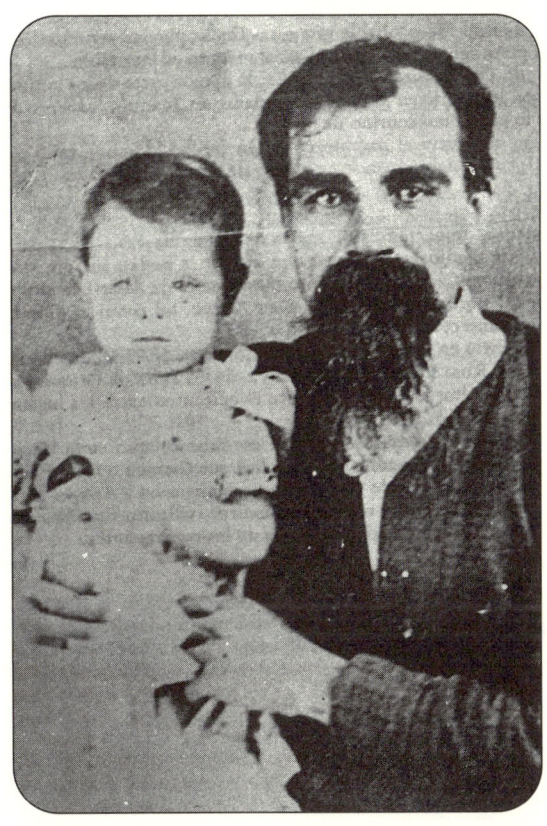

Manuel Rojas
Procopio holds his daughter, Margarita, about 1887.

Just what happened in this incident is unclear, but obviously someone had mistaken the killer for Procopio.

In November of the following year a Los Angeles express office received a report that Procopio had been captured near Tucson, Arizona. When United States Marshal George Gard was notified in California, he contacted Tulare County Sheriff W.F. Martin. Like all good peace officers, Martin's first action was to telegraph the governor and see if the $500 state reward was still in force. A *Los Angeles Times* report said a Tulare County lawman was on his way to pick up the prisoner, but it is not known if he waited for word of the reward.

That report, too, turned out to be a combination of confusion and wishful thinking. Under the heading "Procopio Murieta," the Tucson *Arizona Weekly Citizen* tried to explain the false report:

> The way the report of the capture of this famous California bandit, and nephew of Joaquin, got into the papers was this: A gentleman came up from Hermosillo some two weeks ago, and told a friend that he had seen Procopio, alias Red Dick, convalescing from yellow fever in Hermosillo. Upon such information ex-sheriff [Pete] Gabriel, of Pinal County, telegraphed to Los Angeles to know how much reward was outstanding for him. The reply came back, $600. Mr. Gabriel did not deem the amount sufficient to warrant his going after Procopio, and stayed at home. At the same time a Mexican named Jose Carrisoso, a former partner of Procopio, was arrested by Agent Jackson for attempting to sell cattle to the Indians on the Pima reservation. He was at first thought to be Procopio, from his resemblance to the latter, and was brought to Tucson and registered on the prison books under that name. The mistake was soon discovered, but it gave some color to the report. This is all there was of the alleged capture of Procopio.

That Procopio settled in the Hermosillo area after his flight from California there is no doubt. He married Juanita Armida Bernal sometime in the 1880s, and their daughter, Margarita, was born in May 1886. Frank Latta interviewed Juanita in 1936, when she was eighty-five years old, and from her and several descendants obtained much data pertaining to Joaquin Murrieta. The family was understandably reticent about Procopio's checkered past, but they confirmed that he died as an outlaw sometime in the 1890s at La Lista Blanca, northwest of Hermosillo.

Although few are aware of Procopio's criminal career, he was one of the most notorious outlaws of his time. Riding across the vast plains of the San Joaquin, he was a stirring figure to the Californios and Mexicans who bitterly recalled the loss of their great ranchos and way of life when the Americans came. Even if he hadn't spent his stolen gold in the Spanish cantinas and bordellos of old Livermore and Firebaugh, the Hispaños would have hidden and protected him from relentless officers, just as they had protected his uncle so many years before.

Rightly or wrongly, Procopio was the keeper of the flame. To a new generation he wore well the bloody mantle of Joaquin Murrieta.

4 THE WEST'S MOST INEPT OUTLAW: MILTON HARVEY LEE

1847–1916

The man looked up from his desk; it was late and time to go home. Harvey Lee was a grizzled old fellow, nearly sixty years old, but looked closer to seventy. As a boy he had helped his carpenter stepfather, and the smell of sawdust and lumber perhaps reminded him of those days long ago—and of his time in prison. He had worked at carpentry, coopering, and furniture making in San Quentin. His present employer, the Fresno Cooperage Company, manufactured and repaired tanks, casks, and barrels for much of California's great San Joaquin Valley. Everything had changed. Here he was in his twilight years, doing the kind of work he hated when he was a boy.

Maybe there was something to honest, hard work after all. He had made some progress in his job, and although he was not getting rich, he was getting by. At least bookkeeping did not involve the painful stooping and bending that carpentry and barrel-making required. In a long and ugly life, he still had much to be grateful for. Most of all, he was free and alive.

Born near Clarksville, Arkansas, in 1847, Milton Harvey Lee grew up with three older brothers—Jasper, William, and George—and six sisters. His father, Mark Lee, owned a large farm and distillery where his wife, Nancy, helped out when she wasn't having babies. Life was hard, and when news of the California gold discoveries reached Clarksville, Mark Lee saw an opportunity for a new life in the far West.

Fired with gold fever, the young farmer soon talked Nancy into moving. Selling their farm and properties, the Lees outfitted with ox teams, stocked up on supplies, and headed for California with their ten children. They took the southern route through Arizona and Mexico. The journey was long and dangerous, but they arrived safely in San Diego, where Lee sold his teams and equipment. The family then took ship for San Francisco, where they arrived in early 1850.

Mark Lee died soon after reaching the Bay City, the cause of death noted as "brain fever." Whatever his affliction Nancy found herself alone, friendless, and far from home with her children to care for. The raw and rowdy San Francisco did not appeal to her. Luckily she had enough money to see her through that trying period, and after some inquiries, she decided to move south and settle in the San Jose area.

San Jose had been founded in 1777 and had grown up near the old Santa Clara mission. When Nancy moved there in late 1850, the town was fast becoming an agricultural and stock-raising center. Americans were rapidly settling in the area, and in time Nancy married a busy carpenter named Archibald W. Naylor. They had a daughter, Ellen, in 1854, and another, Anna, two years later. The boys all kept the name Lee and the family grew up in the farming communities of Santa Clara County. Nancy Naylor seems to have been a loving mother who took good care of her brood. In those days girls pretty much took care of themselves, but she worried about her boys.

The trip west and the deadly diseases of the age whittled down the ten Lee siblings. The 1860 San Jose census lists only six children—the two Naylor girls (the Lee girls had apparently died young or were married) and Jasper, William, George, and Harvey Lee. Jasper, the oldest, worked as a cowhand on local ranches and was the wildest of the boys. William and George were ranch hands also, but maintained their home ties. Harvey was still in school and undoubtedly envied his brothers and their stories of life on the cattle ranges.

Harvey helped his stepfather at an early age, but he probably resented the heavy carpentry work which often taxed his weak frame and quickly wore him out. As a teenager he dodged work whenever possible and enjoyed the company of other loafers in the local saloons and billiard halls.

Nancy must have sympathized with her son's frail constitution and lack of interest in carpentry, yet she could not condone his developing laziness and lack of direction. She worried constantly about his association with others of the same disposition.

In the fall of 1862 George enlisted in the army and saw action with the Second Massachusetts Cavalry. He was captured, and after spending the remainder of the war in Andersonville prison, he returned home to California.

Jasper, meanwhile, seemed headed for trouble. He was traveling with a tough crowd, and when Harvey didn't show up at home for a few days, it usually turned out that he had been riding with Jasper and his pals. Nancy had no control over her oldest boy any longer and she worried that he might be leading his younger brother astray.

Her concerns came to a terrible realization when a deputy sheriff called on her in late December 1866. Harvey was in jail. The *San Jose Mercury* reported, "Harvey Lee was brought from Indian Valley to this city last Friday and delivered over to the custody of the sheriff. He had in his possession two stolen horses, one of which belonged to Mr. McCrea of San Jose. Lee is a resident of this city. His recent disappearance simultaneously with several valuable horses from this vicinity aroused the suspicion in the minds of some who knew him that the two circumstances were in some way connected, whereupon Sheriff Adams dispatched Messrs. Lard and Lovell on his track who made the capture as above."

Nancy must have been horrified to have her son spend Christmas in jail. Just how Archy Naylor handled the situation is unknown, but he could not have been happy—not with the prospect of legal fees before him.

Visiting her son as often as possible, Nancy saw to it that he had a nice Christmas dinner. But she was heartsick to see her youngest boy in jail. Why couldn't he be more like George? George was also a ranch hand, but not wild like Jasper. He worked hard during the day, but at night he studied and read books, trying to compensate for the schooling he had missed in his youth. In Andersonville he had been locked up with many educated men and came to realize the importance of gaining knowledge.

Tried in the district court, young Harvey was convicted of grand larceny on February 9, 1867, and sentenced to two and one-half years in state prison. He was also convicted of petit larceny, however, and had to first serve six months in the county jail.

As the weeks turned into months, Nancy visited her son often and noticed he was becoming increasingly nervous and irritable. He was quite pale from his confinement and she was upset to see him pick with disinterest at his food.

On May 1, 1867, Nancy was dismayed to learn Jasper had been arrested near Antioch on a horse-stealing charge. He joined Harvey in the San Jose jail, and we can only imagine the anguish of the mother with two sons in jail, both headed for state prison.

Jasper was tried and convicted in late May and sentenced to four years at San Quentin. As he left jail in custody of a deputy sheriff, Jasper shook hands with Harvey and said he would see him in a few months. There was little he could say to his crying mother. He entered San Quentin on May 31, 1867, as prisoner number 3560.

Harvey continued to appear ill. By the time he was to leave for San Quentin in August, Nancy was seriously concerned about her frail son's health. Crossing the bay on the ferry, the ominous walls of San Quentin, flanked by canister-filled cannon, loomed up before Harvey. After passing through the gate, he exchanged his clothes for prison stripes and was given the number 3615. He was assigned to the prison cooper shop and given a windowless, cramped cell which he shared with several others.

He probably saw Jasper soon after entering, especially if

they had the same work detail. They had little opportunity to talk, however. Even when walking together, convicts had to be in single file, never abreast of one another.

Nancy was horrified at the thought of the fragile Harvey in prison, and she wrote various letters to state legislators and other officials to see what could be done. Just before Harvey's departure for San Quentin she engaged two physicians to examine him. She hoped the doctors might be able to secure Harvey a pardon for health reasons. On August 26, 1867, Doctor A.J. Cory and his brother, also a physician, reported their findings:

> This is to certify that we...have examined Harvey Lee. Our opinion is that he has no organic disease either of the heart or of any other vital organ. There is however a *changed condition* from the *normal* functions of the heart and stomach. This changed condition is characterized by the following symptoms: fickle appetite, indigestion, wakefulness, at times palpitation of heart, pain over the region of the heart, great falling off in weight, etc., etc. Withal, he is possessed of a highly nervous temperament. In view of these symptoms, we herein state that the above mentioned Harvey Lee is in very poor health and we believe that if he should continue thus one year longer—organic disease of the heart or stomach will be established—either one of which is improbable of a cure.

Nancy knew there was a good opportunity for a pardon now. Enlisting the aid of Santa Clara District Attorney D.W. Harrington, who had prosecuted Harvey, Nancy went to work. Harrington sympathized with the family and thought the boy might very well straighten himself out if he could be kept away from his old associates. At Nancy's earnest request, Harrington wrote a letter on November 26, 1867. He enclosed a petition that Nancy had gotten up, bearing a number of signatures, and sent it to Governor Frederick Low in Sacramento. A series of newspaper notices appeared in the *San Jose Argus* notifying the public of the pardon application.

Harrington and the people who signed the petition went

out on a limb for Harvey, blaming bad associations for causing him to stray "from the path of rectitude." Nancy was very grateful—and hopeful. She waited for some word, but when new governor Henry Haight took office in early 1868, she was afraid the petition had been lost in the shuffle. By the end of January she had penned a plaintive letter to the new governor concerning her son:

> Permit me to make an enquiry [sic] of you as the mother of Harvey Lee with regard to a petition sent to Gov. Low a few days before his time expired for the Pardon of said Harvey Lee for grand larceny convicted in Santa Clara County and sentenced for two years & a half in the States Prison. Whether it was handed over to you when you entered upon the duties of your office and if you received it.
>
> I would like to know whether you intend to Pardon him out or not—and if not—the reason why you refuse the Executive clemency so as to relieve my suspense and anxiety for my unfortunate Son. I refer you to Mr. Moore & Ryland Representatives of Santa Clara County for any particulars you wish to know. We regard the unfortunate Boy with high esteem.

Meanwhile Harvey was introduced to his new prison home. He quickly learned that prisoners could obtain almost any contraband through the guards, providing they could pay for it. Gambling games flourished in the yard, with new prisoners making particular targets. Many lost all their personal possessions during the first day.

Manufacturing went on in various large buildings at the prison—so much so that some San Francisco companies complained about the unfair competition of prison labor. The Mission Woolen Mills of San Francisco manufactured the striped material that convicts tailored for their prison clothes. The prison also manufactured flannel shirts and the convict's shoes as well. It cost $12.41 to clothe a prisoner for one year, while the cost of feeding a convict for a year was $45.62.

The climate of Marin County was ideal and quite healthful, yet new prisoners quickly noted the abundance of consumption cases. Many of the prisoners were in the initial stages of the deadly disease when first admitted, and, as nothing was known of its contagious character, close confinement with cell mates quickly condemned others to the same inevitable fate. At times the prison must have seemed like a pest hole, terrifying the frail and weak Harvey Lee.

Finally the governor approved Harvey's pardon. On April 9, 1868, Haight signed the discharge papers, and on April 14 Harvey left prison a free man. When he returned home, Nancy did her best to see that her son returned to a normal life, free of the temptations that had condemned him in the past. Nothing is known of this period of Harvey's life, but he was probably morose and bitter at the expectations of his mother and family. He undoubtedly worked for a time, then one day disappeared. Meanwhile, Jasper was released in October 1870, too late to further influence his younger brother.

Harvey probably headed up over the stage road, through Pacheco Pass and drifted down into the desolate west side of the San Joaquin Valley. After crossing the San Joaquin River at Firebaugh's Ferry, he would have passed over the Fresno Slough and traveled through barren alkali country.

At Hawthorn's stage station Harvey would have found a brief respite in the middle of the alkali desert. From there the stage road crossed the Kings River at Bliss' Ferry and ran down into Visalia.

Perhaps Harvey worked at odd jobs along the way as he steadily drifted south. Somewhere along the way he picked up a pal named J.B. Crandall, and together they appeared in San Bernardino during the late summer or fall of 1870. The pair were not long becoming enmeshed in some serious trouble.

On the evening of October 16, Lee and Crandall stole three horses and some equipment from ranchers William Davis, James Stewart, and William Standifer and headed east for the Arizona border. The ranchers sent one of Standifer's cowboys, a man named Donnelly, to follow the thieves while they sought the San Bernardino sheriff. Donnelly was pursuing the outlaws when he had the good fortune to meet the sheriff returning from an Arizona visit. A rancher himself, Sheriff Newton

Noble had little sympathy for stock thieves. With Donnelly accompanying him, the lawman picked up two fresh horses and galloped after his quarry.

Thinking the thieves might stop at the Agua Caliente stage station, the canny sheriff circled around and arrived from the other direction so the outlaws would not think they had been followed. Tying their horses, Noble and Donnelly explained their mission to station keeper Jack Summers. Summers pointed out a campfire across the road. He told the lawmen what he knew of the men who were riding two horses and herding a third. Both the animals and saddles fit the descriptions, and Donnelly nodded at the sheriff. Noble was confident he had his men.

Checking his pistol, Noble walked across the road to where Crandall was bending over a fire with a six-shooter in his lap. Noble identified himself, put his hand on Crandall's head, and told him that he was under arrest. The outlaw froze for a second, then got to his feet with the pistol in his hand. Backing away, the horse thief raised his weapon to fire, but Noble was faster. Crandall fell with a pistol ball in his forehead.

The sheriff's approach alerted Harvey Lee. As the flame from Noble's pistol lit the area, Harvey dodged behind some wagons only to be greeted with a blast from Jack Summers' shotgun. Screaming as several buckshot ripped across his face, Lee sprawled on the ground as Summers ran up. Seeing the outlaw bleeding profusely, the station keeper assumed he was dead. Powder smoke hung in the light of the campfire when Summers joined the sheriff, who was searching the mortally wounded Crandall for identification. Apparently Noble, Donnelly, and Summers left the horse thieves where they had fallen, then congratulated themselves over their luck while opening a bottle in the station bar.

At 9:00 P.M. Harvey groaned and managed to sit up. He looked around and quickly pulled himself together. He had no idea how badly he was hurt, but he managed to get to his feet and moved off into the desert. All night he staggered through the rocks and scrub brush, and by dawn he had reached the home of a rancher named Moore. Exhausted, he sat down to rest.

Harvey looked in several windows and determined the house was empty. He was preparing to break in when Sheriff Noble suddenly stepped around the corner of the building. He had tracked the wounded horse thief all night. After a quick examination, Noble assured the surprised prisoner his wounds were only superficial. With his hands cuffed, Harvey mounted and the men began the ride back to Agua Caliente.

Crandall died after lingering for about twelve hours, while Harvey soon found himself in the San Bernardino county jail. The *San Bernardino Guardian* acclaimed the sheriff for his prompt and efficient work. "Too much praise cannot be awarded to our sheriff for his promptness in dealing with these scoundrels, and we hope the death of Crandall may deter fellows of his class from falling in love with other people's horseflesh."

Giving his name as James Lee, Harvey waited glumly in his cell. On November 7, 1870, a grand jury indicted him for grand larceny. On December 26 the *Guardian* reported, "The prisoner plead guilty and the Court sentenced him to four years in the state prison."

Harvey had plenty of time to think on the trip to Los Angeles. He was going back to prison, and there was nothing he could do about it. He had given a false first name to keep the judge from discovering he was a second-termer, but most of all he probably wanted to keep it from his mother if possible. He undoubtedly hoped he could serve his time without his family ever learning he was again in prison.

At San Pedro, Harvey and his escort took the steamer for San Francisco. Soon he was back in prison stripes with a new number—4640. He had been free a little over two years, and some of the old convicts recognized him. He was only twenty-three years old, certainly one of the youngest second-term horse thieves in the place. Nothing much had changed, and he probably was assigned again to the cooper shop.

Harvey did his time and kept his nose clean; he wanted his "coppers," credits for good behavior. Whether he was able to keep his incarceration from his family is uncertain, but unless a convict was quite notorious it was easy for him to remain just a number. If he chose not to have a lawyer, friends, or family working for him on the outside, he might as well have dropped off the face of the earth.

If Harvey had no visitors, in good weather there were always Sunday excursions from surrounding cities. Since 1860 it had been customary to throw open the prison to visiting groups who prowled about the grounds hoping for a look at the convicts. The prisoners must have felt like animals in a zoo, but they seemed to enjoy the visitors, who sometimes brought along a band for entertainment. The prison log for April 7, 1871, recorded "Pic Nic Excursion of the Lone Star Social Club, first of Season."

Released on April 17, 1874, Harvey Lee promptly disappeared. He probably returned to San Jose, told his family some cock-and-bull story of the past few years, then got on with his life. He may have tried woodworking, but it would have only reminded him of San Quentin. He probably did various kinds of work while roaming around the area.

Harvey was apparently married during the mid-1870s, but his wife has not been identified. A daughter, Grace, was born shortly after the marriage and another girl, Rose, arrived sometime in 1879. Harvey, however, was not cut out to be a family man.

In January 1884 Harvey was working as a laborer on a stock ranch in the hills near San Jose. Walking near his cabin one morning, he was startled to see the skeletal feet of a man sticking out from a washed-out creek bank. A little digging, in what proved to be a disagreeable task, produced more bones. "There was considerable stench when I dug it up," Harvey later told a reporter, "and it made me sick." He told of the McSkimmins brothers, ranchers of the area who had mysteriously disappeared. One vanished in 1863 and Harvey had heard that the other died in an accident in San Bernardino. "There is a deep mystery about the whole affair," noted the *San Jose Herald*, "that will probably never be explained."

If Harvey had engaged in any larceny after being discharged from prison, he had not been caught. Whatever the case, by the spring of 1884 he was feeling his old, lawless urges again. Restless, or perhaps bored, he talked his friend John Herbert into helping him rob a stagecoach. After listening to Harvey's adventures, Herbert, who worked on a nearby ranch, yearned for the exciting life of a road agent. Bandits, both in and out of prison, enjoyed telling romantic and exaggerated tales of their days on the road. Harvey had heard many such stories and no doubt enjoyed telling them himself. Madera highwayman Tolman Terhune, who was interviewed in his prison cell that same year, said, "For a man who wants a real good business and an easy sort of a life I would advise him to go to work on the Yosemite route. Living is comparatively cheap and good in that vicinity, and stages just plenty enough....You don't want to tackle every stage that comes along, for that would spoil the whole thing. People would not ride, and after awhile there would be no stage line at all."

Terhune elaborated on how he had stopped a coach on the Calaveras road, only to find it empty of both treasure and passengers. After a friendly drink with the driver, the outlaw got up on the box and rode a few miles while the reinsman discoursed on why the coach was empty. "You have ruined the business on this road, ruined yourself and ruined the company. Nobody travels here anymore. You have scared them all off. Now you might as well git yourself, too. There's no money here, and won't be til you restore confidence....You must hold up a stage and then take a rest. Go over to San Francisco for a few weeks and enjoy yourself. Mingle in society and seek diversion. Then when you feel like it come out and take another crack."

It all sounded easy enough to Harvey. The tourist season was opening in Yosemite Valley and visitors from all over the world would soon be making the dusty trek to that already famous landmark. Heading east out of San Jose, Harvey and John Herbert rode over to the Sierra foothills, made a dry camp, and worked out a plan. They were just going to rob the passengers, but if there was any treasure aboard they would take that too. The weather was already getting hot in the valley; it would be cooler in the evening and they would run less risk of identification.

MILTON HARVEY LEE

John Herbert, Lee's stage-robbing partner.

Both: Greg Martin Collection

Harvey Lee's portrait, taken after his 1884 arrest for stage robbery, was found in an old Wells, Fargo mug book.

As they took up positions on either side of the road, Lee carried a shotgun and Herbert had a pistol shoved into the waist of his trousers. They could hear the coach rattling and creaking as it came down out of the hills and into the valley. Soon it loomed before them. Stepping into the road the two highwaymen commanded the driver to stop, and he pulled his lathered horses to a halt.

The robbery was over quickly. The bandits relieved a passenger named Davis of a thirty-dollar silver watch, while John Dappello coughed up a five-dollar gold coin. The disappointed bandits were afraid to spend any time searching for other valuables and motioned the driver to move on. In a few minutes the coach was on its way to Madera and had almost disappeared.

The outlaws realized the victims would soon alert authorities. Reluctantly they headed for San Jose and home. First notice of the robbery appeared in the *Fresno Weekly Expositor* on May 14, 1884: "The Yo Semite stage returning from the valley on Saturday evening was stopped at Cape Horn, near Bates Station, about 23 miles from Madera by two men, and the passengers robbed. The robbers got about $60 and 3 watches. The stage driver and one passenger claim that they can identify the robbers. [Fresno County] Deputy Sheriff Witthouse went to the scene of the robbery yesterday."

Witthouse was a good officer. After obtaining detailed descriptions from the passengers and stage driver, he sent notices to officers in surrounding counties. Santa Clara County Sheriff Benjamin Branham quickly isolated Lee and Herbert as prime suspects. Branham arrested Lee on June 7 and by that evening also had Herbert in custody. "Lee is well known in this city," commented the *San Jose Mercury*, "but Hubbard [sic] had been here only a short time, although it is said he formerly worked in the Mount Hamilton region."

On the evening of June 11 Deputy Witthouse arrived to take charge of his prisoners. He soon had them deposited in the Fresno County jail and their preliminary hearing was set for June 24 before Justice S.H. Hill.

Fresno was the county seat of a rich agricultural area

between San Francisco and Los Angeles. The town was just emerging from its frontier days, and the impressive courthouse was visible for miles on the flat plains surrounding the town. Harvey could only shake his head at the prospect of yet another term in prison. The *Expositor* reported, "The men under arrest for robbing the Yo Semite stage some weeks ago, were bound over by Justice Hill in the sum of $5,000 each to appear for trial in the Superior Court. In default of bail they were remanded to the custody of the Sheriff. Lee is said to be a pretty hard character, having already spent a term or two in San Quentin."

Lee and Herbert retained Fresno attorney Walter D. Grady as counsel and began preparing for the trial in early September. Despite numerous witnesses from Merced and Santa Clara counties, including Harvey's brother George, evidence left little doubt of the defendants' guilt. They were convicted on September 8, 1884. Insisting that new witnesses who lived in the coast range could prove his alibi, Harvey tried desperately to obtain a motion for a new trial but failed. He and Herbert were sentenced to twenty years in San Quentin.

George had apparently brought Harvey's wife and the two girls to Fresno, although newspapers do not mention them. The Fresno press, like so many frontier newspapers that did not want to scare off settlers, gave scant mention to crime. Nothing is known of Harvey's family at this point, but chances are his wife decided to stay in Fresno. George may have helped her as best he could.

Harvey had himself to worry about and plenty of time for thinking on the train to San Francisco. He had failed again. He did not even have the satisfaction of making a good haul. For a watch and a few dollars, he was returning to that hellhole of a prison for twenty years. His portrait in a Wells, Fargo mug book of the time shows a singularly meek and unhappy young man. His hair was prematurely gray and he looked much older than his thirty-seven years.

Harvey didn't know what to expect at the prison, either. The 1870s had been years of depression with violent labor demonstrations in large cities throughout the country, including San

California State Archives

San Quentin mug shot of Harvey Lee, probably taken in the late 1880s.

Francisco. With many men out of work, people howled about the unfair competition of convict labor at the state prison. Private contractors employing convicts at San Quentin had been under fire for some time as they produced farm implements, woodwork of all kinds, wagons, brick and stone building materials, boots, shoes, and other products which competed directly with private industry.

With a large group of the new "Workingmen's Party" as delegates to the California State Constitutional Convention in 1878, it was inevitable that the prison contract system would be modified. Accordingly, the new constitution mandated that no contract convict labor could be used for the benefit of the state after January 1, 1882.

To maintain some kind of labor for the convicts, the prison established a large jute mill for the manufacture of low-cost grain bags for California farmers. Only Chinese had been engaged in such work up to that time, and because of tremendous agitation against Chinese throughout the West, white labor approved of the mill. Despite the new $219,000 jute mill, which went into operation in April 1882, prison directors left other factories in operation, maintaining that they were primarily competing against large eastern manufacturing concerns.

When he was again admitted to San Quentin on September 19, 1884, Harvey might very well have been assigned once again to the cooper shop. Hoping to influence his assignment, he listed "cabinet maker" as his occupation. His new number was 11386.

Harvey easily slipped back into prison routine. The cells were still overcrowded and the food was still bad. Flogging had been abolished, but other punishments were just as cruel. Although third-timer Harvey may have impressed some of the younger convicts, he was probably self-conscious as he looked around. Charles E. Boles, the famous Black Bart, was working in the prison pharmacy. Bart's closest pal was Charles Dorsey, a murderous burglar and thief who had killed a passenger in an 1879 Nevada County stage robbery. George Shinn, a handsome ex-gambler, had wrecked a train in an attempted robbery in 1881, while the noted stage robber Bill Miner had been in and out of San Quentin for years and was currently doing time for a Tuolumne County stage stick-up in 1881. They were veteran highwaymen who had stolen thousands of dollars in one haul. Every time he noticed one of them in the yard, Harvey perhaps thought of the measly watch and gold coin that had resulted in his current imprisonment.

Harvey saw a succession of wardens come and go over the years. The prison had undergone many reforms since the 1860s, and some critics grumbled that San Quentin had become a country club for criminals. When William E. Hale became warden in 1891, he and Captain John Edgar, second in command of the prison, continued a firm, but humane policy. San Quentin was still a prison, though, tough and austere. Food was more varied, but it was not much better than the early days and remained a constant source of complaint. The convicts seemed to steadily test how far they could push their masters. Opium smuggling into the prison also became a serious problem.

In March 1891 a burglar named Ed Martin arrived in San Quentin. Originally from Pennsylvania, Martin had left home at an early age and claimed to have traveled the world. He had recently landed in San Francisco from Australia and drifted down to the southern California desert country. In Riverside young Martin found work doing odd jobs around a local hotel. Used to living by his wits, when he saw the opportunity he stole over $200 from one of the rooms and quickly skipped town. An alert constable picked him up at nearby Colton. Martin pleaded guilty and was sentenced to two and a half years in the state prison.

In San Quentin, Martin met Harvey Lee, who was apparently always on the lookout for some young fellow he could dominate. Martin was impressed with the old outlaw and listened to his tales of shootings and robberies with wide-eyed interest. Harvey needed someone to work for him on the outside. His family had probably given up on him after the stage robbery, but Harvey hoped young Martin might be able to help him.

As Martin's prison term was ending, Harvey asked if he

would go to Fresno and look up his children and lawyer. His wife had remarried a man named Hutchinson, who had also taken in the two girls. Grace, the oldest, had recently married Jim Hutchinson, her step-brother, and the whole family apparently lived in a house on C Street. Rose Lee was now thirteen and lived there also with two younger Hutchinson brothers.

Martin agreed to meet with Lee's children and his lawyer, Walter Grady, and see if a pardon could be secured. He was discharged on March 27, 1893, and left immediately for the San Joaquin Valley.

At the time of Martin's release, the exploits of two outlaws, Chris Evans and John Sontag, had been generating much excitement. The two men were accused of a series of train robberies in the San Joaquin Valley and killed three lawmen who had pursued them. Now they were the quarry of dozens of detectives, peace officers, and bounty hunters in the hills above Visalia.

Martin apparently yearned for the exciting life of outlaws such as Chris Evans. He was using the name Ed Morrell now and rather than going to Fresno, he went to Visalia, probably hoping to somehow join Evans and Sontag. When Evans was captured in June and locked up in the Fresno County jail, Morrell soon followed him.

Morrell later claimed he worked for railroad detective Will Smith in a ploy to get Harvey Lee released. He may have, but the time frame is shaky. After assaulting a local blacksmith, he was in the Fresno County jail himself for several months, beginning on September 22, 1893. Released in December, just in time to sit in on the closing days of Chris Evans' murder trial, Morrell watched as the famed outlaw was sentenced to life imprisonment on December 14.

Then Morrell finally sought out the Hutchinson family and discussed Harvey Lee's parole. He also called on Walter Grady, but the attorney did not think there was anything he could do in the matter. Morrell found the Hutchinson children to be a tough crowd. Jim and his two brothers had all seen the inside of the local calaboose, and Morrell felt right at home.

Whether Morrell had talked to Chris Evans in jail, or Jim

Hutchinson had already made plans of his own, a daring plot was hatched to break Evans out of jail. Two small-time losers such as Hutchinson and Morrell could not plan and carry out a sophisticated jail break; Evans himself masterminded the affair. In late December 1893, the men put their plan in motion.

A Hutchinson confederate "confessed" to authorities in Fresno County that he was involved in a plot to rob a train in the south valley. A trainload of deputies quickly headed for the site. Meanwhile, in Fresno, the conspirators rented a buggy and placed it near the jail. Morrell then called at the jail with a meal for Evans from a local restaurant. With the sheriff out of town and the other deputies in the south looking for nonexistent train robbers, the jailer was alone when he admitted Morrell to Evans' cell on the evening of December 28.

Wielding a pistol that had been covered with a napkin, Evans and Morrell were soon out and headed for their buggy. When City Marshal John Morgan tried to grab Morrell, Evans shot and wounded him. Morrell took Morgan's pistol, and the outlaws fled up an alley, stole a newsboy's cart, and were soon lost in the fog blanketing the city.

The escape startled the state. Officers quickly arrested the Hutchinson boys and Rose and Grace Lee. In the justice court on January 10, Rose testified about Jim Hutchinson's acquaintance with Ed Morrell. She had seen Morrell wearing a pistol and told of his driving up to the Hutchinson home in a rented buggy the day of the break. Jim Hutchinson had given Morrell a valise that was later found in the buggy. Investigators had little to connect the Lee children and the Hutchinsons to the jail break, however, and soon released them all.

Morrell and Evans eluded posses for some time but were finally captured on February 19, 1894, when Evans visited his family in Visalia. It was a sullen Morrell and a resigned Evans who were returned to Fresno. Evans was quickly shipped off to Folsom state prison.

Morrell had a speedy trial and was given a life sentence for stealing Marshal Morgan's pistol—a high price for a few months of glory. His efforts to obtain Harvey Lee's parole never got off the ground. On April 13, 1894, he was admitted to Folsom.

One way or another, Harvey undoubtedly learned the whole story and resigned himself to finishing out his term. He had to keep his nose clean; he wanted those credits for an early release. When Morrell was transferred to San Quentin on May 18, 1896, he no doubt told Harvey all about his exciting time with his family and Evans.

On the morning of Thursday, May 27, 1897, the 720 convicts of the jute mill crew marched in and stood at their machines. As the machinery roared into motion, the power belts started slapping and the jute dust began filling the air. None of the convicts moved. Guards looked at each other, then walked briskly to the work stations ordering the operators to begin work. Still, the convicts did not move. When the machinery was finally shut down, the workers became a yelling mob. Only with great difficulty did the guards and a previously formed strike committee of convicts prevent damage to the mill equipment.

At a meeting with Warden Hale, the committee made a series of demands pertaining to the bakers and cooks and various prison personnel. By the time the noon meal siren sounded, prisoners thought Warden Hale had acceded to most of the demands. As all the prison inmates proceeded to the mess hall and finished their meals, the warden and Captain Edgar had an idea, albeit a long shot, for getting them back in their cells and barring any chance of violence.

Instead of sounding the back-to-work siren after mealtime, they gave the evening lockup signal. Creatures of routine and habit, the convicts marched back to their cells and were locked up without incident.

Once the prisoners were secured in their cells, the warden and his men all heaved a sigh of relief. Then they went into action. They put more guards on the walls and jammed some 400 of the strikers into a ground floor row of cells where they would be easier to control. Others were thrown into the dungeon cells. Feeling betrayed, the prisoners broke up furniture in their cells and began a howling and pounding that one newsman described as a "hysterical frenzy and cursing like demons of the pit."

The *San Francisco Chronicle* noted, "The villagers who live on the peninsula cluster on the heights overlooking the prison and listen to the tumult with the greatest interest. It is the biggest sensation the little settlement has had for many a day."

On Saturday, May 29, about seventy of the mutinous convicts in the dungeons managed to tunnel out of their cells and barricade themselves in the entrance room. Piling heavy iron doors in the entryway, the convicts threw bricks and furniture as the guards battered their way into the room. A volley of rifle shots announced the guards' attack as they rushed upon the convicts and quickly subdued them. The guards then promptly isolated the prisoners in other cells.

To control the mutineers, Warden Hale reduced their food, and on the evening of May 31 he ordered guards to turn hoses on the remaining troublemakers among the still shouting and defiant prisoners. As the high-pressure jets shot through the small grates in its steel doors, each cell slowly filled with water and the inmates thrashed about inside. When the hose finally moved on to the next cell, the convicts shivered and watched the water gradually recede as it ran out under the heavy door. "If I live a hundred years," wrote Ed Morrell, "I shall never forget the horrors of that night with the water trickling out but slowly under the bottom of the door, packed together like sardines." Starved and worn out, the soaked and shivering strikers finally gave in.

The exact reasons for the trouble remained as muddled as ever. "These opium hoodlums are at the bottom of the whole affair," stated Warden Hale, and even Ed Morrell admitted the prison had a serious drug trafficking problem. In all likelihood, however, a number of complaints, coupled with the constant testing of the convicts and a strike that got out of control, had resulted in the trouble and extensive damage.

Harvey Lee did not participate in the strike, but he was terrified that all the convicts would be punished and he would lose his credits. He finally was able to check on his status and was assured he had not lost his credits. He would be released on time. When he was discharged on June 18, 1897, the last of the strikers had only been out of their bread-and-water tanks for a few days.

Lee had put aside a little money from the minimum wages he earned in prison, and he must have richly enjoyed the ferry trip across the bay. Taking in the streets and saloons of San Francisco made him feel the full impact of being on the outside again. He was free, but what did that mean? Perhaps he considered his wasted life now as he gazed at his reflection in a dusty barroom mirror. His hair was nearly white and most of his teeth were gone. The lines of his face and scraggly, gray mustache aged him far beyond his fifty years. The face that looked back at him surely asked questions he could not answer: "Where will you go? What can you do?"

Harvey's movements for the next few weeks are unclear. He probably did not visit Fresno; his wife had divorced him and his children were strangers. Old friends and family still lived in San Jose and he may have visited his brother George, who was janitor at the Empire Street school there. If so, George would have told him about the death of their mother, Nancy, on June 20, 1893. She had died of heart disease at the age of seventy-eight.

By early August Harvey was back in San Francisco where he met twenty-three-year-old Charles Williams. Williams may or may not have been his real name, but he was undoubtedly a petty thief who had been on his own for years and was perhaps looking for a father figure. Harvey probably entertained his new young friend with stories of his life as a robber and his years in San Quentin. Perhaps lured by high adventure and easy money, Williams asked to go along on Harvey's next robbery.

Harvey had indeed been thinking about a robbery, but not an ordinary job. He wanted to get out of California, where officers knew him too well. He was thinking of going to Oregon, not to stop a stagecoach, but to rob a train.

The men bought two shotguns and two pistols, probably at a pawnshop, then purchased steamer tickets for Portland. By then it was mid-September and their money was running low.

Packing their guns and few belongings in a satchel, Lee and Williams boarded the steamer and began the long journey up the coast.

On September 22, 1897, they walked down the gangplank at Portland. Situated on the Willamette River, which flowed into the Columbia, Portland was no longer a frontier town but home to some 30,000 people. As Harvey and his young companion looked over the city, they were impressed with a bustling business community which spread out from the waterfront and into growing residential areas filled with both pretentious and tract homes. The streets were paved and all the conveniences of San Francisco seemed to be present.

The two stayed at a hotel that night and looked for a boarding house the following day. After scanning the newspaper they called at James and Jenny Hamilton's home at 83 Seventh Street. The room seemed to be all they needed, and it had a nice bay window looking out on the street. Harvey gave his name as George Jackson, paid a week's rent, and the two again went out to finalize their operations.

Renting a buggy, Harvey and Williams checked the local schedule of the Oregon Railway and Navigation Railroad, then drove to the outskirts of the city. They selected a spot about five miles east of town in a relatively open area. A doubling spur on the tracks made a wide spot between a slight cut through a hill. Brush and small trees lined the tracks for cover and only a few homes were scattered nearby. A more isolated site would have been preferable, but Harvey was unfamiliar with the country and probably thought they had to be able to get back into town quickly to hide.

Next, they needed dynamite. They called at the California Powder Works and told manager John Willman they were heading for the new Whatcom gold excitement in Washington State and needed explosives. For some reason they did not buy anything at that time, but later purchased twenty sticks of dynamite at Avery & Company's hardware store. Then they were ready.

Evidence indicates at least two others were involved in Harvey's plan, although their identities were never discovered.

Since Lee and Williams had been in town only a few days, they had no time to line up trustworthy locals. Any accomplices must have come from San Francisco, probably on the same boat.

The men selected Saturday, September 25, for the holdup. That evening Harvey rented a buggy at the Fashion Stables. He returned for Williams, and after loading their guns and dynamite in the vehicle they proceeded to the robbery site. Express Number Two was due out of Portland shortly after 9:00 P.M., and after hiding the horse and buggy in the brush, the two outlaws anxiously looked around for their tardy companions.

Harvey must have been close to panic when he heard the train in the distance and the accomplices still had not appeared. Telling Williams to keep an eye out for their partners, Harvey lit a lantern and stepped into the middle of the tracks. As the train approached he began waving the light and was relieved when the big express engine ground to a halt before him. Still looking around frantically for their accomplices, Harvey stepped around to the cab and commanded the engineer to climb down.

"No," blurted out engineer Charles Evans, "I'm not going to do it."

"You won't?" returned Lee and he let go one barrel of his shotgun up into Evans' general area. The engineer quickly jumped down to the tracks.

Meanwhile Williams was addressing fireman Marion P. Wilkes in a similar scenario. When Williams told Wilkes to get down, he asked what was going on. Williams answered with a warning shot that whizzed by the fireman's head and buried itself in the baggage car. At that, Wilkes also climbed down onto the tracks. Keeping his pistol leveled, Williams walked the fireman down the tracks and into the train's headlamp. In a few minutes Harvey joined him, prodding Evans into the lamplight.

Standing in the light with their two captives, both bandits looked around and Lee made several remarks about undependable accomplices. Meanwhile, brakeman J.W. Casey came walking down the tracks to see why the train had stopped.

When he heard the two shots fired he pulled his bulldog revolver and rolled under the baggage car, just behind the engine. After exchanging several shots with the bandits, Casey retreated.

The outlaws and their two captives now stepped out of the light and into the brush to make a less inviting target. Seizing the opportunity, Casey climbed into the cab and succeeded in backing the engine some distance to the rear.

Frustrated and cursing, Lee and Williams saw their scheme falling apart. With no help to dynamite the express car and with the trainmen and passengers all alerted, they could do little except abandon their plans. Determined not to leave empty-handed, Lee told Evans to shell out and seized the engineer's proffered watch, chain, and coin purse containing five dollars. Williams gave the fireman the same order, but obtained only eight dollars. Ordering the trainmen to walk back to the engine, the outlaws vanished into the surrounding brush.

The holdup caused a sensation in Portland. When railroad Superintendent James P. O'Brien received the news, he promptly contacted Captain James Nevins of the local Pinkerton National Detective Agency office. Nevins and two assistants rushed to the scene of the crime, arriving about four o'clock the following morning.

A careful investigation yielded a number of shell casings and about fifteen sticks of dynamite, all fused and ready to go. The explosives had obviously been meant for the express car safe. Carefully prowling along the tracks, the detectives found the bandits' trail into the brush, where a horse and buggy had been secured. They carefully noted the horseshoe marks, and the buggy tracks seemed to lead back towards town.

Confident they had done all they could at the holdup site, Nevins and his men followed the buggy tracks. For a mile or so the tracks were clear enough, but near the city, milk wagons and other vehicles obscured them. Obviously their quarry was headed for town, and the lawmen concentrated on locating the source of the outlaws' horse and rig.

Checking the local stables, Nevins struck pay dirt at the

Fashion. A lone man had indeed hired a rig the previous evening, and the timing fit perfectly with the robbery. After obtaining a description, Nevins set out to find the bandits.

Meanwhile Superintendent O'Brien had also alerted the chief of police, a man named Barry. Dispatching four of his detectives to canvass the lower end of town for suspects, Barry and Detective Al Cody began walking to the robbery scene. They hoped to look for clues along the way and maybe even run into the escaping outlaws. Nevins and his men had already gone over the robbery site thoroughly, so there was little for the chief and Cody to do. Barry did notice the buggy and horse tracks, however, and retracing his steps to town, he too directed his men to search for a stable that had rented a horse and rig that evening.

The lawmen were out in force when the big break came. A day before the robbery, Jenny Hamilton had been cleaning her new boarders' room when she noticed a bundle marked "caution" under the bed. Opening one end of the package, she was sure the contents were dynamite. Nosing about the room, she discovered two shotguns and a pair of pistols wrapped in newspapers in a bureau drawer. When she told her husband what she had found, they decided to terminate the arrangement the moment Jackson's rent was up.

Reading about the holdup in the *Portland Oregonian*, Jim Hamilton immediately thought of his wife's discovery. She also had seen their two mysterious boarders loading something into a buggy that night. The timing added to the couple's suspicions, and Hamilton was soon telling his story at police headquarters.

Certain they had their men, investigators devised a plan whereby the officers would keep out of sight and follow their informant home. If the two outlaws were in their room, Hamilton was to signal by raising his hand. Chief Barry, Captain Nevins, and Detectives Joe Reilly and one Maher made up the posse and were waiting in concealment when they saw the signal.

Fearing the outlaws might try to escape by jumping through the bay window, Barry and Nevins waited outside while Reilly and Maher slipped in through the front door. Kicking open the door with pistols at the ready, the detectives shouted "hands up" and took the two bandits completely by surprise. Both moved for the bureau, and Williams had his hand in the drawer when one of the detectives thrust a pistol under his nose and warned him again to put up his hands. In a moment the men were in custody—and Harvey Lee was on his way to prison again.

At the city jail the prisoners gave their names as George Jackson and Charles Williams and insisted they were innocent of the charge against them. The *Oregonian* reported, "Jackson is 50 years of age, has a countenance suggestive of a reflective mind, and would be taken for an ordinary business man. His blue eyes wander restlessly when addressed, especially when denying the grave charges now confronting him. He impresses the observer that he has remarkable coolness, which was demonstrated thoroughly during the robbery and arrest.

"Williams is a younger man, giving his age as 23. He has not the thoughtful expression characteristic of his senior companion, and would quickly be selected as the instrument of the latter."

The prisoners continued to insist they were innocent, but a grand jury indicted them on September 28. Evidence against them was strong and accumulating fast. Ironically, they could not be tried for mail or train robbery, but only for armed robbery and assault with deadly weapons against the two trainmen.

Although the shooting aspects of the incident were serious enough, the whole business was such a bungled, comic-opera affair that the *Oregonian* couldn't resist some jocular editorializing:

> The Association of United Trainrobbers should petition the court to incarcerate these men for life for bringing a profession that has heretofore boasted a distinct purpose and cleverness and courage in its execution into disrepute, and making it a laughter to common pickpockets. With the exception of the effort to secure a handsome reward through the robbery of a grave in Riverview cemetery a few

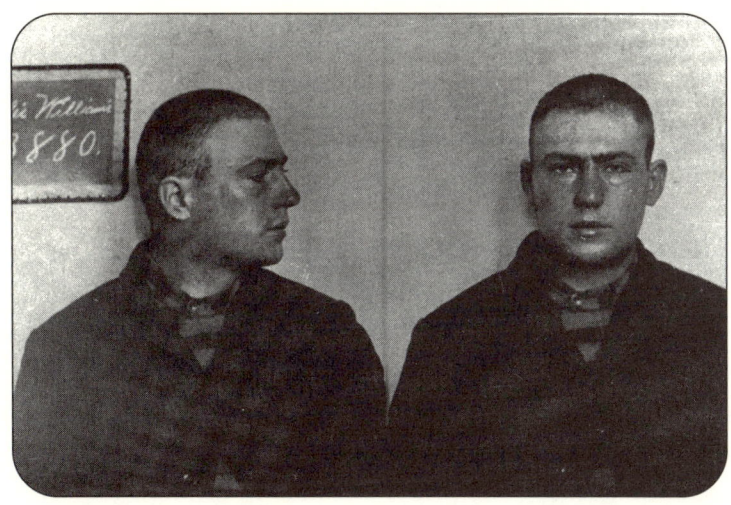

As he posed for his Oregon prison mug shot, Charles Williams must have wondered why he ever got mixed up with Harvey Lee.

Portland police detective Joe Reilly was among the officers who arrested Lee and Williams for the Oregon train robbery.

months ago, the attempt at train robbery will go upon the records as the most abortive aping of the tactics of the skilled desperado by the witless amateur in crime that has ever found its way to the criminal calendar. If this thing continues, an embecile [sic] ward will become a necessary adjunct to the state penitentiary.

Lee and young Williams made their trial appearance on the afternoon of October 8, 1897, in the Multnomah County Circuit Court in Portland. Harvey had done some thinking—it was no use trying to avoid the inevitable. Using the name Jackson had prevented local investigators from uncovering his past, and perhaps the judge would go easy on him. If he took the blame himself, Williams might be acquitted and could work on the outside for Harvey's parole. Through his counsel he asked to change his plea from innocent to guilty. The court agreed and set the following week for sentencing.

Meanwhile the court proceeded with the Williams trial. Prior to calling the first witness, District Attorney Charles Lord made a startling announcement. "Your Honor, there is a box full of dynamite in the courtroom. It is right here alongside the jury and any slight jar might explode it. It was found near the scene of the holdup and was brought here by the police as evidence. As for myself, I would rather it was somewhere else."

As the jury stirred uneasily in their seats, the explosives were removed to the county clerk's office and the trial continued. Although Harvey insisted Williams was not at the holdup, other evidence refuted his testimony, and Williams was easily convicted. On October 12 both men received concurrent sentences of twelve years and three months and eighteen years and four months in the Oregon penitentiary. The stiff sentence startled Harvey. He had gambled and lost and now faced another long prison term.

In his San Francisco office, relentless Wells, Fargo detective chief James B. Hume read of the Portland train robbery attempt. Like all good detectives, Hume's eyes naturally sought out such articles in the press. Something clicked in his mind. That man Jackson—the description sounded familiar, but he

Milton Harvey Lee's mug shot as he entered the Oregon State Penitentiary.

just could not place him. He was probably an old convict and he looked through his wanted circulars, mug books, and clippings to see if anything would jell. Finally, various references to Milton Harvey Lee seemed to add up. He wrote to the Portland chief of police and asked for photographs of the prisoners. When he received the mug shots he failed to recognize Williams, but definitely identified Lee. Either Hume did not communicate with Portland about the true identity of their prisoner, or his message was lost. When Lee entered the Oregon state prison on October 16, 1897, he was still known as Jackson.

Originally established in 1851 in Portland, the Oregon penitentiary was shifted to Salem in 1866. It was a drab, granite fortress surrounded by forests that greeted Harvey. He knew what to expect. Like most such institutions the prison had a variety of work programs for the inmates, who numbered around 300 at any given time. The Loewenberg-Going Company operated a foundry manufacturing stoves, and a brickyard was fast falling into disuse because of exhausted clay deposits. Trusties did road work and maintained government grounds, while extensive vegetable gardens were cultivated for prison use and private sale. Prison maintenance provided endless chores, while warehouse work details unloaded or shipped supplies and goods.

While exchanging his clothes for prison stripes, Harvey submitted to a close examination which disclosed all pertinent marks on his body. He had numerous "pit scars" indicative of an early pox infection, while several abscess marks on the groin suggested bouts with venereal disease. Various scars on his hands testified to his carpentry work. Curiously, his lack of teeth is not mentioned, nor is a scar "at the base of his neck where a tube has been inserted in an operation for lung trouble" as recorded in a Portland newspaper. He weighed 146 pounds.

Harvey and Williams were assigned to the same cell. A former San Quentin inmate quickly identified Lee and spread the word that he was an old California stage robber who had served several previous terms. His recent train exploit was also the talk of the yard. The petty thieves and grifters, who had no idea how unsuccessful Jackson had been as a bandit, were soon calling him "the Old Hero" and other grandiose names. Despite all that, prison authorities did not discover Jackson's real identity.

According to Joseph "Bunco" Kelley, an inmate at the time, Jackson and Williams kept to themselves for several years, the old man refusing to associate with anyone but train robbers. Kelley recalled that after two years of prison life the Old Hero was ready to make a break, but that was about as successful as his other law-breaking ventures.

Over a period of time Harvey and Williams managed to smuggle various tools into their cell—probably in pieces. They began cutting their way out through the ceiling one night and had reached the roof when one of them dropped a drill which clattered to the floor. Hearing the noise, a prisoner called to a guard who quickly sounded the alarm and summoned reinforcements. The two convicts were ordered to return to their cell immediately or be shot.

"We will come down," shouted Harvey. "We have no arms."

Guards seized the men when they dropped to the floor and took them to the dungeon to await punishment. Warden Gilbert ordered Lee and Williams to each receive thirteen lashes, and the following day they were stripped and tied to the whipping post. "Old Jackson," recalled Bunco Kelley, "never made a cry, but every time the Man of Flogs came down on his back he would groan. Look out for the man who does not yell. Young Williams cried for mercy very hard."

The beating must have caused Harvey to reflect on his course of action. Stories circulated that Deputy Warden Charles Sherwood, who had flogged Harvey, had killed men with the lash. Harvey was too frail to bear up under many such whippings, and he determined on another approach to seek his freedom.

Bunco Kelley recalled Harvey's going to work with him in the prison warehouse. "This was the first time I was close to him, and as I looked at him a shiver went over me. There was something unnatural about him. His face looked like that of a corpse from the many years he had served in penitentiaries. Jackson would go all day without speaking to anyone."

Harvey was anxious to put his new plan into operation which included cozying up to the new superintendent, Joseph D. Lee. His scheme involved planting the idea that a big break was imminent, then implicating some of the convicts and making himself enough of a hero to win a pardon. The plan was good, but Harvey was playing a dangerous double game as he also told his fellow convicts he was planning a large-scale break-out. At that time Bunco Kelley was not aware of Harvey's scheming, but he later figured it out. He said:

> One day Jackson saw me speaking to Superintendent Lee and he came over to where I was working and asked me if I knew Mr. Lee on the outside. I said I knew him slightly, and Jackson asked what had been Lee's business. For a josh I replied "I think he is a minister." Jackson answered: "Well, he looks like one, but the reason I asked was because I wanted to know. I think he is a relative of mine. My name is Lee. This Jackson is only a penitentiary name."
>
> After this Jackson tried to become very friendly with me.

Harvey continued with his plan, talking to convicts in the yard, then later telling a guard they were in on the escape plot. The officials probably were not sure just how far they could trust old Jackson, yet they could not afford to ignore him, either. Kelley called on Superintendent Lee at the prison chapel one morning and began telling him of Jackson's machinations. When the official gave him the "glassy eye," Kelley turned and left. The superintendent obviously did not believe him.

Later Harvey asked him what he and Superintendent Lee had talked about. Kelley just laughed and told him he had been promised a pardon.

"I wish you would go and tell him these fellows are talking of a break," Harvey mused.

"What fellows?" queried Kelley.

"These long-timers."

Entrance to the Oregon State Penitentiary, about 1899. Here, Harvey Lee finally decided he had seen enough of prison bars.

"You're crazy," declared Kelley.

Later he found himself "hung up" for four hours when Jackson told guard Jack Stapleton that Kelley had called him a stool pigeon.

Harvey's scheme began to pay off when his accusations resulted in a group of lifers being singled out to wear Oregon Boots. The steel devices, often weighing up to twenty-eight pounds, were locked onto a man's ankle forcing him to work, eat, and sleep with them.

Harvey thought his freedom was imminent now for preventing a break, but nothing happened. He begged Superintendent Lee for a pardon, saying the prison was no longer safe for him, but still no pardon came. Angry and frustrated, he next tried to talk some of the convicts into helping him burn down the prison.

Harvey tried various other ploys to gain his release. When he announced he had taken up religion, he made it credible as he really had learned the Bible backwards and forwards at some point in his life. "He could tell any passage in the Bible," recalled Bunco Kelley, "and when the old plotter was talking to a minister he could make a fool of the clergyman on the Scripture." Harvey was taken down to the creek one Sunday and baptized, but several of the guards were on to him and they made him wear his wet clothes the rest of the day.

One of the convicts forced to wear a "boot" as a result of Harvey's scheming was an obscure stick-up man and burglar named Harry Tracy. When Tracy was placed in his "boot," Harvey told him to "keep a stiff upper lip."

Bunco Kelley maintained that Harvey's plotting and scheming put the idea of escape in Tracy's mind. "Neither Tracy nor [David] Merrill would ever have thought of anything like it had Jackson not given them the plans," Kelley said, but that was probably overstating the case. Tracy was a desperado who was bitter towards several guards and had already escaped from the Utah State Prison in late 1897. The Oregon Boot incident may have stiffened his resolve, but he undoubtedly would have attempted escape at the first opportunity—with or without the prompting of Milton Harvey Lee, alias George Jackson.

At 7:00 A.M. June 9, 1902, Tracy, his pal Merrill, and a group of other convicts were marched to the prison foundry to begin work. Suddenly shop guard Frank B. Ferrell saw Tracy with a rifle in his hands. "Oh my God!" he gasped as the convict shot him through the heart.

Merrill also grabbed a rifle that had been secreted in the foundry and the two prisoners, each with a bag of ammunition, prepared to make their escape. They fired at two other guards who had fled toward the chapel, then turned to the windows to see where the guards were on the walls. As they shot from the windows, convicts and guards were running in all directions in the prison yard.

Rushing to another room in the foundry where a ladder was stored, Merrill ran into convict Frank Ingram and covered him with his rifle. As Ingram pushed the muzzle down, Merrill fired and Ingram collapsed with a bullet in the leg.

Tracy rushed in at that point, and the two convicts began raking the southwest and northwest guard posts with gunfire to clear the area where they wanted to scale the wall. Guard S.R.T. Jones was shot and killed, while two other guards returned the fire and ducked for cover. Tracy and Merrill rushed through the yard to the wall with the ladder and were quickly on top amid a flurry of whistling bullets. In a moment they had jumped to the ground.

Two guards followed the escapees, but the convicts got the drop on them and took them as hostages. After more guards opened fire from the prison, one of the hostages, B.F. Tiffany, fell dead. The other hostage, a man named Ross, feigned death, and the convicts left him as they fled into the surrounding forest. Heading north, the fugitives crossed the Columbia River into Washington, where Merrill's body was later found. Tracy had supposedly killed him.

Posses gathered in both states as the desperate Tracy shot and killed several more lawmen in his frantic flight. He was heading for Wyoming when he was cornered at an eastern Washington ranch on August 3, 1902. After a gun battle with several posses, the badly wounded outlaw killed himself and his body was returned to the Salem penitentiary.

It would be interesting to know Harvey Lee's reaction as Tracy's corpse was carried through the prison yard. All the convicts viewed the body as it lay in the prison chapel, the guards hoping it would be a lesson the convicts would never forget. Bunco Kelley was bitter over the escape, blaming all the deaths on Harvey for instigating the affair. Whoever was to blame, Harvey Lee decided to give his pardon plan a little more time. He would have to wait nearly four more years.

A series of events that would ultimately help Lee gain his freedom had begun several years earlier and many miles to the south. On a bitterly cold evening in late January 1898, Ike Ruiz was tending bar at his F Street saloon in Fresno's tenderloin district. A neighbor rushed through the swinging doors and told him he must get home in a hurry. Turning the bar over to a patron, Ike ran out the door. At his home several blocks away, he found his mistress lying in the front yard. She was groaning and obviously in great pain. When several neighbors told him she had taken carbolic acid, Ike picked her up and rushed her into the house. He gave her a cup of sweet oil, and as he held her hand she seemed to relax. Meanwhile, frantic telephone calls went out to several local physicians.

When a Dr. Davidson finally arrived, he cared for the young girl for some time before he was certain he had done all he could. Luckily she had taken a small dose of the acid, and the sweet oil undoubtedly saved her life.

About midnight a *Fresno Morning Republican* reporter called at the Ruiz home to inquire about the incident. He found the patient much improved and talked to her briefly. "I was tired of living and wanted to die," she said. "I am sorry I did not succeed." The girl would say no more, other than that she and Ruiz, with whom she had been living for nine months, were having no trouble. She had tried to kill herself on several previous occasions. The reporter, however, learned more from the neighbors, and his story appeared in the paper the next day. "Rose Lee has lived in Fresno for years and is the daughter of Harvey Lee, who was sent to prison from this county about ten [sic] years ago for robbing a stage. Lee's sentence for this crime ended about one year ago, and then he went to Oregon and was implicated in the robbery of the Oregon Express. He was sentenced to thirty years in the penitentiary for this offense. It is reported that Lee committed suicide a short time ago and it is believed that the daughter became despondent because of this."

The *Republican* article leaves no doubt that Rose was a prostitute. The Ruiz home was in the red light district and flanked by cribs, whorehouses, and saloons.

One way or another Rose may have discovered that her father was still alive and initiated a correspondence. Harvey had ignored her all her life, but then he could do little else as he had spent most of his own life in prison. When he made contact with her, he saw a chance to use her for his own purposes and began scheming with renewed vigor.

Playing every card he could think of, Harvey reminded prison officials of his services in ferreting out convicts who were planning escapes. He obtained a promise from former Superintendent Lee to vouch for his services, and he convinced Judge A.F. Sears, who had sentenced him, that he was ill and would lead a reformed life if released. He even solicited and obtained the cooperation of W.W. Cotton, the attorney for the railroad he had attempted to rob.

When Rose Lee promised to take Harvey in and look out for him, Oregon Governor George E. Chamberlain finally relented. On July 16, 1906, he signed a document restoring citizenship and a full pardon to "George J. Jackson." Chamberlain granted the pardon because, according to the document, "the prisoner is now an old man, in feeble health, and the prison physician certifies that he cannot live but a short time; and...his conduct as a prisoner has been exemplary since his imprisonment and his daughter is willing to take him to her home and care for him."

When he stepped out the front gate of the prison, old Harvey Lee had served less than nine years of his thirty-year sentence. But he was weary. He was actually looking forward to seeing his daughter and settling down as he caught the train for California. Besides, what else could he do?

Rose met him at the station in Fresno. The town had changed greatly since he had seen it last. The vast plains surrounding the village he remembered were still evident, but ornate banks and professional buildings gave the city an almost cosmopolitan appearance, and trees were everywhere. Rose had gotten him a small room on R Street, where she would stay and look after him until he got on his feet. She really didn't know how ill he might be, but he assured her he would look for work in a few days. He must have savored his new liberty as he walked about and surveyed the town.

The world Harvey entered was new to him. Men drove automobiles on the streets and flew airplanes through the sky. He liked Fresno. July was hot, with temperatures soaring to 100 degrees, but bands played evening concerts in courthouse park and the Novelty Vaudeville Theater showed motion pictures on the Cinematograph and Novelscope.

Harvey found work at the Fresno Cooperage east of town and was amazed at how mechanized the industry had become. When he first learned coopering in the 1870s, men plied the trade by hand after many years of apprenticeship. The work was exacting and backbreaking and a skilled craftsman could turn out only one barrel a day. Now machines did the work. Operators fed lumber into stave-cutting equipment, and hydraulic pressure then shaped the staves. Yet another machine then assembled the barrels.

The United States manufactured some 300,000,000 barrels annually; the cement business alone required 35,000,000 barrels. In the great San Joaquin Valley of California, people used barrels for a variety of packing and storage uses. Also, large, gravity-feed water tanks supplied most homes and farms, while wineries and breweries used all sorts of tanks, kegs, and casks.

Harvey moved several times in the next few years, finally settling at 328 Mary Street. He worked hard at the cooperage and became shop foreman. Later he was promoted to keep the firm's books. He was undoubtedly glad to get away from the machinery and the physical work required to keep the equipment stoked. As he gazed out the cooperage window from time to time, he must have contemplated his wasted youth.

Seated in the middle of the Fresno Cooperage shop in 1916, Harvey Lee had found a place for himself at last.

Graphic Technology Company

What had ever made him think he could make a living as a bandit? His plunder had been pitiful and he had been quickly caught after every robbery. He shook his head. He had always considered himself a misfit, and as a wayward youth there seemed little else he could do.

Milton Harvey Lee died on July 19, 1916, at the Fresno County Hospital. Neither Grace nor Rose are noted on the death certificate. He is listed as a "widower." The local press gave no notice of his death and there was no estate. Few people were aware of the old outlaw who had lived in their midst and finally redeemed himself by discovering the nobility of work at the end of a lifetime of crime. He lies in an unmarked grave in Fresno's Mountain View Cemetery. In obscurity and death Harvey Lee had found peace at last.

5 THE STRANGE AND BLOODY SAGA OF ABE MAJORS
1880–1957

Outlaw Abe Majors' story is one of waste, tragedy, and deceit. Plagued by the memory of a murderous father who died on a California gallows, Abe betrayed everyone—his mother, his brother, and all who tried to help or reform him. Yet Abe had the type of character and magnetic personality that generated hope in people around him. Most of his friends and family refused to give him up to the underworld that pulled him down.

Born in San Jose, California, on April 2, 1880, Abraham Majors was the second child of Lloyd and Lucinda Majors. Lloyd was born in Illinois and reportedly fought in a Missouri cavalry unit during the Civil War. He claimed to have a law degree from the University of Michigan, but his crude surviving letters indicate little more than a rudimentary education at best.

Lucinda was a beautiful woman of delicate disposition and frail health. Many people wondered what she saw in the gruff, rough-looking Lloyd Majors, but the couple seemed to be happy.

When they married at Council Bluffs, Iowa, Lloyd was a bible-thumping evangelist thought to have great potential in the Methodist church. The couple lived in Missouri for several years, then moved to California in 1875 with their young son, Archibald. Lloyd was active in his San Jose church and seemed to be popular locally.

After moving to the West Coast, however, Lloyd lost much of his missionary zeal and settled into other work. As his wife lavished loving care on their two boys, Lloyd cut cord wood in the nearby mountains, operated a wagon business, and built houses in the area. He was still prominent in his church, however, and often orated at special events in the community.

Apparently a poor businessman, Lloyd never seemed to have enough money. He moved to nearby Los Gatos, where he operated a saloon which did a lackluster business. When fire destroyed the place, he began building a hotel but stopped after completing only the saloon portion. That venture also met with little success. Discouraged, with his wife pregnant again, Lloyd cast about for other means to improve his situation. He must have been in dire straits, for he settled on a desperate scheme.

The few patrons of Lloyd's saloon were sleazy locals who had little money to spend. A recent arrival was an illiterate painter named Joseph Jewell. In talking to Jewell over the bar in February 1883, Lloyd found him morally obtuse enough to be an ideal pawn for his scheme. After business hours one night, Lloyd confided his plans to his new partner.

William P. Renowden, an old recluse who lived in the nearby hills, was rumored to be quite wealthy. Though locals knew he had property and earned a good living, Lloyd discovered he had no accounts in the local banks. Obviously, he was hoarding his wealth at home.

Lloyd's plan was simple. Jewell was to go to the old man's cabin one night, torture him into revealing his treasure's location, then kill him and make the crime appear to be that of an itinerant assassin bent on plunder. Jewell was agreeable, but hesitant about being the lone participant. The men searched for a suitable partner and selected a dull-witted local named John Showers. He would not only aid in the crime, but afterward Jewell would kill him, too. Showers' body would suggest

Lloyd Majors' endless scheming brought despair and tragedy to his family.

California State Library

This newspaper sketch of Abe Majors (left) and his brother, Archie, was drawn from a photograph. San Francisco Call, *August 23, 1895*

that old Renowden had killed his attacker just before he had died. The plan seemed to get better and better.

To explain Jewell's suddenly improved circumstances, Lloyd began a rumor that his associate had recently inherited some money in the East and would be investing it as a partner in Majors' saloon. The two men next made a reconnaissance of the isolated site of their projected crime. Taking a buggy ride through the hills, they stopped at the Renowden cabin and struck up a conversation with the owner. The old man graciously asked them to stay for an evening meal, and incredible as it seems, the two heartless plotters actually accepted the offer.

The night before the crime, Showers and Jewell stayed in an abandoned cabin one-half mile from Renowden's place. Early on March 11 they crept up to the cabin, but were startled to see their intended victim and a Canadian friend of his, Archibald McIntyre, standing in the yard. Disconcerted, the two returned to their cabin and decided to go back that evening and kill both men. At sundown they again approached the cabin and knocked at the door.

When Renowden came out, Jewell asked for directions and the two strolled down the path. When Jewell suddenly told him to hold up his hands, the old man threw himself on his assailant and called out to McIntyre. As the Canadian came running to his aid, Showers appeared and shot him. Mortally wounded, McIntyre staggered back into the cabin and collapsed. Showers then clubbed the struggling Renowden to the ground.

The two thugs now dashed water in their victim's face and slapped him back into consciousness. "Where's the money?" they demanded over and over. The old man refused to say anything, despite threats of being burned alive if he didn't talk. When they poured some turpentine on Renowden's leg and set it on fire, he screamed and fainted. Again resuscitating him, they repeated their demands for the hidden money, but he stoically refused. Screaming and battering him with their fists, Jewell and Showers finally became so frustrated they pressed revolvers to his chest and shot him dead. Frightened that they might be discovered, the murderers fled without even searching for the victim's money.

Returning to Los Gatos the two killers explained what happened to a furious and disgusted Lloyd Majors. The scheming saloon owner saw his whole carefully orchestrated plot falling apart, and all three nervously discussed what to do next. Knowing the crime might be discovered at any moment, Lloyd gave his two henchmen some money and whiskey and ordered them to steal two horses and head south immediately. Majors then returned to the saloon and closed up as soon as possible without arousing any suspicion.

By then it was late at night, and he had to get up to Renowden's cabin and try to salvage the botched crime. Saddling his horse, he galloped furiously into the hills and rushed into the cabin. Mistaking McIntyre's body for Renowden, he piled furniture on the corpse. In a few moments a fire was blazing, engulfing the small shack. In his rush to destroy evidence of the murder, Lloyd overlooked Renowden's body laying outside the burning building. Finishing his dreadful task, he galloped back toward Los Gatos.

Just nineteen days later Lloyd Majors and his two partners were in custody, charged with the double murder. The discovery of Renowden's body the morning after the murders resulted in a manhunt that netted Showers in nearby Gilroy. He quickly confessed and implicated his two partners. Authorities had ample evidence to prosecute the trio, and both Jewell and Showers were convicted. Jewell was executed, while Showers was given a life sentence for his testimony. Lloyd Majors, however, was a different story.

Tried in the Superior Court of Santa Clara County, Lloyd was convicted on May 27, 1883, and sentenced to life in prison. His counsel made no appeal, recognizing his client had received the lightest sentence possible for such a heinous crime. He arrived at San Quentin on June 4 but was returned to the custody of the Santa Clara County sheriff on July 21, when he was charged with the McIntyre murder.

Lloyd's counsel fought to establish that he could not be

tried on the new charge while serving a life sentence, but when a writ of habeas corpus was issued, the superior court dismissed the writ.

Lloyd filed for a change of venue to Alameda County, which he received in early October. While he took up residence in the Oakland jail, Lloyd's counsel again appealed to the supreme court on the grounds that he was being tried for a crime of which he was already convicted. The court heard the case on October 26 but again refused the writ. Lloyd went to trial for the McIntyre murder in Oakland on October 31, 1883.

The trial lasted sixteen days, resulting in a conviction and death sentence. Before the date of hanging had been set, however, a new flurry of appeals began. The execution was finally set for January 18, but because the supreme court was to review his case after that, Governor George Stoneman granted a reprieve until March 14, 1884. The state supreme court refused the latest appeal on February 12. The following day the *San Jose Herald* announced, "Majors must hang." However, as the appeals dragged on the execution was again put off to May 23.

On the night of May 16 two deputies closely watched Lloyd pace in his cell. When the prisoner called for some salts, jailer Pete Lahr opened the cell doors to bring it in. As Lahr stood admiring some flowers, he looked up to see the prisoner bringing a heavy slat down on the head of a guard named Cummings. A desperate fight ensued, and a third deputy ran into the cell when he heard the commotion. Lloyd swung his club with such ferocity that he beat back all three of the deputies. When a blow knocked out the gas light, Lloyd demanded the keys from Lahr, who quickly gave them up. Rushing from the cell, Lloyd fled down the stairs and burst out onto the street just as Lahr began shouting from an upstairs window, "Majors has escaped! Majors has escaped!"

A group of firemen heard the noise and rushed to the jail, where they confronted the escaping prisoner. They recognized him immediately, and fireman Bill Connors knocked Lloyd down with a solid punch to the jaw. Two others seized his arms, and they quickly took him back into the jail.

Physicians were summoned to patch up the battered guards and set Lloyd's broken arm and finger. His only other injuries were a series of scratches on his hands and nose. The *San Jose Herald* was appalled at the escape attempt:

> Majors sat quietly in his cell while the dark cell was being prepared to receive him....He was the coolest man in the room, and endured the pain from his broken arm without a wince or murmur, and said that after leaving the jail he met a policeman and approaching him asked that he take his pistol and shoot him as he preferred to be killed rather than return to the jail.
>
> That one man could overpower three guards as Majors did, would seem almost impossible. In explanation the guards say the attack was so sudden and violent they had no time for any action before they were struck and partially stunned.

Juan Edson, a Santa Clara deputy sheriff, accompanied Lloyd Majors to the gallows on the fateful day, March 14, 1884. The condemned man walked with an unfaltering step, looking neither to the right or left as he strode through the crowd of some 250 spectators. After climbing the steps, Edson stood by Lloyd's side as the noose was adjusted around his neck. When the rope kinked, Edson barked, "turn the rope the other way." In a moment the hood had covered Lloyd's coarse face. As the condemned man swayed slightly, the sheriff waved his hand, and Edson cut the string which triggered the trapdoor. Lloyd shot through to his death.

In San Jose Lucinda Majors had struggled desperately to cope with the tragedy that had engulfed her family. One-year-old Maud, the family's youngest child, had recently died, adding to Lucinda's distress. The *Herald* noted on May 27, "It is reported that Mrs. Majors, the wife of Lloyd L. Majors, is now lying at the point of death at her residence....Mrs. Dr. Curnow, who is taking an active part in assisting her, says that the probabilities are that she will not live until morning. Mrs. Majors did not hear of the execution of Majors until Sunday, and it is said to have given her such a nervous shock—being in delicate health anyway—that she will never fully rally. She is said to be a refined and estimable woman and never deserved such a fate."

Somehow Mrs. Majors held on and put the shattered pieces of her life back together. She managed to keep her two boys oblivious to their father's fate, carefully shielding them from the damning news.

Lucinda married Joseph A. Wagner in 1886 and the family moved to San Francisco, where she happily looked forward to beginning a new life. Young Abe and Archie attended the public schools there, while Lucinda had two more sons by Wagner.

But misery seemed to be Lucinda's fate. Joseph soon proved to be unfaithful and the couple divorced in 1893. Doing whatever she could to earn a small income, the frail woman was forced to remove Abe and Archie from school so they could help provide for the family. Abe worked in a warehouse office for a time, and when he obtained a better position with a news dealer, the family moved to Oakland to be closer to his new job.

Whenever she could, Lucinda sought the comfort of her church and a small circle of new acquaintances. She worked at a local mission with a Mrs. Willmore and the two became close friends. When he had the time, Abe sought the company of Mrs. Willmore's son, Bert, and took a fancy to Bert's ten-year-old sister, Ina. In March 1895 he presented the girl with a gift which upset his mother considerably. Lucinda considered the gift improper and insisted Abe retrieve it. When he refused, they had an argument and Abe ran away from home. Lucinda later claimed that Mrs. Willmore was weaning Abe away from his own family, and that was the cause of the argument.

Angered and humiliated, Abe fled to the San Joaquin Valley, where he found work in a vineyard near Hanford. His mother, heartbroken over the rift with her son, was having difficulty making ends meet. In late August she saw a brief item in a San Francisco newspaper announcing the engagement of her ex-husband to a San Mateo girl. Wagner had been ignoring alimony payments for many months despite Lucinda's attempts to collect through the Humane Society, a children's

San Jose, California, as it appeared when the Majors family lived there. The Santa Clara County courthouse, where Lloyd Majors was tried, is the large white building at left center.

welfare organization. To make matters worse, instead of working on Wagner, a Mrs. Sanford of the Humane Society constantly pressured Lucinda to put her children in foster homes because of the family's poverty. She even located Abe in Hanford and had him returned to Oakland and jailed for vagrancy. Lucinda was horrified, as the *San Francisco Call* reported on August 23. Lucinda said, "I consider Mrs. Sanford's conduct in the matter extremely uncalled-for and most heartless. When it was proved my boy was working he was allowed to go free, with the disgrace of having been arrested hanging over him, and most of all, while there he was told for the first time how his father had met his death, a terrible revelation to him."

Abe returned to San Francisco, where he got a job at the Beresford Hotel. He was still depressed over learning of his hideous heritage when the hotel was sold in December and he found himself out of work and broke.

Returning to Oakland, he took up residence with the Willmores, where he and his friend Bert ostensibly looked for work. Ashamed of his father, Abe used the name Ford. He also sought to make it more difficult for his mother to find him.

But the evil that seemed to hover about the family settled on Abe. He could not dismiss the shock of his father's death. Not only was he a murderer, but he had been hanged in that very city.

Finding jobs scarce and disliking the only types of work open to them, Abe and Bert Willmore began thinking about burglarizing some local stores. Young Majors found it easy to rationalize such work now. Was he not the son of a murderer who had paid for his crime on the gallows? Was it not natural that a son follow in his father's footsteps? The two boys began making plans.

On the evening of February 6, 1896, three Oakland police officers were standing at the corner of Fifth and Washington streets when they noticed two boys walking towards them. After a series of recent break-ins and safe burglaries, the police were being roundly criticized for their lack of arrests. This night the officers had orders to stop and question anyone on the street, suspicious or otherwise.

The policemen first dismissed the figures as newsboys, but stopped and searched them. To their great surprise they found the boys were carrying burglary tools, a coil of fuse, and pistols. The officers lodged the boys at the station house.

Bert Willmore admitted his name, but Abe gave his as Ford. He was promptly identified, however. Scared and discouraged, the boys showed the incredulous officers where their loot had been hidden at the Willmore home.

The *San Francisco Chronicle* was as amazed as the rest of the bay area over the arrests:

TWO YOUNGSTERS AS SAFE-CRACKERS

> The Oakland police have arrested the burglars and safe crackers who have been terrorizing the town, looting stores and blowing and drilling safes for the past month, and the strange part of it all is that there were only two persons in the jobs and they were not old hands at all at the business, but mere stripling boys, one aged 17 and the other 16 years. One of them is well known in Oakland.
>
> They were reticent at first, and denied all knowledge of the burglaries, but by close questioning, separately, they finally confessed to being the authors of all the Oakland, Alameda and Berkeley robberies, including the blowing open of Girard's piano-store safe.

The "Boy Burglars" caused a sensation when they appeared in police court on February 7. A hearing was set for the following week.

Police suspected Mrs. Willmore knew of the boys' activities, although both vehemently denied it. She claimed Abe had told her the money came from an eastern relative, but she lied when she said she had only known Abe by the name of Ford. Lucinda Wagner had no doubts about her former friend, however. "All is due to Mrs. Willmore," she cried. "I feared it all along. The woman had a bad influence over my boy and I had forbidden his going to her house....I saw him going into that house the other night, and many times since have I walked past there crying and praying that he would come back to me.

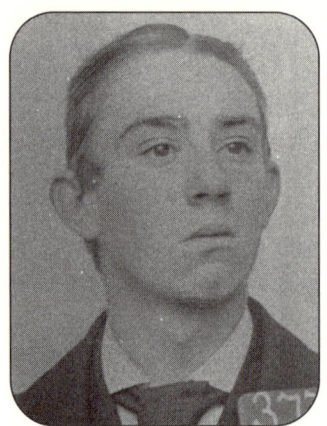

Both: California State Archives

Folsom Prison mugshots of Bert Willmore (above) and Abe Majors (right).

California State Library

The fearsome granite walls of Folsom must have terrified young Abe Majors, but he quickly adapted to prison life.

He never came, and here is where it has all ended."

Abe had given Ina Willmore an engagement ring and hoped they could marry when he turned eighteen. Mrs. Willmore had encouraged the relationship. When Mrs. Willmore blamed Abe for Bert's criminal activities, Abe saw his association with the Willmores disintegrating. Now he had nowhere to turn.

While police questioned him, Abe bitterly complained about his troubles at home. "I left my mother because she made my life unbearable for me at home. She took every cent I earned. I went to live at the Willmores after this, but Mrs. Willmore did not entice me away, as claimed by my mother."

Adding to her troubles, Lucinda was evicted from her home for non-payment of rent and was now staying with friends. She wept bitterly as she stood beside Abe at his February 26 preliminary hearing in superior court. Her older son, Archie, was also in court watching the proceedings; he, too, had turned against his mother. "While Mrs. Wagner was led away half-fainting by friends," commented a newspaper report, "Archie, cold and immovable of countenance, left the courtroom without giving her a passing glance."

In a superior court hearing on February 28, 1896, the boys pleaded guilty. By then Abe was accusing Mrs. Willmore of being fully aware of the boys' crimes. Despite their lawyer's plea to send them to the boys' reformatory at Ione, Judge Waldo York sentenced the young defendants to the state penitentiary at Folsom for ten years each. The judge remarked that the boys' record of crime was one of the most remarkable that had ever come to his knowledge, but he stressed that by good behavior they could be transferred to Ione in a few years. Lucinda nearly collapsed as Abe was taken away on March 3.

Just why Judge York gave the teenaged first offenders the maximum sentence allowed is unknown. Certainly, the Preston School of Industry at Ione would seem to be the obvious place to send them, not Folsom, although from ten to fifteen percent of California prison inmates over the years had been under twenty years of age. Apparently, the merchants who had been robbed lobbied hard for the boys' harsh punishment. The pistols and dynamite they carried at the time of their arrests indicated they were dangerous characters despite their youth, and the fact that Abe's father was the notorious Lloyd Majors did not help his case any. Just where Abe had learned the use of dynamite in blowing safes was never disclosed.

At Folsom Abe Majors became number 3770. Other convicts pitied the boys and treated them well as they went about their assigned work projects. In prison Abe quickly learned how important it was to have someone on the outside working for his release. Whether his confinement suddenly rekindled an appreciation of his mother or more practical reasons dictated his affection is open to question. In any case, a letter Abe wrote on March 6, 1897, reflects, among other things, the young man's shattering realization of his loss of freedom.

> Dearest Mother:
> Received your welcome letter of 26th inst. this evening, although it was brief you may be sure it was appreciated for your letter[s] always are, in refering [sic] to your letters Mr. Roberts are included for when he writes I know it for you as well as for himself.
> Your letters tend to break the monotony of my confinement, they remind me that I am not altogether forgotten by the outside world.
> You do not know how often I think of you all and wish for your health. Dear Mother how I long to show you how I value your love and devotion, how I wish to show my love in return. Oh, if I had relized your love before I left home, if I had known how you sacrificed your self for me—Oh! why was I so infatuated that I could not relize your benignant [intentions], if I had but relized [sic] this before I would never have caused you or myself this misery & suffering. You do not know how I preserve and revere the memory of our happy home, it certainly was happy before that first cloud of troble [sic] threw its shadow across our threshole [sic].
> Well dearest mother enough of this reminiscence, I fear I have already made you mellancoly [sic], if I have you will have to excuse me for I am inclined to be [so] my self tonight.

> Well dearest of mothers I will now close hopeing [sic] this
> will find you, the children & friend Harry as well as it leaves
>
> > Your Devoted Son
> > Abe Majors

Lucinda Wagner, with her frail health and poverty, drove herself desperately in her son's behalf. She was particularly distraught to think of her sixteen-year-old boy living among hundreds of thieves and murderers. She launched a vigorous campaign calling attention to Abe's age as the most vulnerable point of attack in his case. She initiated a petition even before the boys had left for Folsom.

Fighting back her despair, Lucinda located the physician who had delivered Abe in San Jose. Doctor George Bentley provided a notarized statement that Abe had been born on April 2, 1880. That was conclusive evidence the boy was indeed under sixteen years old when sentenced to prison. A San Jose friend, Mrs. Alice Shaw, supplied a statement testifying to Abe's birthdate, while Lucinda also had her own statement notarized.

As she collected other affidavits Lucinda sought out various agencies that might work in her behalf. Lydia Prescott, of the California Society for the Prevention of Cruelty to Children, lent a sympathetic ear but hesitated to take any action until a period of time had elapsed and the boys' records could be properly evaluated. Lucinda's tearful pleading finally won Prescott over, and she visited Governor James H. Budd on Lucinda's behalf in June 1896. The governor was understanding, but insisted it was too early for any action.

Though barely surviving on the charity of friends, Lucinda kept up her work on Abe's behalf. She wrote government representatives, contacted newspapers, and wrote anyone who might help in her fight. Mrs. Ella Clune, a family friend, wrote a typical deposition:

> To whom it may concern I would say I first knew Abe Majors when he was between 14 and 15. I saw a great deal of him in his home life and considered him a model boy. In fact I always spoke of him as a noble little fellow. His mother

told me he was her main support. He had a steady position at good pay, but would neither get him flannels or overcoat as he always said his mother needed every dollar to help pay the rent and feed his two little half-brothers, who were neglected by their *own father*.

I spoke to Mrs. McChesney, wife of the principal of the girls High School. I told her of the manly spirit of this very young boy. She was so pleased to hear of such a brave little fellow, that she sent him her son's over-coat.

He must have been strictly honest as I remember on one occasion he brought home a large sum of his employment money to keep over night. He got his mother to hide it in different parts of the house, but that boy was so conscientious, and the responsibility so great, that he had nightmares all night. His mother in singing his praise told me all this next day....There are thousands in this city who would be glad to see him free and helping his mother again. She is not physically strong and the support of two small children is too much for her alone.

Day after day Lucinda kept up the fight. In August Mrs. Prescott wrote to the governor and included a collection of affidavits. By then Governor Budd had received a favorable statement concerning Abe's prison record, but it was still too early to stir him. Continuing her campaign, Lucinda wrote letters, contacted friends, collected more depositions, and talked to prosecutors. She called on the robbed merchants and obtained their forgiveness. In February 1898 she wrote J.E. Baker, the Folsom general overseer, for a report on her son. Baker responded that, "Your son, Abe Majors, has behaved himself exceedingly well during his imprisonment here and has no punishment record against him and therefore has a clear record. He is in the best of health."

In April Lucinda had the pastor of her church write the governor while she kept up the pressure on all fronts. That same month she received a letter from Abe:

Dearest Mother:
Received a most welcome letter from you last week. Was

very glad to hear of your recovered health, and that my dear little brothers retain theirs.

You mentioned in your letter that you would send me a clipping from a paper. If you have not already sent it, do not, for daily State journals, or clippings therefrom are not allowed the prisoners here, you also mentioned the petition to be presented to the Governor, you can not imagine the hope it imbibes me with, not only hope, but ambition, the one desire of my heart is to be free once again, and to prove that I am a man and not a criminal.

When I look back to the time when I committed the crimes for which I am now confined here, it seem[s] to me that I must have been suffering from aberation [sic] of the mind, the only excuse I can offer is that I did not relize [sic] the enormity of the crimes I committed. When I once more have my liberty, I will exemplify that I have good morals and that I can follow their dictates.

Before I close allow me to offer a suggestion in regard to your movement for a pardon for me. I think it very expedient that an application be made to the Prison directors for a recommendation of good conduct and etc. to be presented with the petition to the Governor.

Well dear mother I will now close, sending my love to the little ones and yourself and my best regards to all my friends I remain

Your Devoted Son Abe Majors

Lucinda's improved health was probably due to her frenzied work on Abe's case. She hardly had time to think of herself and her problems seemed insignificant when compared to her son's miserable situation. Finally, all the effort and heartbreak paid off. A petition and dozens of other statements and depositions were forwarded to the governor and prison directors, who scheduled a meeting for June 18, 1898, to consider recommendation for executive clemency. But the hearing was a disappointment. Both Abe and Bert Willmore's cases were rejected.

Lucinda was crushed, but redoubled her efforts when reminded that a pardon was still possible. She received a favorable letter from Folsom Warden Charles Aull, and Alameda District Attorney Charles Snook joined the campaign and forwarded Aull's letter to Judge York, who had sentenced the boys. On September 30 Judge York wrote saying he, too, would recommend a parole. However, parolees had to have jobs awaiting them, and Lucinda's group secured several offers of employment. Lucinda was ecstatic when she received word the prison parole committee had recommended parole. "As we state in the case of Willmore," warned the report, "unless proper restrictions and supervision is thrown around these boys, they will certainly be returned to prison." But Lucinda did not care—her boy would be free.

On December 28, 1898, Abe Majors returned home. He showed great affection for his mother and was delighted to be among friends and family again. He had never fully realized the joys of walking the hills of Oakland and gazing out over the bay.

His brother Archie had married the previous year and had been living with his wife in Seattle, Washington. Archie had always traveled, and he spent most of 1895 working as a cowboy in Texas. He had returned home just before Abe's trial but was broke and in rags, and his mother had to clothe him. After his brother left for Folsom, Archie met a young Salvation Army girl named Lena Stone and swept her off her feet. They decided to move away and get married, but Archie had no money. Taking everything of value from his mother's house, he and Lena went to Sacramento, where they were married. They finally settled in Seattle and soon had a child.

Archie probably had not known that Lena was an orphan who had been rescued from a Utah brothel as a young girl. Later she had joined the Salvation Army and was serving in Oakland when Archie met her. The marriage went bad, however, and Archie reportedly abandoned his family. Some stories maintained that he had learned of his wife's previous occupation and insisted she again take to the streets to support him. Whatever caused the breakup, Archie showed up in Oakland shortly after Abe's parole.

The brothers revitalized their kinship, but Abe appeared

unsettled for some reason, as if trying to make a serious decision. Perhaps Archie was plying him with stories of the wild, free life of a cowboy—of bandits and outlaws he had met in Texas. At the same time he belittled Abe's low-paying job and the strictures of his parole.

Lucinda may have seen the tell-tale signs. Abe seemed happy, however, and she had her family back again. When the boys didn't show up at home for a few days in late March 1899, she worried but assumed they had merely taken a brief trip. Abe had to report to the local police headquarters on April 1 under the terms of his parole, and when that day came and passed she knew something was wrong. Friends again noticed her haggard face and the vacant look in her eyes.

Late Saturday, April 29, 1899, the telephone rang at the Ogden, Utah, police headquarters. When Captain William A. "Billy" Brown picked up the receiver, he probably assumed it was just one of his patrolmen needing help with a rowdy drunk. Instead, the call was from nearby Box Elder County. Brown listened attentively as a deputy sheriff reported a gun battle with two highwaymen near Brigham City. The lawmen had the men hemmed in, but wanted reinforcements when they pressed the attack again in the morning. Brown agreed to assemble a posse and join the other lawmen at the Hot Springs some miles north of the city.

Getting permission from his chief, Brown called Weber County Sheriff Layne and deputies Joseph Belnap and Bailey, and they met on a downtown street corner. Sheriff Layne and Deputy Belnap started their buggy up the North Ogden road, while Captain Brown and Bailey headed up the Harrisville road. The four Ogden lawmen met the Box Elder County officers at the Springs just before daylight.

The two outlaws had been hanging around Brigham City all day Saturday. That evening they robbed milk peddler James Hampton on the road. They took a trivial amount of cash, a watch, and even Hampton's shoes. After tying him up, they drank the bucket of milk he had been carrying, then moved on. Hampton soon freed himself and promptly alerted the officers at Brigham City.

Box Elder County Sheriff Cardon, a deputy and a local constable intercepted the bandits at the Hot Springs. They were walking down the railroad track, but when the officers told them to halt they took off at a run up a road. The lawmen chased the outlaws into the hills, where a pistol duel erupted. After exhausting their ammunition, the officers retreated and called for help.

Splitting into three parties of two men each, the lawmen tracked the outlaws into the hills and soon found their camp. Joining forces again, Sheriff Layne and Deputy Bailey took their buggy around a mountain the outlaws were crossing as Joe Belnap, Captain Brown, and Sheriff Cardon followed the tracks on foot. Soon the tracks appeared quite fresh.

"Here are their tracks," shouted Belnap, "and they are as fresh as ours."

Billy Brown dashed ahead, and soon the two fugitives raced down the steep side of the mountain. Cardon yelled for Brown to wait, but he plunged on. Belnap called for the outlaws to halt when they were about seventy-five yards away. Only fifty yards separated Brown from his quarry as both parties drew their pistols. The officers called for the bandits to surrender, but they opened fire instead, just as all three lawmen also began shooting. With little cover on the steep mountainside, Brown held onto brush to keep his balance. The larger of the two outlaws dropped as his partner fired at Brown and missed. Belnap later recalled the exciting scene:

> As the young robber started to shoot again Billy was off his balance, but he and Cardon shot and missed and I pulled my Winchester on him and pulled the trigger, but I had forgotten to throw the old shell out and the hammer struck the exploded cap and just at that second the robber fired and Billy gave a sharp cry and fell forward. The robber had aimed with his revolver resting on his left arm and took steady aim. Cardon and I both shot at him as he dropped behind the rock near where his brother lay, and I fired again as he raised his head, chipping the rock and throwing it in his face.

San Francisco Call, *May 14, 1899*

A newspaper sketch by noted California artist Maynard Dixon portrays a romanticized, inaccurate concept of the fight in the Utah hills.

Cardon called out for the outlaw to surrender, but he yelled back that his brother had been killed. "You have killed a better man than half a dozen such as he," responded Belnap.

Finally, the bandit put up his hands and stood up. Belnap immediately ran over to Billy Brown and found him dead. The one bandit was dead also and Belnap tossed his cuffs to the sheriff to put on the sullen prisoner. The party then returned to Brigham City with the sad news of Captain Brown's death.

Billy Brown's funeral cortege was over a mile long and included some 2,000 people. The president of the Mormon Church was scheduled to speak, but was held up in Salt Lake City. "A braver man never lived," commented Joe Belnap. The popular officer left a wife and five children.

In the Brigham City jail, the prisoner claimed his name was James Morgan and that he and his dead brother were from Chicago. He identified two photographs found on the dead bandit as his sister-in-law and niece who lived in British Columbia. By early May the jig was pretty much up, however.

Oakland authorities had put out bulletins on Abe Majors when he missed his parole appointment on April 1. By May 8 Sheriff Cardon had identified Archie Majors and was sure his prisoner was his brother Abe, the noted "boy burglar" of Oakland, California. Abe still tried to maintain his alias, but by the time his first-degree murder trial commenced May 9, 1899, authorities had firmly established his true identity.

The San Francisco and Oakland papers had picked up the story as early as May 1, and within a week the two bandits' identities were known. The *San Francisco Call* reported the effect of the news on the boys' mother. "As soon as Mrs. Wagner was told of the suspicion that the murdered bandit was one of her sons and the bandit charged with murder was the other, she went into hysterics and was under medical attendance for hours. She persisted in declaring that her boys were not murderers and that she would never believe they had committed the crime unless she had proof of it by letter from the son that is said to be now in a Utah jail charged with murder."

The lawmen in the gunfight had seen Abe fire the shot that killed Brown, and the coroner's jury came to the same conclusion, but throughout his trial Abe maintained that Archie had been the killer. The trial itself was uneventful except for the third day. Sheriff Cardon had just finished his testimony and left the stand when he laid his pistol on the floor. When the courtroom cleared at the end of the day, the attorneys, officers, and the prisoner were the only ones left. As Abe walked over to get his hat, he suddenly saw the sheriff's pistol still laying on the floor. Taking a circuitous route back to his chair, he suddenly quickened his pace just before grabbing for the weapon.

A man named Allison, one of the prosecuting attorneys, saw the move and promptly grabbed Abe. "What are you going to do with that gun?" he asked. The prisoner stammered and grinned weakly, but quickly regained his composure. "There will be no more guns left lying around," commented the *Ogden Standard*. Abe's action didn't help his case any, and Sheriff Cardon and several other witnesses gave a full account of the incident in court the next day.

At 8:45 P.M., May 12, 1899, the jury began deliberations. After three hours they returned a guilty verdict. An appeal was immediately refused. The courtroom was filled to capacity on May 16 when Abe appeared before a Judge Hart for sentencing. The *Ogden Standard* recorded the dramatic moment, reporting, "The prisoner was...told to stand up, and every eye in the court room was centered upon him. The silence was oppressive as Judge Hart asked him if he had anything to say why sentence should not be passed upon him. He was very cool, and answered 'no.' Asked if he had any choice as to the manner of death, he said he chose 'shooting.'"

Abe was sentenced to be shot by the sheriff of Box Elder County on July 7, 1899. Until that date he was to be confined in the state prison at Salt Lake City. "The prisoner," reported a newspaper, "never showed the least emotion, and he has said that he would never break down."

In California, Lucinda Wagner's friends tried desperately to keep the news of Abe's impending doom from her. She was under the care of several physicians, her right side paralyzed, and one newspaper described her mind as "wrecked." Abe refused to write home and well-meaning friends censored any news she received. The county was supporting Lucinda and she had no money to visit Abe, even if her health had permitted such a trip. A newspaper noted, "The fact that her son Abe was yesterday convicted of murder with the death penalty will not be told Mrs. Wagner till she can stand it, which may be never."

Late on the day of his sentencing, Abe received word of a murder at Folsom prison in California. Just before noon the previous day, John Showers, the man whose testimony had convicted and hanged Lloyd Majors and Joseph Jewell almost twenty years earlier, had been standing in the doorway of a cell. Suddenly a tough convict named George Puttman savagely attacked him. Wielding a knife made from a prison file, Puttman slashed Showers across the face, opening a gaping wound in his cheek and neck. As Showers tried to protect himself, Puttman ripped him again across the throat. Staying on his victim as he slumped, Puttman stabbed him in the armpit and chest, penetrating the lower heart. As Showers lay gasping in a spreading pool of gore, Puttman ran off. He was still holding the bloody knife when a guard and several prisoners seized him.

Showers died about twenty minutes later. Puttman was a thug who was often in trouble and speculation concerning the cause of the murder immediately arose. Some said young Abe Majors and Puttman had been friends in prison, but Abe denied it. Another rumor said that Showers had made a deathbed confession that he had sworn falsely against Majors and Jewell, but the story was not verified.

Just before Showers' death, Abe decided to write to his mother. He again realized he must have all the help he could muster if he was to survive his latest predicament. He insisted in the letter that he and Archie were not highwaymen and had committed no robberies. However, Abe said Archie had killed Captain Brown; his own pistol had remained unfired. That was just the straw Lucinda was seeking. The letter buoyed her spirits considerably and she quickly convinced herself Abe had been railroaded. She complained bitterly to a reporter of the

San Francisco Call who wrote:

> Mrs. Wagner does not believe that her boy had a fair trial, She has received information that on account of prejudice against him he was rushed to trial; he had no money with which to procure an attorney, and no one even took the trouble to open communication with the boy's only parent and guardian. Within seventeen days of the time that the murder was committed in the Utah hills Abe Majors was arrested, had a preliminary examination, was tried in the Superior Court, sentenced to death and chose to be shot....Abe has assured his mother of his innocence, and Mrs. Wagner firmly believes him.

Abe no sooner arrived at the state penitentiary than things began looking up. The Salt Lake City Woman's Club decided to appoint a committee to call on the governor and ask that Abe's sentence be commuted to life imprisonment. Many of the convicts also took an interest and petitioned for clemency. Before the month was out the local chapter of the Women's Christian Temperance Union and the Ministerial Society were showing concern. By the time Abe's execution date arrived there had been enough interest to raise money for an appeal and show probable cause to stay the execution.

In California the Majors case raised a furor against the parole system. The situation did not improve any when a burglar died in a gunfight with Oakland police. Just after midnight on October 9, 1899, police officers surprised three burglars at work in a local jewelry store. In a running shootout, police killed one of the burglars then captured another. Several of the lawmen suffered minor wounds. The following day, the captured burglar identified his dead partner as Bert Willmore. At an inquest City Marshal Conrad expressed regret to Bert's sister, Ina Willmore, that he had not been able to capture Bert alive. "I'm glad you didn't," she replied. "I would rather see him dead than to see him go back to prison."

In Utah, however, Abe's boyish looks and charm—and his attorney's efforts—won him a new trial. This time he was convicted of second-degree murder and sentenced to life imprisonment on October 8, 1901. His term was to begin that same day.

Even though the death penalty no longer loomed over him, Abe quickly began looking for a way out of a grim life behind the walls. "The first day you are locked up is the hardest," recalled Utah convict Jack Black. "There comes a feeling of helplessness when the prison gates swallow you up—cut you off from the sunshine and flowers out in the world—but that feeling soon wears away if you have guts. Some men despair." Meanwhile, Abe received his work assignment and number 1123.

Warden George Dow and thirteen guards presided over the Utah State Penitentiary, a sandstone fortress on the outskirts of Salt Lake City which housed only about 165 convicts at the time. Inside, inmates manufactured clothes and shoes for the convicts and cotton socks, brushes, saddle cinches, and various other items for outside sale. Convicts also worked several farms in the surrounding area.

Abe's new home was a modern, three-story brick cell block completed in June 1888. Inside were 120 all-steel, state-of-the-art cells, opened and closed with levers at the end of each of the three tiers. Every cell contained an odorless night bucket and the whole building was "nicely heated by steam," as an inmate reported. The builder, the Pauly Company, had also constructed prisons at Fort Smith, Arkansas, and Walla Walla, Washington.

Abe met every kind of thief, killer, and con man in the prison, but he also met various Mormons convicted of having too many wives. These "cohabs," as Jack Black called them, were "a very decent lot of men—they were never complaining of persecution, always ready to help their fellow prisoners, and freely dividing the food, money and tobacco with which they were well supplied by friends and relatives."

But Abe did not seek the counsel of the "cohabs." Instead, he became friendly with one Harry Waddell, a burglar serving a seven-year term. After becoming well acquainted, they began laying plans for an escape.

Both men were aware of the many items being smuggled

A 1909 photograph of the Utah State Penitentiary cellblock from which Majors made his desperate escape attempt.

Utah State Historical Society

into the prison—food, drugs, tobacco, and forbidden reading material; it was just one step further to bring in guns. By July 1903 the escape plans were well enough along that prisoners were passing rumors around the yard. When the tales reached the authorities, they dismissed them as idle chatter after making a futile search for guns.

Convict Jack Penglass, due to be released on October 3, was the key to the planned break. Abe and Waddell prevailed on him to secure two pistols, wrap them in newspaper, and throw them over the wall onto a good sized ash pile. Abe was on the ash-hauling detail, and he could easily pick up the contraband weapons.

The break was scheduled for early October, but Abe and Waddell had to secure everything at the last minute to avoid discovery. A primitive conical mold was constructed and lead was obtained. Working secretly in the boiler room, lead weights were molded and wrapped in heavy denim. These would serve as deadly slung shots. The convicts fashioned files and other tools into knives, and kept all the weapons in a false-bottomed drawer Abe had constructed in his cell.

On Friday, October 9, 1903, guard Zebulon Jacobs heard the six o'clock bell, summoning prisoners to their cells for the evening lockup. Jacobs took the keys to lock up the courtyard door, but on the stairs leading to the library convict Harry Waddell suddenly confronted him.

"Throw up your hands or I'll kill you," Waddell said.

Jacobs was startled, but he noted Waddell's finger was on the guard of his nickel-plated pistol, not the trigger. Springing forward, he pushed the pistol away and tried to strike the convict with his heavy key ring. Abe Majors suddenly appeared with convicts Frank Dayton and Frank Connors, and all of them began beating the guard.

"Strike him, boys," shouted Waddell, "and strike him hard." Jacobs broke away and ran for the dining room, but the convicts quickly cut him off. Jacobs grabbed a chair and tried to swing it, but the ceiling was too low and Waddell snatched it away. As Abe began beating the guard, Connors smashed his slungshot against Jacob's head, knocking him senseless. The escapees also clubbed a prisoner named Maxwell to the floor when he tried to aid the guard.

Jacobs recovered as Abe and Waddell were dragging him by the heels over the floor. By then Nick Haworth and Jim Lynch had been released from their cells on death row. Ed Mullen was also released and joined the other convicts as Abe and Waddell dumped the battered Jacobs in a heap on the floor.

"Let's finish the old son of a bitch right here," snarled Abe, but Jim Lynch quickly spoke up.

"Stop that! Don't complicate matters and make it worse than it is."

Abe and Waddell turned and ran to a courtyard closet where they secured several ladders. Returning to the cell block, Abe pushed an alarm bell, then quickly stepped to a window in time to see a guard named Naylor come out of his guard box and look in his direction. He motioned to Waddell and both took a shot at Naylor from different windows. As Naylor dodged into the protection of his guard box, the convicts grabbed guard David Wilcken as a shield and started with the ladders down the stairs to the yard.

As they reached the bottom of the stairs all hell broke loose. Wilcken twisted out of a convict's grasp and all made a dash for the wall, with Frank Dayton leading the way. Scrambling up the ladder, Dayton had just reached the top when Naylor shot him. He dropped dead on the other side of the wall. Lynch and Haworth next scrambled over, with Waddell close behind.

Wilcken climbed up the ladder behind Waddell, seized the escaping convict, and grabbed his pistol. Turning, Wilcken then kicked at Abe, who was behind him on the ladder. Abe aimed his pistol at Naylor, but it misfired just as the guard shot him through the arm. As Abe gasped and grabbed his wound, Wilcken heaved him off the ladder.

Other guards ran out to the melee, and one named Bishop took aim at Wilcken, who cried out, "For God's sake, Bishop, don't shoot." Wilcken suffered a bullet wound in the leg, but whether Bishop or Naylor fired the shot is unknown.

Shouts sounded in the distance, but the guns were silent as the guards took stock of the situation. Wisps of gunsmoke hung along the wall. Convict Connors had been captured in the yard, while Ed Mullen took a shot in the leg and was also in custody. Haworth and Jim Lynch had managed to escape in the dusk, but authorities thought Lynch was badly wounded. Convict Frank Dayton lay dead outside the wall. Guards Zebe Jacobs and David Wilcken were quickly placed under a physician's care and taken to Holy Cross Hospital in Salt Lake City. Abe was found under a ladder, groaning and clutching the wound in his arm. He was taken to the infirmary along with convict Mullen.

On October 14 the State Board of Corrections held its regular meeting and investigated the attempted break. Chairman Elias Smith interviewed Abe, Waddell, Connors, and many other convicts and guards. Utah Governor Heber M. Wells also attended the meeting. When questioned, Abe minced no words. According to minutes of the meeting, "Majors stated that all questions he answered, he would answer truthfully, but some he could not answer without implicating other parties, these he would be compelled not to answer. He acknowledged he was the leader in the break and had charge of guns, but would not tell as to how or where he got them, declined to state how long they had been in his possession."

Waddell bargained hard for his testimony, however, and vowed to tell all if he would not be punished for the break. The board determined Abe and Waddell were the main conspirators and the others joined only at the last minute.

A posse captured Haworth Sunday morning, and by the following Wednesday Lynch was also back in custody. As the ringleader, and because of his desperate past, much attention focused on Abe. Dr. A.C. Young, a hard-nosed prison physician, took the opportunity to vent his spleen on Abe and convicts in general, as the *Deseret Evening News* reported. "The doctor then went on to score the ladies and Christian workers who have taken such an interest in Abe Majors and some of the other convicts. 'The prisoners,' he declared, '...work this religion graft and it does surprise me how people are gulled by them. I have never yet heard of a real convert that amounted to anything....This fellow Abe Majors is thoroughly bad: aside from his previous record his actions while in Utah demonstrate that the only place for him is behind bars.'"

The break led to various security improvements at the prison. Ladders were no longer kept in the yard and the alarm system was upgraded. From then on, prisoners could not have close contact with visitors; a wire mesh screen now separated them.

After the break, Abe's promises to reform and take care of his mother were no longer believable. His only hope was to behave himself and someday again apply for parole with renewed credibility. Meanwhile, he knew he could count on his mother to keep up the pressure once he had established a suitable period of good behavior. The long, grim years of waiting had begun.

Over the years Lucinda worked tirelessly for her boy. She interested Salt Lake people in her son and gradually worked up a scenario for a case dulled by time. Abe had not killed Captain Billy Brown; instead one of the other possemen had probably accidentally shot him. Jurors who had been interviewed agreed that they had voted the boy guilty because of his previous prison record. In any case they only expected him to be convicted of robbery and receive a brief prison term. Always Abe's youth at the time worked for him as affidavits of his innocence were being collected.

Over the years Abe seems to have charmed everyone he met. All of his acquaintances, from the governor on down, took an interest in him. They could hardly believe that such a sincere young man could be a hardened criminal. He convinced anyone who would listen that all he needed was a chance to make good.

In early 1918, after years of pressure from Lucinda, officials, and various social agencies, Abe had a successful parole hearing. Samuel Newhouse, a prominent Salt Lake realtor, had taken an interest in the case and guaranteed Abe a job if he was released. He was formally discharged on January 22, on condition he remain in the state and successfully fulfill a period of time at a job. Lucinda managed to go to Utah for Abe's release and met him at the prison gate.

The world outside those cold, sandstone walls was new to Abe. A great war engulfed Europe and technological changes were astounding. "Why, Warden," Abe remarked to Warden George Storrs, "it is like being born again to even look at the outside world."

Automobiles vied with horses and buggies on the streets of Salt Lake. The theaters of the city must have intrigued Abe also, especially those showing the popular new motion pictures. Pauline Frederick was playing at the Rialto in *The Hungry Heart*, while the beautiful Mary Garden starred in *Thais* at the Salt Lake Theater. Abe took his mother to various entertainments in the city before she had to return to California.

Newhouse got Abe a job with a mining company, and Abe's new employer, a man named MacLease, put him to work at the Copper Mountain Mine near Milford, nearly 200 miles from Salt Lake. Abe wrote his friend Newhouse on February 6, 1918, "I have not yet begun to work. Although I have been to the mine, Mac did not leave me there because he wishes to be present when I begin to work....The MacLeases took me into their apartments here and treat me as if they regard me as their best friend, which I hope to be someday."

When Abe finally went to work at the mine, a general strike was in progress and no one was there. He looked after the property alone for several months, but when the company decided not to work the mine he had to return to the prison. Warden Storrs obtained a position for Abe at the Salt Lake City Telephone Company, where he worked for about a year.

As early as September 25, 1918, Abe wrote a long letter to California Governor William D. Stephens, explaining his troubles with the law and begging for a full pardon so he could return to California. His Folsom prison sentence was the result of the mischievousness of a fourteen-year-old boy, whined Abe. "My God," he wrote, "think of it! Sending a child of fourteen years to that hell." Certainly the sentence was unduly harsh for a teenage first offender, but Abe was lying again. He was fifteen when he was arrested and had turned sixteen by the time he entered prison.

Abe continued his letter. "When I am exonerated here, I

desire to go home. My home is in California. Dear Old California calls me as a mother calls—the call to a son of the Golden West to come home. But my natural mother, she that presents this letter to you, calls me also. She calls with a voice tremulous with love for me. Her heart, broken by the grief of twenty-two years, yearns for me....For her sake, pardon my wrong-doing as a child."

Utah's governor and Warden Storrs both sent letters supporting Abe's request, as did various Utah residents. Lucinda kept up the pressure with her own pleas and visits to the governor's office. Abe had fulfilled all his obligations in Utah and was waiting for the pardon board to meet and release him when he received word that his mother was ill. Knowing the board's decision would be favorable, Governor Simon T. Bamberger allowed the ex-convict to go to California ahead of schedule.

In Los Angeles Abe looked after his mother as best he could. His half-brother Ralph lived with them also and apparently provided enough income for the three of them—at least until Abe could find work. Lucinda was quite feeble and, neighbors recalled, Abe was home nearly every night taking care of her. Despite his nursing duties, Abe was soon in trouble again.

On March 5, 1919, Abe ran into Leon Saulard, an ex-convict he had known in the Utah prison. The two were talking on a Los Angeles street corner when a police detective named Woods walked up and arrested Abe as a suspect in some recent burglaries. Insisting he was innocent, Abe gave the officer a false name as he was escorted down the street. The *Los Angeles Times* reported, "Arrested by Detectives Wood and Murphy after they are said to have pawned jewelry identified as the property of residents in the fashionable Westlake and Wilshire district, whose homes have been burglarized, two men giving the names of James Wilson, 29 years old, of Salt Lake City, and Leon Saulard, also 29, of San Francisco are in the city jail.

"At police headquarters they refused to give any information about themselves, but according to Detective Wood, the officers will be able to connect them with nearly a dozen burglaries the last month."

Woods took Abe to the pawn shop of Samuel Levy, where some jewelry from a recent burglary had been found. The theft had occurred at the home of George D. Varnum on February 11 and Woods hoped to tie both that, and several other burglaries, to his suspect. Levy readily identified Abe as the one who had accompanied another man to the store and sold him the jewelry. When he was booked into the Los Angeles County jail on March 10, it was under his real name, and Abe realized he was again in serious trouble.

On June 17 Abe was released on bond. His lawyer, R.T. Walters, undoubtedly warned him that he must secure a job at once to make a good showing in court, and he quickly found work at the Ideal Radiator and Body Works, an automotive repair shop. He worked hard and favorably impressed owner Dwight S. Person, who was no doubt shocked to learn of his impending trial.

On December 8, 1919, Abe went to trial in Los Angeles Superior Court for the robbery of one Madaline Bridges' home. The court reversed a prompt guilty verdict on the basis of alleged misconduct by the prosecuting attorney, rather than the flimsy evidence produced.

The Varnum case was more substantial, and was tried between January 8 and 13, 1920. The prosecution based its argument on Levy's identification of Abe and the testimony of a handwriting expert, who identified Abe's signature on Levy's receipt book.

While out on bond, Abe and his attorney visited Levy's shop on the pretense of buying a tie clasp. Levy did not recognize Abe, however, as he had before. They did the same at another pawn shop where stolen jewelry had turned up, but that proprietor also failed to recognize Abe. When Abe's attorney, Paul Schenck, tried to introduce those results into evidence, the court ruled them inadmissible. Knowing the prosecution would bring out Abe's record, Schenck could not even put Abe on the stand. Abe had lost. Lawyer and client stood stoic and grim as the jury foreman recited the verdict—"Guilty."

Lucinda must have been crushed, but she had few tears left

San Quentin mug shots of Majors taken after his Los Angeles burglary conviction. He was a handsome, lean, and hardened criminal by now, yet seemed to have reformed.

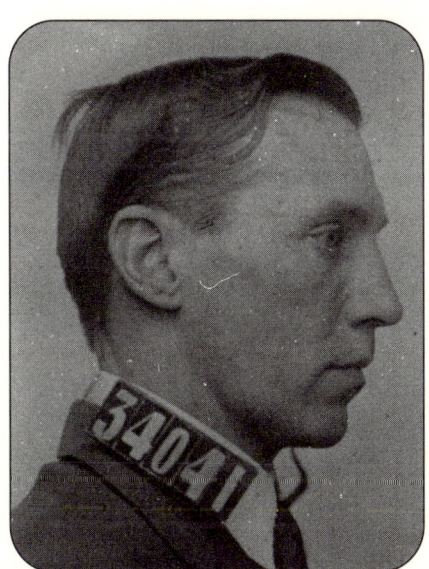

Both: California State Archives

to shed. When the appeals all failed and Abe left for San Quentin in mid-September 1920, Lucinda took the train for Yuma, Arizona, where Ralph then lived.

Utah prison warden Storrs, who had taken quite an interest in Abe, visited him in prison and ultimately wrote several letters to California authorities on his behalf. He also had the Los Angeles County undersheriff investigate Abe's conviction. The undersheriff reported that he was "absolutely sure that Majors was innocent of any wrong doing there, but that he was foolish in being found in the company of this other fellow."

Regardless, Abe was back in prison. Recognizing Abe as a third-term potential troublemaker, prison authorities transferred him to Folsom on October 25, 1920, to begin his five-year term. He seems to have been a model prisoner and worked in the tailor shop, a trade in which he by then had considerable experience. He continually applied for gardening and road camp jobs, but as a third-termer he was not eligible. Undaunted, he enlisted the aid of prominent Los Angeles residents to intercede for him, but to no avail.

Lucinda returned to Los Angeles where she dictated a plaintive letter to the state prison board in late March 1921 concerning Abe's application for parole. Attorney Schenck and many others wrote in Abe's behalf also, but it was too early and the application was denied.

Worn out and weary, Lucinda could do no more. After a brief illness, she died on January 29, 1922. Her death certificate listed organic heart trouble as the cause of death.

Abe remained in the prison tailor shop, where, to his credit, he was appointed head tailor in early 1923. His term was to expire on April 15, 1924, but he wrote a long letter to Warden J.J. Smith detailing the efficient and cost-effective way he had managed his shop and asked that extra credits be awarded for his service.

His letter bore fruit. When the parole board met on January 12, 1924, Abe was not only given his parole, but was awarded three months' additional credits. He could hardly believe it. He would be discharged on January 16.

An ecstatic Abe sent a telegram to Miss June Westerbeck, a

Los Angeles prison reformer who had worked actively for his parole. The extent of their relationship is unknown, but the telegram, which may suggest a romantic liaison or just a meeting with an old friend, said, "Free Wednesday morning 8:30. At Oakland hotel, Oakland, 4 P.M. Abe Majors."

When he left Folsom that January morning, Abe effectively disappeared into the mists of history. He was only forty-four years old, and perhaps had at last decided crime did not pay. At least he never returned to prison. With his beguiling personality he would have had no trouble prevailing on his host of supporters for a job.

Many people had put their reputations on the line for Abe Majors over the years and were anxious for him to make good at any stage of his life. Governors, wardens, lawyers, legislators, and many others had expressed faith in Abe, only to be disappointed time and again. Many never lost faith, however, and maintained his innocence in Brown's death and the Los Angeles burglaries.

From time to time, newsmen wanting to write about Abe's career wondered what had happened to the former outlaw. But he had disappeared. "Discharged prisoners," Folsom's warden replied to one such request, "very seldom inform their fellow inmates or the officials...of their intentions."

The California State Library death index records Abe's passing in Los Angeles on November 6, 1957. The Old West was long since dead, and Abe's long trail of crime, deceit, blood, and broken promises had ended at last.

NOTES

Chapter 1
The Bullet-Riddled Ballad of Cherokee Bob, 1833–1863

The reconstruction of Henry Talbot's early years in Georgia is based on various sources. There seems little doubt he was one of the Wilkes County Talbots, prominent residents since the eighteenth century. Henry himself once referred to his father as a "Georgia planter" and "Superior Judge" and there are references to Henry in two early Wilkes County wills. Still, the 1840 census and other sources of Wilkes County and Talbot history make no reference to his immediate family. See Eliza A. Bowen, *The Story of Wilkes County, Georgia* (Marietta, Georgia: Continental Book Company, 1950); Virgil Talbot, *The Talbots* (Colcord, Oklahoma: privately published, 1983); Mary Bondurant Warren, editor, *Chronicles of Wilkes County, Georgia* (Danielsville, Georgia: Heritage Papers, 1978).

My grateful thanks to Mrs. Sarabelle O'Daniel, Monmouth, Illinois; Robert Scott Davis, Jr., Hanceville, Alabama; Ruth Mather, Sunnyvale, California; and Mrs. Kathy Best, Atlanta, Georgia, for their efforts in trying to sort out the Talbot ancestry. The March 12, 1855, *California Courier* published a personal interview with young Talbot that was most helpful, as were the Wilkes County United States Census population schedules for 1840.

Many works contain descriptions of early San Francisco. They include William Perkins, *Three Years in California: William Perkins' Journal of Life in Sonora, 1849–1852* (Berkeley and Los Angeles: University of California Press, 1964) and Frank Soulé, John H. Gihon, M.D., and James Nisbet, *The Annals of San Francisco* (New York: D. Appleton, 1854). The January 26, 1850, *San Francisco Alta California* chronicled Henry Talbot's police court appearance.

Talbot mentioned his sojourn in the Sonora area in the *Los Angeles Star*'s December 29, 1855, issue. Perkins contains excellent descriptions of life in early Sonora. The description of Cherokee Bob appeared in Milicent Washburn Shinn's "Cherokee Bob, the Original Jack Hamlin," *Overland Monthly,* July 1890. The article consisted of stories told to her by Bret Harte.

The Los Angeles reference to Cherokee Bob appeared in Horace Bell, *Reminiscences of a Ranger* (Santa Barbara, California: Wallace Hebbard, 1927). The bloody fracas at Melones is noted in Perkins and the June 18, 1851, Stockton *San Joaquin Republican.* Bob related the story of the fight in the restaurant in the *California Courier* article.

Historian Carlo M. De Ferrari of Sonora provided the Tuolumne County inquest record on the killing of hotel man Brown at Jamestown. Mr. De Ferrari kindly copied all the pertinent details of the affair for me, but no newspaper account of the incident has been located (letter from De Ferrari, August 1, 1983). Bob related details of the Mariposa scrap and the Velasquez duel in the *Courier* article. A letter from Millerton published in the March 3, 1854, *Mariposa Chronicle* gives an account of the capture of Talbot and his two friends. The Horace Snow quote is from his *"Dear Charlie" Letters* (Fresno, California: Mariposa County Historical Society, 1979). Court records and documents in the Mariposa County Courthouse provided details of the trial, noted in the March 17, 1854, *Mariposa Chronicle.* Thanks to my brother, Dr. James Secrest, of Mount Bullion, and Jim Snyder, United States Department of the Interior, Yosemite National Park, for help on Talbot's Mariposa adventures.

For a general history of San Quentin, see Kenneth Lamott, *Chronicles of San Quentin* (New York: David McKay, 1961), and Tirey L. Ford, *California State Prisons* (San Francisco: James H. Barry, 1910). For a more contemporary view of the prison, the personnel, and inmates, see California State Assembly, "Report of Committee Relative to the Condition and Management of the State Prison," Assembly Journal appendix, Document Number 26, 1855 session (Sacramento: B.R. Redding, State Printer, 1855).

The description of Cherokee Bob is in the *List of State Convicts on Register of State Prison at San Quentin* (Sacramento, California: State Printing Office, 1889; hereafter cited as San Quentin List). Accounts of work details, escape attempts, and convict life are reported in a long article in the November 27, 1854, *Sacramento Daily Union.* The *San Francisco Alta California* published James M. Estell's annual report about San Quentin on February 22, 1855. On December 29, 1854, the *San Francisco Herald* and *Alta California* published detailed accounts of the mass escape from San Quentin. The *Los Angeles Star* published

Bob's comments on the break in its December 29, 1855, issue.

The October 22, 1856, *San Francisco Evening Bulletin* and October 23, 1856, *San Francisco Herald* published Bill White's confession. Several documents in White's San Quentin pardon file (now in the California State Archives) verify his confession.

Bob recounted his movements after his prison escape in the December 29, 1855, *Los Angeles Star.* The January 5, 1856, *Star* gives the story of his long trip from the San Francisco Bay area to Los Angeles in much detail. The route down the old mission highway is easily identified by the towns, missions, and sites mentioned. The above-cited issues of the *Star* noted Bob's activities in San Gabriel.

The December 22, 1855, *Star* reported Bob's arrest at San Gabriel. His examinination before Judge Benjamin Hayes is fully detailed in the same paper's January 5, 1856, issue. The Wall and Williamson murders are a noted incident in the tale of the Roach-Belcher feud over the Sanchez estate. The November 17, 1855, *Monterey Sentinel* first reported the killings. The real murderer, Anastacio Garcia, was later captured in Los Angeles, as reported in the November 1, 1856, *Santa Cruz Sentinel.* For a full account of this bloody episode of California history see Paul P. Parker, "The Roach-Belcher Feud," *California Historical Society Quarterly*, March 1950. The January 12, 1856, *Monterey Sentinel* mentions Bob's Los Angeles hearing and arrival at Monterey.

The building and cost of the new wall around San Quentin is fully detailed in California State Legislature, "Report on State Prison, by Joint Committee of Senate & Assembly," Legislative Journal appendix, 1856 session (Sacramento: James Allen, State Printer, 1856). A description of Bob while in prison was given in the March 12, 1855, *California Courier.* His letter to Governor Weller is in the Governor's Pardon Files, California State Archives, Sacramento. The prison register and other records indicating the several release dates are also in the California State Archives.

For a rousing—if somewhat glamorized—history of the Nevada mining excitement, see George D. Lyman, *The Saga of the Comstock Lode* (New York: Charles Scribner's Sons, 1934). Lyman gives a good description of the trip from Placerville across the Sierra Nevada to Genoa and Carson City. J. Ross Browne describes the same trip in early 1860. His account is found in *J. Ross Browne: His Letters, Journals and Writings,* edited by Lina Fergusson Browne (Albuquerque: University of New Mexico Press, 1969). The newspaper quote is from the August 10, 1861, *Placerville Mountain Democrat.*

As the brother of the secretary to Nevada's territorial governor, Mark Twain (Sam Clemens) was in Carson City at the same time as Cherokee Bob. His description of the area and inhabitants is taken from a letter to his mother in *The Selected Letters of Mark Twain*, edited by Charles Neider (New York: Harper & Row, 1982). Twain's description of the town is in *Roughing It* (New York: Harper & Brothers, 1913). Data on the Carson City area are in Henry DeGroot, *The Comstock Papers* (Reno, Nevada: Grace Dangberg Foundation, 1985). DeGroot was also there at the time. Much good information about the area is in Hubert Howe Bancroft, *History of Nevada, Colorado and Wyoming* (San Francisco: The History Company, 1890).

Little is known of Bill Mayfield except that he went to California from Missouri in the late 1850s, then joined the rush to the Comstock. See the January 24, 1892, *San Francisco Chronicle* for some details of his life as reported by a contemporary, Joe Goodman. A less reliable account, written by J.L. Considine, appeared in the November 16, 1941, Reno *Nevada State Journal*. (Letter from Lee Mortensen, Nevada Historical Society, August 4, 1993.) A description of Mayfield appeared in the March 25, 1862, *Sacramento Daily Union*.

The account of the Gardner-Mayfield-Talbot fracas appeared in the August 14, 1861, *Sacramento Daily Union*. The 1860 United States Census population schedules for Genoa list the twenty-one-year-old William H. Gardiner, constable, as a native of Ireland. The August 10, 1861, Carson *Daily Silver Age* noted the defendant's appearance before Justice Dixson. Unfortunately, only a few scattered issues of this newspaper exist for the period. My thanks to Bob Ellison of Minden, Nevada, who provided much insight and documentation for Cherokee Bob's brief Nevada residence. Ellison, the above Joe Goodman account, and Bancroft provided information on Sheriff Blackburn. Blackburn's death and the resulting inquest are reported in the November 23, 1861, *Sacramento Daily Union*.

The Downey shooting scrape, reported in the September 27, 1861, *Sacramento Daily Union*, referred to Talbot as "alias Cherokee Bob of California." A copy of the first grand jury report of January 1862, in the Nevada State Library, Carson City, does not mention Talbot—indicating he had fled the area.

For Idaho mining history I have relied on Merrill D. Beal and Merle W. Wells, *History of Idaho* (New York: Lewis Historical Publishing Company, 1959); Robert G. Bailey, *River of No Return* (Lewiston, Idaho: R.G. Bailey, 1947); and Byron Defenbach, *Idaho: The Place and Its People*, Volume I (Chicago and New York: American

Historical Society, 1933). I have also utilized recollections of the period such as William Goulder, *Reminiscences* (Boise, Idaho: Timothy Regan, 1909).

Bob's connection with the California Volunteers is in *The Golden Frontier: The Recollections of Herman Francis Reinhart*, edited by Doyce B. Nunis, Jr. (Austin: University of Texas Press, 1962). For data on the volunteers see Aurora Hunt, *The Army of The Pacific* (Glendale, California: The Arthur H. Clark Company, 1951), and Richard H. Orton, *Records of California Men in the War of the Rebellion* (Sacramento, California: State Printing Office, 1890). The October 17, 1861, *Red Bluff* (California) *Beacon* has a long article about the volunteers. Many other California newspapers of the time also covered them.

The October 16, 1861, *San Francisco Daily Evening Bulletin* reported the "over-lively" activities of the volunteers. The *San Francisco Alta California* of October 17 and 18, 1861, gives the military preparations for the departure of the volunteers, while a letter published in the October 30, 1861, *Alta* relates incidents of the trip to Portland. Another letter from a volunteer was published in the same newspaper's November 12 issue. The *Portland Daily Oregonian* of October 25 and 26, 1861, reports on the arrival of the troops at Vancouver.

An attempt to locate a passenger list for the steamer *Pacific*'s trip to Vancouver and Portland was unsuccessful. (Letter from David W. Hastings, chief of archives, Washington Archives and Records Management Division, July 14, 1992; letter from F. Glover, reference librarian, Sutro Library, San Francisco, September 18, 1992.)

A notice in the February 3, 1862, *Oregonian* that a letter was being held for Bob at the local post office gives positive indication of his route north. Typical notices of the booming Idaho gold country appeared in the *Oregonian* issues of October 28 and November 14, 1861. Freight and passenger rates from Portland to Lewiston are in Oscar Osburn Winther, *The Old Oregon Country: A History of Frontier Trade, Transportation and Travel* (Lincoln, Nebraska: University of Nebraska Press, 1950). The January 30, 1862, *Oregonian* noted the hardships of the bitter winter and frozen river.

Despite extensive efforts, Cherokee Bob's brief sojourn at The Dalles has not been substantiated. There is no doubt that he passed that way, and it is reasonable to assume he would stop over for a few days and see if he could find a good game. The Dalles visit is based wholly on the Shinn article. Written in the style of the day, without documentation, Shinn's tale features real people and seems to be second-generation oral history, with at least some basis in fact.

Much information on the early days of The Dalles and nearby Fort Dalles can be found in Priscilla Knuth, *Picturesque Frontier* (Portland: Oregon Historical Society, 1968). The Oregon Historical Society provided much help in researching this period of the story. (Letters from Knuth and Sieglinde Smith, reference librarian, April 7, April 28, June 2, and June 16, 1992.)

A display ad for the Mount Hood Saloon in the August 14, 1861, *The Dalles Weekly Mountaineer* touted tables that are "the best in Oregon." (Letter received from Sieglinde Smith, April 7, 1992.)

An effort was made to identify the deserter in the Shinn article, but without success (letter received from DeAnne Blanton, Military Reference Branch, National Archives, Washington, D.C., July 16, 1992). A likely candidate would be a "Lieutenant Young" of the California Volunteers who was then stationed at Fort Walla Walla. The April 28, 1862 *Oregonian* reports the officer as deserting on a government mule "recently."

The March 15, 1862, *Oregonian* noted the breaking up of the river ice, enabling the resumption of travel on the Columbia. The steamers *Julia, Idaho, Colonel Wright,* and *Tenino* traveled between Portland and Wallula on the trip to Walla Walla, as reported in the Portland press.

The description of Walla Walla inhabitants is from the December 18, 1861, *Oregonian*. The California Volunteer troops stationed at Fort Walla Walla are listed in Orton, and the Reinhart quote is from Nunis. The quote referring to Walla Walla whiskey is from the October 3, 1863, Walla Walla *Washington Statesman*. Bob's boast of how he could whip the Yankee army is first reported in Nathaniel Pitt Langford, *Vigilante Days and Ways* (Chicago: A.C. McClurg & Company, 1927).

Nunis reports on the theater benefit and gives an account of the fight. Reinhart apparently knew some of the soldiers and names them correctly, give or take a few vowels. The April 19, 1862, *Washington Statesman* devotes much of a page to the theater riot and the resulting friction/correspondence between the mayor and Colonel Lee. W.D. Lyman, *History Of Old Walla Walla County* (Chicago: S.J. Clarke, 1918), touches on the incident. A search of the early post records for Fort Walla Walla in the National Archives produced only one letter of Mayor Whitman (letter received from Richard F. Cox, Military Reference Branch, Military Archives Division, Washington, D.C., January 29, 1986). An obituary of Whitman in the August 9, 1899, *Oregonian* also recounts the incident (letter from Howard Kaseberg, Walla Walla Valley Pioneer & Historical Society, November 9, 1985).

Orton lists both the dead soldiers as members of Company A. Each is reported as having died from a "pistol shot received in theater at Walla Walla."

The May 23, 1862, *Oregonian* and the November 6, 1862, *Washington Statesman* describe Lewiston during this period, as do Defenbach and Bailey. The description of the traffic moving into the gold country is from a letter of miner W. Augustus Knapp, dated May 26, 1862, and in Beal and Wells.

The description of the *Nicaragua* is from an address by Justice Robert D. Leeper, quoted in Defenbach. Although all sources suggest that Mayfield and Talbot met for the first time in Lewiston, they had previously become friends in Carson City, as noted in the text. Mayfield merely followed Bob to the Northwest after escaping jail in Nevada.

Joe Goodman's previously-cited article in the *San Francisco Chronicle* is an extensive account of the Blackburn killing. DeGroot's account is also good and gives some interesting details. Both agree with the contemporary account in the March 25, 1862, *Sacramento Daily Union*. The November 25, 1861, *Union* reports Mayfield's capture and Blackburn's funeral. Wells Drury tells the story in *An Editor on the Comstock Lode* (New York: Farrar & Rinehart, 1936), as do most of the Nevada histories. The Mayfield quote is from Goodman's account.

Bob Ellison turned up the February 3, 1862, document showing the grand jury indictment of Mayfield for the Blackburn killing (Second Judicial District Court minutes, 1861–1865; in microfilm collections of the Nevada State Library and Archives). The minutes give every indication that Mayfield and his attorney were satisfied with the final jury (letter from Ellison, August 14, 1993).

A check of the 1860 United States Census population schedules for Walla Walla County failed to locate an enumeration for a Jacob or Cynthia Williams (letter received from Howard Kaseberg, May 11, 1992).

Barney Owsley's quote is from Fritz Timmen, "Deadly Belle of the Ball," *True Frontier*, May 1970. Owsley had earlier contributed material incorporated in Bailey. He is also the subject of a 1936 article in the *Walla Walla Union-Bulletin* (letter received from Howard Kaseberg, November 9, 1985).

The Florence miner's quote is from the November 6, 1862, *Washington Statesman*. Descriptions of Florence are in the previously-cited Idaho histories. Langford and other early chroniclers note the presence of Cyrus Skinner and other California thugs and outlaws in

Florence. An example was William "Brockey" Winters, a San Francisco thug and thief who served a term in San Quentin while Bob was there, then escaped in 1859 and made his way to the Northwest. Shortly after a shooting scrape in Florence, he was killed by a man he assaulted at a ferry (author's files on early California badmen, San Quentin List and *California Police Gazette*, July 23, 1859).

Bob's acquisition of the Florence saloon is reported by both Langford and Owsley, who also give the sequence of events leading up to Bob's final shootout. They disagree in some details, however. Owsley maintained Bob escorted Cynthia to the dance, but she had not been snubbed as the only women in town were prostitutes. Actually, the town had been established during the fall of 1861 and was in a decline at this time. Many decent women resided in Florence and attended that New Year's ball.

The January 17, 1863, *Washington Statesman* briefly accounted Bob's death, and many Idaho histories chronicle the incident. Langford reports Williams at first fled from the two badmen in order to avoid trouble, but soon turned and fought, joined by Robbins and other friends. Bob's comment on Williams' and Robbins' shooting is from W.J. McConnell, *Early History of Idaho* (Caldwell, Idaho: Caxton Printers, 1913). The account of the hearing before Justice Rand is from the old court docket book as published in Sister M. Alfreda Elsensohn, *Pioneer Days in Idaho County* (Cottonwood, Idaho: Idaho Corp. of Benedictine Sisters, 1978).

For information on Anton Roman and the *Overland Monthly*, see Franklin Walker, *San Francisco's Literary Frontier* (New York: Alfred A. Knopf, 1939), and Ella Sterling Cummins Mighels, *The Story of the Files* (San Francisco: Co-operative Print Company, 1893). A brief biography of Anton Roman appears in James D. Hart, *A Companion to California* (New York: Oxford University Press, 1978).

The information on the *Overland Monthly* and the comparison between Bret Harte characters and Cherokee Bob is taken from the previously-cited Milicent Washburn Shinn article and based on the author's conclusions.

Chapter 2
A Bad Seed: The Deadly Charles Mortimer, 1834–1873

The September 11, 1864, *San Francisco Daily Morning Call* contains Mark Twain's comments about Mortimer. I became familiar with

California's early criminals while researching *Lawmen and Desperadoes: A Compendium of Noted Early California Lawmen, Badmen and Outlaws* (Spokane, Washington: The Arthur H. Clark Company, 1994) and my biography of Isaiah W. Lees, the famous San Francisco police detective, still in manuscript.

Details of Mortimer's early life are exclusively from his memoirs, Charles J. Flinn, *Life and Career of the Most Skillful and Noted Criminal of His Day, Charles Mortimer...* (Sacramento, California: William H. Mills & Company, 1873). Because Mortimer mentions few dates or names in his memoirs, verifying his reported activities in the East is next to impossible. A check of the 1840–1860 index to the Massachusetts convict register reveals no inmates with the name of Charles J. Flinn, Flynn, or Mortimer. He undoubtedly used an alias at the time he was arrested. (Letter from Richard C. Kaplan, reference archivist, Massachusetts Archives at Columbia Point, Boston.)

The February 6, 1862, *San Francisco Daily Alta California* reports the Conrad Pfister robbery. A police record book in the Christian de Guignè Collection, San Mateo, California, has specifics about Mortimer's arrest.

The contemporary description of San Quentin is from the February 6, 1862, *Red Bluff* (California) *Beacon*. Mortimer's prison number and other data are from the San Quentin List. For details of the prison and its cell blocks see Ford, Lamott, and Nancy Ann Nichols, *San Quentin Inside the Walls* (San Quentin, California: San Quentin Museum Press, 1991).

For Mike Brannigan's rape of actress Ellen Mitchell, see the *Sacramento Daily Union* of June 25 and July 2, 1861. He was admitted to San Quentin on January 30, 1862. Mortimer's quote is from his memoirs.

The April 24, 1856, *Sacramento Daily Union* reports the capture of Adolph Newton. His trial is noted in Rosena A. Giles, *Shasta County California: A History* (Oakland, California: Biobooks, 1949). Information about Jim Smith's outlaw days is in the December 8, 1879, *San Francisco Chronicle*. The July 13, 1864, *Sacramento Daily Union* gives information about Isaac McCullum's criminal career. Mortimer mentions all of them in his memoirs, and the San Quentin List shows all of them incarcerated there during Mortimer's term.

Lamott lists the various industries operating within San Quentin, as does the California State Senate "Report of Committee on Commitments," Statistical Reports, Senate Journal appendix, 1860 session (Sacramento: State Printing Office, 1860). The November 14,

1861, *Red Bluff Beacon* reports the prison tailor shop manufacturing army clothing and sacking.

The convict snitch to whom Mortimer refers is apparently the same Charles Harmon admitted February 12, 1861, from San Joaquin County on a grand larceny conviction. The Chellis break is covered well in Lamott and the contemporary press.

Several of Mortimer's Virginia City pals were ex-San Quentin convicts; others are more difficult to identify. The "Pete Goodwin" he names in his memoirs was undoubtedly the Peter Goodwin admitted to San Quentin November 2, 1859, on a grand larceny conviction from San Francisco. Likewise, John "Black Jack" Bowen was a prominent highwayman and burglar who first entered San Quentin on August 19, 1853, and escaped numerous times (see the April 11, 1877, *Sacramento Daily Union*). Several convicts named "Wright" were in prison at the same time as Mortimer, but nothing more is known about the Wright he speaks of and the two other nicknamed characters.

The Wiggins robbery is reported in the September 7, 1864, *San Francisco Alta California*. Mortimer claims that special detective George Rose, who had been his partner in various previous crimes, put him up to the Wiggins robbery. Indications are the near-fatal fight between the two men was over the loot and Rose's determination to arrest Mortimer. Mark Twain's articles pertaining to the incident appear in the *San Francisco Call* of September 11, 16, 25, and 29, 1864.

The man Mortimer refers to as "Shanks" might be the stage robber George Shank, or Shanks, whom Steve Venard killed on May 15, 1866. Shank was reportedly a pressman on Horace Greeley's *New York Tribune* before arriving in California. One account gives his real name as Shamacks and says he worked as a stage groom at the Strawberry stage station near Lake Tahoe, where he was accused of robbing a passenger. Whatever his name and background, Venard killed him and two companions after they robbed a Nevada County stagecoach on May 15. Pat Jones of Chicago Park, California, furnished copies of the May 17, 1866, *Nevada Daily Gazette*, and the Wells Fargo Bank History Room, San Francisco, has a series of undated contemporary clippings about the incident.

Tom Boulton had received a seven-year sentence in the Nevada state prison for robbing a church in Virginia City. He was a forty-two-year-old native of Ireland and began his sentence on November 15, 1863. He escaped in August 1864 and fled to California, where he eventually took up with Mortimer. He was arrested in Yreka on the night of October 21, 1864, on a charge of drunkenness and riotous conduct. Eventually he was returned to the Nevada state prison, where a reward of $500 on his head was still outstanding. (*Yreka Semi-Weekly Union*, November 16 and 26, 1864; an 1864 list of Nevada state prison convicts; and Boulton's pardon file in the Nevada State Archives, Carson City, copy supplied by Bob Ellison.)

Constable James M. Luttrell described William Richardson, the fugitive from the Oregon penitentiary, as about thirty years old, with long, light hair and sandy whiskers. He was wearing light-colored trousers, a dark coat, and a plaid woolen shirt. (See the February 18, 1865, *Yreka Weekly Union.*) Oregon penitentiary indexes fail to disclose a "William Richardson" as a convict in that state; perhaps he had escaped from a local jail. (Letter from James Clark, reference archivist, Oregon State Archives, Salem, Oregon, May 7, 1993.)

For descriptions of the Klamath River country and the Sciad Ranch, see William Brewer's *Up and Down California in 1860–1864*, edited by Francis P. Farquhar (New Haven, Connecticut: Yale University Press, 1930).

The November 26, 1864, *Yreka Weekly Union* reports Mortimer's robbery of the Rosenburg store on McAdam's Creek and his capture. Harry L. Wells, *History of Siskiyou County, California* (Oakland, California: D.J. Stewart, 1881), the February 17, 1865, *Yreka Journal* and the February 18, 1865, *Yreka Weekly Union* chronicle Mortimer's escape from the Siskiyou County jail. (Correspondence with Mona Payne of the Siskiyou County Library and Mike Hendryx of the Siskiyou County Museum, Yreka, California, March 1987.)

Judge A.M. Roseborough, who tried and sentenced Mortimer, was a prominent pioneer and a member of the Yreka legal firm of Steele, Roseborough and Berry before becoming county judge in 1856. He served as Indian agent and was a good friend of the local Indians. He died in Oakland in 1900 at an advanced age. Information about Roseborough is in Jeff C. Riddle, *The Indian History of the Modoc War* (Medford, Oregon: Pine Cone Publishers, 1973). Notice of Mortimer's and Ferry's trial and sentencing appears in the February 11, 1865, *Union.*

George Rose's discovery of Mortimer in the San Francisco city jail is reported in the March 15, 1865, *Alta California*. Mortimer's second-term San Quentin number is in the San Quentin List. Prison routine and convict regulations are in Lamott and the California State Senate's "Annual Report of the Board of State Prison Directors for the year 1858," Senate Journal appendix, 1858 session (Sacramento:

State Printing Office, 1859).

Mortimer also gives interesting details of prison life in his memoirs and describes the so-called "mush break." His account tallies fairly well with that in the January 16, 1866, *Alta California* and the January 15, 1866, *San Francisco Bulletin*. Neither account, however, mentions a slaughter at the prison gate such as Mortimer recalled. For prison food served at the time see California State Legislature, "Report of the State Prison Committee of the Assembly," Senate Journal appendix, 1858 session (Sacramento: State Printing Office, 1866).

The January 21, 1871, *Alta California* notes Mortimer's release and his arrest by Detective Towle. Mark Twain's comments on George Rose appear in the July 21, 1864, *Call*. Mortimer himself remarks on Rose's Salt Lake City "trouble" in his memoirs but gives no specifics. The San Jose interview appears in the February 13, 1873, *San Francisco Bulletin*. Although he apparently was not indicted or tried, Rose's connection with a Salt Lake train robbery is reported in the *Call* of September 21 and October 26 and 27, 1876. The best evidence that Rose and Mortimer were partners is in Detective Edward Byram's "Record Book No. 1," a journal in which he lists the names and brief biographies of San Francisco criminals. Although Byram did not join the force until 1875, he obtained information from police records and newspaper clippings of many criminals who were active before he joined the department. In his brief recital of the Mortimer-Rose affray, Byram notes, "It was afterwards generally concluded that Rose and Mortimer were in league with each other." Byram's journals and two such "Record Books" are in the collection of John Boessenecker, Foster City, California.

George Washington Tyler represented Mortimer on various occasions and was probably the most well-known criminal lawyer in California. A brilliant but erratic barrister, he arrived in California in 1849 and was a county judge in Stockton for a time. He was counsel for many criminals, but his temper and bizarre courtroom antics constantly caused him trouble. When he died in April 1895, he was trying to overturn his disbarment for withholding funds recovered for a client. He died in Alameda, California, at the age of sixty-eight. See Jackson A. Graves, *California Memories* (Los Angeles: Los Angeles Times-Mirror Press, 1930) and the April 10, 1895, *San Francisco Chronicle*.

Little is known of Carrie Spencer, but Mortimer says she was twenty-two years old in 1871 and had previously lived with a father and brother near Healdsburg in Sonoma County. She apparently had a reckless nature and a previous consort had led her into a life of crime. The 1870 United States Census for Sonoma County does not list Carrie's family.

San Francisco Chief of Police Patrick Crowley was born in New York in 1831 and went to California with the 1850 gold rush. After engaging in various pursuits, he was elected constable in 1858 and succeeded Martin Burke as police chief in 1866. He served until 1873 and was reappointed by the board of police commissioners to the same office in 1879. He retired in 1897. (See March 17, 1896, *San Francisco Chronicle.*)

The details of Mortimer's travels are from his memoirs, which contain few dates. Specific events in the newspapers, however, allow a fairly accurate timing of his movements.

Mortimer's account of the robbery of the county treasurer's office closely parallels the initial account published in the February 10, 1872, *Santa Cruz Sentinel.* The treasurer, S.W. Blakely, was almost immediately arrested as a suspect.

The crowd attending the laying of the cornerstone for the new San Francisco city hall was an ideal target for pickpockets, as were theater concerts, parades and other public gatherings. The new city hall, incidentally, wasn't completed and turned over to the city until July 1, 1899, following nearly thirty years of construction. See Gladys Hansen, *San Francisco Almanac* (San Francisco: Chronicle Books, 1975).

The May 2, 1872, *Chronicle,* details Carrie's lifting of "Yank's" watch. An account of the Caroline Prenel murder is in the May 26, 1872, *San Francisco Chronicle,* while the report of the coroner's inquest is in the May 28, 1872, *Call.*

Edward Byram's "Record Book" reports Mortimer "Arrested June 1st/72 for robbing Henry Marshall of a watch at a circus. June 6/72 the case reduced to Petit Larceny and he was sent to the County Jail for 3 months." The attempted robbery is reported in the June 2, 1872, *Chronicle.*

Mortimer sometimes uses aliases for friends in his memoirs. According to Byram's "Record Book," Mortimer's "Blackwine" was really named "Redwine." Carrie settled her case with Redwine and he was one of the men arrested with her in Alameda, according to both Mortimer and Byram.

Sacramento police detective Leonard Harris was born in New York in 1827 and served in the Mexican War before arriving in California in 1849. He took up residence in Sacramento, where he was a constable and deputy sheriff. After serving as turnkey at San Quentin, he had returned to Sacramento by late 1871 and was employed as a city police detective. By 1874 Harris was working for the Central Pacific Railroad as a detective under Fred Burke. He continued with the railroad for the next twenty years, gaining a reputation as a brave and clever officer who captured many outlaws and thieves. A train station robber fatally wounded him in 1894, and he died at the Alameda home of a daughter. See William B. Secrest, "Brave Len Harris Is Dead," *True West*, December 1992.

The conversations in the Gibson house, and throughout this story, are from Mortimer's memoirs. Mortimer says Carrie was largely responsible for both of the murders he mentions in his memoirs, and my text reflects that position. Readers should realize, however, that Mortimer's version of events may not be true. The degree of complicity of Mortimer and Carrie is impossible to assess. I have taken Mortimer at his word, bearing in mind that he was under sentence of death at the time of the writing. The parts of his memoirs that can be checked are quite accurate; still, as punishment for testifying against him, he might have portrayed Carrie as more culpable than she was in order to get her indicted as an accomplice.

The September 20, 1872, *Sacramento Bee* details the Gibson murder; the following day the Bee reported Mortimer's arrest. The description of Mrs. Gibson's body is by E.B. Willis, city editor of the *Sacramento Daily Record* and special deputy sheriff, in his introduction to Mortimer's memoirs. The conversation in the undertaking parlors is also from that source.

The *Santa Cruz Sentinel* of February 3, 8, 15, 22, and March 1 and 8, 1873, covers Mortimer's connection with the Blakely trial. See also the *San Francisco Bulletin* of January 28, 31, February 4 and 5, 1873. Blakely was acquitted the following year, due in part to Mortimer's testimony.

The first indication that Mortimer had been tied to the Prenel murder is in the November 18, 1872, *Bulletin*. Later, when Carrie testified at Bec's trial, his innocence became obvious and he was released.

Mortimer's trial for the Gibson murder receives good coverage in the *San Francisco Bulletin* of March 13, 14, 15, and 17, 1873. His sentencing is reported in the March 29 edition. The *Sacramento Bee* reports Mortimer's entrance into the courtroom in its March 12, 1873, issue. The reference to "frequent bloodletting" refers to Mortimer's several attempts at suicide the previous November, as related in Willis' introduction to the memoirs. Carrie Spencer's courtroom entrance is from the March 14, 1873, *Bee*, as well as the trial transcript in Mortimer's pardon file (California State Archives).

The description of Mortimer watching Carrie in court is from the March 14, 1873, *Bulletin*. The March 17 *Bee* reports the jury's verdict and Mortimer's singing prowess. Carrie's last conversation with Mortimer is from his memoirs. The March 29 *Bee* gives a long and detailed account of the sentencing.

William Flinn's attempted rescue of Mortimer and Flinn's resulting death are described in great detail in the April 16, 1873, *Bee*, with follow-up articles appearing in the May 6 and 10 issues. The *Bulletin* also gives full coverage to those events on April 16, 17, 18, and 21, 1873. Family information appears on May 7 in the same paper.

Mortimer's comments after identifying his brother's body are from his memoirs. He was quite bitter over his brother's death, maintaining Deputy Cross should not have shot to kill as he did. His family, however, bore no ill will towards the officer.

Thomas Flinn's letter is in the May 7, 1873, *Sacramento Daily Record*. The arrival of Frank Flinn in Sacramento and his meeting with Charlie is noted in a long May 12 *Bulletin* article. The same edition reports the visit of Governor Newton Booth and Dr. Benjamin Shurtleff, as well as Frank Flinn's quote about Mortimer's state of mind.

Mortimer's execution is fully reported in the *Bulletin* and the *Bee* on May 15, and in the *Daily Record* on May 16, 1873.

Carrie Spencer's later life is from the November 13, 1873, *Bee*; the May 11, 1874, *Bulletin*; and the June 10, 1876, *Call*. Other information is found in Edward Byram's "Record Book," where he lists her as "Mortimer, Carrie alias Spencer alias Stevens alias Butler alias Jones alias Marshall alias Williams alias Wardell alias Willis." A final reference is her portrait in the 1884 San Francisco police mug book (Special Collections, Henry Madden Library, California State University, Fresno).

Information on the Flinn family plot in Lynn, Massachusetts, is from Pine Grove Cemetery clerk Frances M. Jarvis, who provided a record of the family burials there. Mary E. Paine died in March 1890; Frank Flinn in December of the same year; Louisa L. Flinn, the mother, in July 1893; and Edward D. Flinn in May 1906. William Flinn is listed as buried there also, but no record exists of either Charlie or his brother, Thomas.

Chapter 3
The Nephew of Joaquin Murrieta:, Procopio, 1840–1892 (?)

Information about Procopio's lineage and early years is almost exclusively from Frank Latta, *Joaquin Murrieta and His Horse Gangs* (Santa Cruz, California: Bear State Books, 1980). Latta visited Mexico and interviewed Procopio's widow and other family members, but he was primarily interested in Joaquin Murrieta. The dateless bits and pieces of the Procopio story are incomplete at best. Latta says Procopio was four years old in 1853 when his uncle Joaquin died, but Procopio's prison record reports him as twenty-one when admitted to San Quentin in 1863. If true, that would make him ten or eleven in 1853.

Information about Joaquin Murrieta is from Latta's *Murrieta* and my collection of miscellaneous data on the subject. For prejudice in the mines, see Sister M. Collete Standart, O.P., "The Sonoran Migration to California, 1848–1856; A Study in Prejudice," *Southern California Quarterly* (Fall 1976). For the confusion over Joaquin's death and his head see William B. Secrest, "The Horrifying History of a Highwayman's Head," *The Californians*, November–December, 1986.

Information about Sonora Town in old Los Angeles is found in Harris Newmark, *Sixty Years in Southern California, 1853–1913* (Boston: Houghton Mifflin, 1930) and Richard Griswold del Castillo, *The Los Angeles Barrio, 1850–1890* (Berkeley and Los Angeles: University of California Press, 1979). Attempts to find Procopio or his family in the 1860 United States census for Los Angeles proved unproductive.

Typical notices of horse stealing appear in the *Los Angeles Star* of March 29 and September 6, 1862. Indictment notices of Procopio and his partner Antonio Rodriguez are in the March 1, 1862, issue. The March 15 *Star* notes the continuance of Procopio's case and according to the March 29 edition, Rodriguez left for San Quentin on March 22.

For the story of John Rains and his Rancho Cucamonga see Esther Boulton Black, *Rancho Cucamonga and Doña Merced* (Redlands, California: San Bernardino County Museum Association, 1975). The November 29, 1862, *Star* announces Rains' death; a funeral notice and report of Judge Hayes' investigation appear in the same issue. Hayes' letter to Cave Couts is dated December 10, 1862, and is in the Couts Collection, Henry E. Huntington Library, San Marino, California. Details of the murder, and the capture and disposition of

Cerradel and other suspects, are in the *Star* of February 14 and 24, 1863. The Carlisle letter is also in the Huntington Library.

Details of Cerradel's lynching are in Newmark and in a letter from William Gouvernor Morris to Cave Couts dated December 11, 1863, in the Couts Collection. Robert Carlisle's involvement in the Rains case and his later death in the King brothers shootout are detailed in Black. See also the June 4, 1864, *Star*.

Although containing some erroneous information, Harry Morse's meticulous recollections of Narcisso Bojorques and Procopio appear in the *San Francisco Morning Call* of May 14, 21, and 28, 1882. Morse was a writer who recited endless details. He sometimes included hearsay in his accounts, but the diaries and notebooks he kept made most of his work quite accurate. Much of his material is in the collection of John Boessenecker, who is working on a biography of Morse. Details of Morse's life are in Charles Howard Shinn, *Graphic Description of Pacific Coast Outlaws* (Los Angeles: Westernlore Press, 1958) and J.M. Guinn, *History of the State of California and Biographical Record of Oakland and Environs* (Los Angeles: Historic Record Company, 1907). Morse's description of Procopio appeared in the May 14, 1882, *Call*.

First news of the Golding murders appeared in the February 2, 1863, *Stockton Daily Independent*. Follow-up articles in February 4, 16, and 17 issues give more details on the murder and the search for the killers. John Boessenecker provided a copy of the official San Joaquin County coroner's report and a typescript giving much information on the killings and possible motives. Morse's articles, noted previously, were also helpful.

The Pope rustling incident and Procopio's confrontation with Constable Wood is recounted in numerous sources, including the July 11, 1863, *San Francisco Daily Alta California* and the August 28, 1871, *San Francisco Daily Evening Bulletin*. The quote is from the February 12, 1872, *Bulletin*. Harry Morse also describes the incident in the previously-cited articles.

The San Quentin Prison Register in the California State Archives contains Procopio's description. A contemporary description of that facility appears in the February 6, 1862, *Red Bluff* (California) *Beacon*. Several early maps of the prison, provided by Richard A. Nelson of the San Quentin Museum Association, show the buildings in and around the prison grounds. For a general history of the prison, see Lamott, as mentioned earlier. Clare V. McKanna, "Crime and Punishment: The Hispanic Experience in San Quentin, 1851–1880,"

Southern California Quarterly (Spring 1990), gives statistics and punishment details of early prison life.

One of the most comprehensive accounts of Tiburcio Vasquez's career is *The California Outlaw, Tiburcio Vasquez,* compiled by Robert Greenwood (Los Gatos, California: Talisman Press, 1960). For Vasquez's escape from San Quentin, see the June 27, 1859, *Alta California.* George A. Beers' *Vasquez; or, the Hunted Bandits of the San Joaquin* (New York: Robert M. DeWitt, 1875), a principal component of Greenwood's compilation, notes the respect other prisoners accorded Vasquez. Beers was a newspaper reporter who, as a posse member, chased Vasquez and later interviewed him after his capture. Although Beers' account is overall an excellent contemporary source, researchers must use it with caution. He places Procopio with the Vasquez gang in several places when, in reality, he was still in San Quentin.

State officials recognized the crime-school aspects of prison early, as noted in the California State Senate's "Annual Report of the Board of State Prison Directors for the Year 1858," Senate Journal appendix, 1859 session (Sacramento: State Printing Office, 1859). The "dog to his vomit" quote is from the August 28, 1871, *San Francisco Daily Evening Bulletin.*

The previously-cited Morse article in the May 28, 1882, *Call* details the fate of Bojorques. Morse viewed the body to identify it positively.

According to an article in the May 19, 1874, *San Jose Daily Patriot,* Procopio and Vasquez were camped some distance away when Morse killed Juan Soto. Vasquez himself, in the May 28 *Patriot,* states that Soto and Procopio had a dispute and that Soto had made Procopio "go down into his boots. If Procopio had not left like a coward Soto would have killed him." Vasquez lied when it suited his purposes. He may have been lying about this since he, too, was angry with Procopio.

The theft of the Arnett cow and succeeding events are related in the *Oakland Daily News* and the *San Francisco Bulletin* of April 26, 1872. An article in the August 19, 1871, *San Francisco Bulletin,* as reprinted from the *San Jose Patriot,* details the Soap Lake stage robbery. Vasquez's own account of the robbery, without incriminating any accomplices, is in Beers.

The September 16, 1871, *Santa Cruz Sentinel* reports Undersheriff Lincoln's encounter with Francisco Barcenas. Vasquez, in a July 25, 1874, *Patriot* interview, calls Barcenas "Bassinez," but that was no doubt a mistake of the reporter. A follow-up article on September 23 reports the Lorenzano incident. See also *Bulletin* accounts on September 15 and 18, 1871.

Most accounts report Vasquez and Procopio's trip to Mexico, although Eugene T. Sawyer, in *The Life and Career of Tiburcio Vasquez, the California Stage Robber* (San Jose, California, 1875; reprinted, Oakland, California: Biobooks, 1944) notes that Procopio did not accompany Vasquez. That information is undoubtedly from a long Vasquez interview in the July 25, 1874, *San Jose Patriot.* Latta's interviews with Procopio's family and others lack dates but leave little doubt that Procopio returned to Mexico; this seems to have been a practical time for him to have made the trip. Procopio's 1872 prison description lists "arrow wounds" on his body, indicating he may have been involved with some Indian fights.

The bay area press reported Procopio's capture with jubilation. See the *Bulletin, Oakland News,* and the *Oakland Daily Transcript* of February 12, and the February 15, 1872, *Alameda County Gazette.* Trial testimony is from a transcript made when the case was appealed; see California Supreme Court Case, File No. 8783, *People v. Rodundo,* in the California State Archives. The trial is also reported fully in the *Bulletin* and *Oakland News* of April 26, and the May 2, 1872, *Gazette.*

The report of the moral instructor and details of work projects at the prison are in the California State Legislature's "Report of the Directors of the California State Prison, July 1, 1871," Legislative Journal appendix, 1871 session (Sacramento: State Printing Office, 1871). A roster of officials and manufacturing firms at the prison is in the Legislature's "Report on the State Prison by the Joint Committee of the Senate and Assembly," Legislative Journals appendix, 1872 session (Sacramento: State Printing Office, 1872).

Procopio's prison files do not indicate why his sentence was commuted, and he was probably freed merely when he had served his time. His release date is on the prison register.

The January 14, 1878, *San Francisco Alta California* details the Dougherty robbery and subsequent events. A long article in the November 17, 1877, *Visalia Weekly Delta* recounts the Grangeville raid, while the December 29, 1877, *Tulare Weekly Times* and the *Delta* of the same date give much information on the Caliente raid and the lynching in Bakersfield. See also Frank Latta, *Saga of Rancho El Tejon* (Santa Cruz, California: Bear State Books, 1976).

The Hanford raid is reported in the December 29, 1877, *Fresno Weekly Republican,* while both the robbery and the fatal aftermath are covered in the *Fresno Weekly Expositor* of January 2 and 9, 1878, and the

January 5 *Delta*. In later years Frank Latta interviewed three of the possemen who pursued Procopio after the Hanford robbery. This account of that chase is from Latta's manuscript materials in the Harold G. Schutt Collection (Special Collections, Henry Madden Library, California State University, Fresno). The January 11, 1878, *Delta* contains the disgruntled comments concerning the posse's shortcomings, while the *Republican* of the same date reports the alibis of Procopio's Firebaugh friends.

The identification of Procopio appears in the January 16, 1878, *Expositor*. A Tulare County petition in the Governor's Reward Files (California State Archives) asks that a reward be offered for Procopio, who had been seen "lerking" [sic] about town just prior to the robbery. Apparently the Whitesides posse knew exactly who they were looking for. The governor's $500 reward proclamation is also in the California State Archives.

Procopio's woodcut portrait and a descriptive article appear in the March 15, 1879, *National Police Gazette*. Ned Buntline's *Red Dick, the Tiger of California*, appeared in a New York weekly popular fiction newspaper in the early 1870s. The New York firm of Street & Smith published it as a dime novel in 1890.

Efforts to obtain more information on the killing of Cantabrana in Hermosillo, Mexico, have been unsuccessful. The Tucson *Arizona Weekly Citizen* of November 10 and 24, 1883, reports the mix-up in Tucson. A telegram from Sheriff Martin asking about the standing reward for Procopio is in the California Governor's Reward Files.

The meager information on Procopio's last years is in Latta's *Murrieta* and in Manuel Rojas, *Joaquin Murrieta, El Patrio* (Mexicali, Baja California, Mexico: El "Far West" Del Mexico, 1986). An inquiry to Hermosillo, Sonora, Mexico, pertaining to a birth or death certificate for Procopio was unproductive (correspondence with Pbro. Teodoro E. Pino, Hermosillo Archdiocese Archives, April 30, 1993).

Chapter 4
The West's Most Inept Outlaw: Milton Harvey Lee, 1847–1916

Lee's musings from his desk are, of course, speculative. They are based, however, on his past life, which is documented in the following pages.

Early family data are from a biography of George Lee in J.M. Guinn, *History of the State of California and Biographical Record of the*

Coast Counties of California (Chicago: Chapman, 1904). For background on San Jose and vicinity see Eugene T. Sawyer, *History of Santa Clara County, California* (Los Angeles: Historic Record Company, 1922), and Benjamin H. Cottle and Theodore F. Wright, *Directory for the City of San Jose for 1878, Together with a Historical Sketch of the City* (San Jose: n.p., 1878).

Information on the Naylor family is from the 1860 United States Census population schedules for Santa Clara County. Although only thirteen years old at the time, Harvey may have been working, for the report lists him as not attending school the past year. However, it does not list him as a "day laborer" like his older brothers.

Guinn cites George's service in the army during the Civil War. These data seem to be based on a personal interview with George, who was alive at the time.

Harvey's arrest for grand larceny is reported in the December 27, 1866, *San Jose Mercury*. The same issue reports a spate of rustling in the area. Although trial records could not be located, various documents in Harvey's prison pardon file give information on his trial. (Governor's Pardon Files, California State Archives; correspondence with M.C. Guerra, deputy county clerk, San Jose, California.)

The May 2, 1867, *Mercury* notes Jasper Lee's arrest; the same paper reports his trial on May 30. His arrival and prison number, along with a description and release date, are in the San Quentin List. A good description of San Quentin at this time appears in the February 6, 1862, *Red Bluff* (California) *Beacon*.

Harvey's medical report by the Cory brothers and various documents, petitions and letters relating to his pardon application are in his previously-cited pardon file at the California State Archives.

Information about prison manufacturing is from the California State Legislature's "Report of the State Prison Committee of the Assembly," Legislative Journals appendix, 1866 session (Sacramento: State Printing Office, 1866). Prison rules relating to convicts are in the California State Senate's "Annual Report of the Board of State Prison Directors for the Year 1858," Senate Journal appendix, 1859 session (Sacramento: State Printing Office, 1859). For the prison gambling problem, see "Report of the Joint Committee on the State Prison," Legislative Journal appendix, 1868 session (Sacramento: State Printing Office, 1868).

Information about life in prison during the 1860s and the diseases within the walls is in Lamott. Prison medical reports of the time are in the contemporary appendixes to the state legislative journals and give a good idea of prisoner health in San Quentin. See also James H. Wilkins, "The Evolution of a State Prison," *San Francisco Bulletin*, July 8, 1918. Work details of the convicts are listed in the California State Legislature's "Report of the Directors of the California State Prison, December 1, 1867," Legislative Journal appendix, 1868 session (Sacramento: State Printing Office, 1868).

The date of Harvey's prison release is in the San Quentin List and on his official pardon, a copy of which is in the previously-cited pardon files in the California State Archives. His pardon was finally recommended because he was "suffering from disease of the lungs." See also the California State Legislature's "Report of the Directors of the State Prison Recommending the Pardon of Certain Criminals," Legislative Journals appendix, 1868 session (Sacramento: State Printing Office, 1868).

For descriptions of the San Joaquin Valley in the 1870s, see *San Joaquin Vignettes, The Reminiscences of Captain John Barker*, edited by William Harland Boyd and Glendon J. Rodgers (Bakersfield, California: Kern County Historical Society, 1955).

The October 22, 1870, *San Bernardino Guardian* chronicles Lee and Crandall's horse-stealing venture. Lee's grand jury appearance and his guilty plea are reported in the same paper on November 12 and his sentencing on December 26. A copy of Lee's grand larceny indictment is in the San Bernardino County Archives (correspondence with James D. Hofer, county archivist, and Chris Shovey, junior librarian, November 9, 1990, San Bernardino County Library, San Bernardino, California).

Lee's new prison number, entrance date, and release date are in the previously-cited San Quentin List. Lamott mentions the Sunday visiting excursions. The January 10 and February 5, 1884, editions of the *San Jose Daily Herald* report Harvey's experience with the skeleton.

The June 8, 1884, *San Jose Mercury* notes John Herbert's presence as a neighbor of Harvey's. Madera stage robber Tolman Terhune's reminiscences appear in the May 25, 1884, *New York Sun*.

The May 9, 1884, *Fresno Weekly Republican* reports Lee and Herbert's robbery of the "Yo Semite" stage. News of the suspects' arrest appears in the June 8 *San Jose Mercury* and the June 11, 1884 *Fresno Weekly Expositor*. Deputy Witthouse's arrival to pick up the two prisoners is recorded in the June 12 *San Jose Herald*. The June 18 *Expositor* reports the arrival of the trio in Fresno and gives the scheduled date of trial. A record of the trial and various court documents are on file in the Fresno County Clerk's office in Fresno.

Walter Grady, Lee and Herbert's attorney, was as colorful as his clients. In the same year as the Lee/Herbert trial, he had a pistol duel in a Fresno theater he owned, and was frequently involved in extramarital affairs and brawls. In 1897 he was accused of biting a chunk from a San Francisco waiter's ear. (From June English, "W.D. Grady, Anti-Divisionist," a typescript in the author's collection, and the January 21, 1897, *San Francisco Examiner.*)

Lee's new prison number, date of admission and other information is in the San Quentin List. For a resumé of the labor and Chinese problems plaguing San Francisco and the rest of the country during the late 1870s, see William Issel and Robert W. Cherny, *San Francisco 1865–1932* (Berkeley and Los Angeles: University of California Press, 1986). Complaints against the competition of prison labor are in the California State Legislature's "Memorial from the Mechanics' State Council in Reference to State Prison Labor," Legislative Journal appendix, 1874 session (Sacramento: State Printing Office, 1874). Other information on this problem and the installation of the new jute mill are in Lamott.

For leniency at San Quentin, see prison director James H. Wilkins' comments in the May 31, 1897, *San Francisco Chronicle.* Opium smuggling had been a problem for years in the prison. The October 14, 1894, *San Francisco Examiner* contains a long article about convicts making burglar tools in prison, then trading them for drugs from the outside.

The March 20, 1891, *Riverside Daily Press* reports "Ed Martin's" southern California burglary. San Bernardino County justice court and superior court records provide detailed summaries of the case. My thanks to Ronald J. Baker, local history coordinator of the Riverside City and County Public Library, and Jim Hofer and Anne L. Brandt of the San Bernardino County Archives, San Bernardino, California. San Quentin prison register information on Martin's term there is in the California State Archives.

Ed Morrell's real name was Martin Delaney, and he details his travels and experiences in and around Fresno in his autobiography, *The Twenty-Fifth Man* (Montclair, New Jersey: New Era Publishing Company, 1924). However, historians must use his writings with caution as he had a decided inclination to make a hero of himself in almost every situation. More accurate information on his movements is found in the December 30, 1893, and January 10, 1894, *San Francisco Chronicle.* The September 24, 1893, *Fresno Morning Republican* reports on Morrell's stay in the Fresno jail. See the *Fresno Daily Evening*

Expositor of January 10, 1894, for Morrell's involvement with the Hutchinsons and his parole errand for Harvey Lee. My thanks to longtime Morrell researcher Jack Fleming of Berkeley, California, for sharing information on these subjects.

For the escape from the Fresno County jail, see the December 29, 1893, *Expositor*. There is much newspaper coverage of Morrell and Evans in the mountains up to their capture, which was reported by the Visalia and Fresno press on February 19, 1894. Morrell was received at Folsom as prisoner number 3097 as noted in the California State Archives' Folsom prison register. For a complete, although not always accurate, account of the careers of Christopher Evans and John Sontag see Wallace Smith, *Prodigal Sons: The Adventures of Christopher Evans and John Sontag* (Boston: Christopher Publishing House, 1951).

Scant information exists on the Hutchinson family. The 1891 Fresno city directory lists a J. Hutchinson as a helper at the Fresno Agricultural Works. That is probably Jim, as newspapers mentioned him as being a molder, or foundry worker. Neither he nor any of his family were found in the 1900 United States Census population schedules for Fresno County.

Lamott devotes six pages to the story of the prison "strike" and its aftermath. Morrell's *Twenty-fifth Man* is interesting as the recollections of one who was in on the strike. His exaggerations and overdone accusations, however, make his story subject to something more than a mere grain of salt. For detailed newspaper accounts, see the *San Francisco Chronicle* of May 28, 29, 30, 31, and June 2, 1897.

Harvey Lee's wanderings after his release from prison are conjectural, of course. The June 21, 1893, editions of the *San Jose Herald* and *Mercury* report his mother's death.

Harvey Lee and Williams' date of arrival in Portland is reported in the September 27, 1897, *Portland Morning Oregonian*. The same issue recounts their wanderings, as the detectives checked every move they had made.

A long article in the September 26 *Oregonian* details the attempted robbery. The September 27 issue describes the prisoners, and an editorial on the bungling train robbers appears on September 28. Notice of the prisoners' indictment appears the following day. The dynamite scare and trial are noted in the same paper in the October 9 and 10 *Oregonian*. Various commitment documents pertaining to the case were obtained from Jim Murchison, circuit court administrator, Multnomah County Courthouse, Portland, Oregon. The October 12,

1897, *San Francisco Chronicle* reports Hume's involvement in the case.

The date of Harvey's prison admittance is in the Convict Record, Oregon State Penitentiary, which lists his number as 3879. (From James Clark, Reference Archivist, Archives Division, Office of the Secretary of State, Salem, Oregon.) Oregon prison history is taken from the *Dictionary of Oregon History*, edited by Howard McKinley Corning (Portland, Oregon: Binford & Mort Publishing, 1989), and a letter from Sieglinde Smith, reference librarian at the Oregon Historical Society, Portland, November 24, 1992.

Much information about the prison operation and convict work details of the time is from Joseph D. Lee, superintendent, *Biennial Report of the Superintendent of the State Penitentiary to Hon. T.T. Geer, Governor of Oregon* (Salem, Oregon: State Printing Office, 1901) and a letter received from James Clark, August 20, 1992. A copy of Harvey Lee's physical examination report was obtained from Sharon L. Christensen, Custodian of Records, Oregon Department of Corrections, Salem, Oregon.

Joseph "Bunco" Kelley, *Thirteen Years in the Penitentiary* (Portland, Oregon: Author, 1908), gives that convict's recollections. He tells of Tracy's noted escape, but the best account is Jim Dullenty's *Harry Tracy: The Last Desperado* (Dubuque, Iowa: Kendall/Hunt Publishing Company, 1989).

The story of Rose Lee's attempted suicide and the attendant circumstances is in the January 29, 1898, *Fresno Morning Republican*. Attempts to find a contemporary record of her have been unsuccessful. Neither Rose nor her paramour appear in city directories of the time or in the 1900 United States Census population schedules for Fresno County.

A copy of Lee's pardon was obtained from James Clark, (letter dated January 11, 1988). Milton H. Lee first appears in the Fresno city directory in the 1907 edition as an employee of the Fresno Cooperage Company. He shows up consistently through 1916, although with various address changes. An ad in the 1913 directory states that the Fresno Cooperage Company manufactures "Tanks, Kegs and Barrels" and was located at the corner of East and California streets. By 1914 Lee is listed as foreman of the company.

For a good description of the American cooperage business at the time see George F. Walsh, "The Life of a Barrel," *Scientific American*, January 21, 1905.

Lee's death certificate is from the Fresno County Clerk's office in Fresno. He was listed as a bookkeeper and widower. The certificate mentions neither of his daughters. Records of Fresno's Mountain View Cemetery indicate only the general area of Lee's unmarked grave.

Chapter 5
The Strange Saga of Abe Majors, 1882–1957

Much material on Abe Majors' life is in his Folsom prison pardon files in the California State Archives. Letters in this collection shed much light on his activities. Abe had an incredible talent for involving people on his behalf, and his files are filled with correspondence from governors, wardens, lawyers, family members, friends, acquaintances, co-workers, and various professional people who all saw something in him worth salvaging.

Lloyd Majors wrote a brief sketch of his early life; it appears in the May 24, 1884, *San Francisco Chronicle*. His many fires and insurance claims are recounted in the March 18, 1883, *San Jose Morning Times*. Other details appear in the May 24, 1884, and May 14, 1889, *San Francisco Morning Call* and the July 1, 1934, *San Jose Mercury-Herald*. See also Thomas S. Duke, *Celebrated Criminal Cases of America* (San Francisco: James H. Barry, 1910).

Besides the local San Jose press, details of the Renowden and McIntyre murders appear in the *San Francisco Morning Call* of March 13, 14, 16, 20, and April 26, 1883. May 1883 issues of both the *Call* and the *San Jose Morning Times* give good coverage to the trials and convictions of Jewell, Showers, and Lloyd Majors. The June 3, 1883, *Morning Times* notes the sentences of the three criminals. Details of the cases also appear in *The Life of David Belden*, edited by John J. Berry (New York: Belden Brothers, 1891). Belden was the judge at the trials. Majors' Alameda trial for the McIntyre murder is reported in November 1883 issues of the *Call*. The same paper notes his death sentence on December 2, 1883. The *San Jose Daily Herald* announced the date of death on January 4, 1884.

The July 25, 1883, *Herald* announces the birth of Majors' daughter, Maud, while he resided in the Santa Clara county jail. The same paper reports Majors' escape attempt in its May 17, 1884, issue and his wife's suffering on May 27. The May 24, 1884, *San Francisco Chronicle* gives extensive coverage to Majors' execution.

Lucinda Majors' remarriage and life with Joseph A. Wagner is reported in the *Morning Call* of August 28, 1895, and May 14, 1899, and the February 8, 1896, *Chronicle*. The troubles with Mrs. Willmore are related in the August 23, 1895, *Call* and the February 8, 1896, *Chronicle*. Mrs. Ella Clune's deposition, found in Abe Majors' pardon file (California State Archives) likewise contains valuable information on these subjects.

Abe's behavior in the Willmore squabble and his life prior to entering Folsom in 1896 are related in a biographical statement he was compelled to write when applying for a pardon. The three-page document is found in his parole papers (California State Archives).

Oakland's consternation over the rash of burglaries is reflected in an article in the February 6, 1896, *Chronicle*. That very night the boys were caught, as the *Chronicle* reported the following day. For Majors' and Wilmore's court appearances, see the *Chronicle* for February 8, 11, 27, 28, and 29, 1896. The superior court commitment papers for the two boys are in Majors' pardon file.

As early as 1858 California Governor John B. Weller was complaining about youthful convicts, but little had changed by the time Abe Majors was sentenced to Folsom. For California prison age statistics and related data, see Clare V. McKanna, Jr., "Crime and Punishment: The Hispanic Experience in San Quentin, 1851–1880," *Southern California Quarterly*, Spring 1990.

Various letters of Abe to his mother are in his pardon papers; she obviously placed them there for the benefit of the parole board. In the same file are the great many letters and documents that Lucinda secured in her efforts to obtain a pardon for her boy. A notarized document in Abe's pardon files is from Dr. George G. Bentley, who notes that he delivered Abe on April 2, 1880. A statement from his mother gives the same date.

Archie Majors' travels and marriage are chronicled in the May 8, 1899, *San Francisco Morning Call* and the May 9, 1899, *Ogden* (Utah) *Standard*. The May 1, 1899, *Standard* announces the death of Captain William A. Brown in a front-page article which details the robbery, ensuing chase in the hills, and events that resulted in the deaths of Brown and Archie Majors. The *San Francisco Call* carries a brief account of the incident that same day, although it was not then known the Majors boys were involved. Follow-up articles in the *Standard* on May 2 and 3 give additional details of the fight, and also report on the coroner's jury verdict and Brown's funeral.

Abe Majors' identity as the "boy burglar" of Oakland was quickly discovered and reported in the May 9, 1899, *Standard*. Lucinda Wagner's hysterics when she received the Utah news are reported at length in the May 8, 1899, *Call.* Abe's trial is reported in the *Standard* beginning on May 10. His attempt to obtain Sheriff Cardon's pistol is related in the following day's issue. The same newspaper reports the verdict on May 13 and Majors' death sentence on May 17, 1899.

The May 14, 1899, *Call* reports on Lucinda Wagner's condition. The *Call* notes the Showers murder on May 16, as does the *Standard.* The *Salt Lake City Deseret Evening News* of May 20, 1899, contains an interview with Abe in which he denies any close association with Showers' killer. Mrs. Wagner's complaints concerning Abe's trial appear in the June 4, 1899, *Call.*

Articles concerning the Salt Lake City Woman's Club and other organizations taking an interest in Abe's case appear in the June 14 and 20, 1899, issues of the *Standard.*

The October 14, 1899, *Standard* reports Bert Willmore's death. The *Alameda Daily Argus* devotes much space to the incident on October 9, 10, and 11, 1899. Ina Willmore's comment is in an article on the coroner's inquest which appeared on the latter date. All these articles spell the surname "Willmore," though it is sometimes spelled with only one *l.* Duke covers Abe's second trial and sentencing.

Jack Black's comments are from his autobiography, *You Can't Win* (New York: Macmillan, 1926). A "List of Prisoners in the Utah State Prison" in the Utah State Archives, Salt Lake City, Utah, lists Abe as "Abraham R. Majors, alias James Morgan, No. 1123." Information on the Utah State Penitentiary when Abe Majors was there is in *Biennial Report of the State Board of Corrections of the State of Utah, for the Years 1899 and 1900* (Salt Lake City: The Deseret Evening News, 1901). A description of the cell block, cells, and the builder is in Fred Harrison, *Hell Holes and Hangings* (Clarendon, Texas: Clarendon Press, 1968). Convict Eli Day wrote the "steam" quote on a drawing he did of the cell block (obtained courtesy of the Utah State Archives, Salt Lake City).

The October 12, 1903, *Deseret Evening News* contains details of smuggling in the prison and of the escape preparations. The State Board of Corrections' thorough review of the incident is found in "Investigation in the Jail Break, Oct. 14, 1900" (typescript, Governor Heber Wells correspondence, 1895–1905, Utah State Archives, Salt Lake City).

Haworth's capture is recounted in the October 12, 1903, *Deseret Evening News*, and Lynch's in the October 15 issue of the same paper. Dr. Young's salty comments appear in the October 13 *News.* The same article reports on the various security improvements.

In a long, undated letter addressed to the Utah State Board of Prison Directors, Abe accuses deputy Joe Belnap of accidentally shooting Captain Billy Brown. At his trial, he had insisted Archie killed Brown. Abe further states that jurors had admitted convicting him primarily because of his previous prison record. In a letter dated April 3, 1921, to the California governor's executive secretary, attorney Paul W. Schenck mentions seeing the transcript of record used in Abe's application for pardon in Utah. He reports the transcript contained affidavits by eight jurors who said they never believed Abe was guilty of the murder charge, but thought he should be punished for robbing the milkman. Both documents are in the Majors pardon file.

Utah Governor Simon T. Bamberger, Warden George A. Storrs of the Utah State Prison, Deputy Warden J.W. McKinney, Samuel Newhouse and others testified to Abe's good character, favoring his parole in Utah and later in California. Their letters are in the Majors pardon file (California State Archives). Majors' parole application is mentioned in the *Deseret Evening News* of January 5 and 21, 1918.

Letters from Samuel Newhouse pertaining to Abe's parole, and a parole document dated January 21, 1918, are in the Utah State Archives, Salt Lake City, Utah. A letter from Warden Storrs to attorney Schenck, dated February 25, 1920, mentions Lucinda Wagner's presence in Salt Lake City at the time of Abe's parole and Abe's comment about being "born again" (Majors pardon file, California State Archives).

The January 21, 1918, *Deseret Evening News* notes the motion pictures playing in town. Abe's letter to Sam Newhouse is in the Utah State Archives. The February 25, 1920, Storrs letter, noted above, describes Abe's work at the mine and later employment with the telephone company.

Abe and Lucinda's letters to California Governor William D. Stevens are in the Utah State Archives, along with communications from Utah officials. While Abe influenced many people in his behalf, he continually lied and stretched the truth to make himself a more sympathetic figure. A case in point is his statement that he was fourteen when he first entered Folsom. He also apparently told Warden Storrs he was illiterate when he entered the Utah state prison and had learned to read and write while there "under mighty trying conditions." That, of course, is a lie. Abe wrote many letters during his prior term in California's Folsom prison. He did, however, become a much better writer in prison while soliciting help in securing a parole. See the previously-cited Storrs letter in the Majors pardon file

(California State Archives).

In a twelve-page autobiography dated February 1, 1921, and written while applying for his parole from Folsom, Abe mentions going to California in early January 1919 because his mother was ill. Warden Storrs mentions that also in the letter cited above. Both documents are in the Majors parole file (California State Archives).

Letters from Mr. and Mrs. Henry Bode, prison reform advocate June Westerbeck, Mrs. J.S. Altice, and others testify that Abe cared for his mother in Los Angeles. Lucinda, of course, also mentions his care in her letter of March 21, 1921. (Majors pardon file, California State Archives.)

Abe's own story of his arrest in Los Angeles is in his aforementioned three-page biographical statement. His assertion that "two detectives of the Javert type" arrested him indicates how well-read he was at the time. An April 3, 1921, four-page letter from his attorney, Paul Schenck, gives much detail on the case, as does a March 21, 1921, letter of June Westerbeck. Los Angeles Police Chief Lyle Pendergast, in a January 7, 1921, note to the California State Board of Prison Directors says Abe was "arrested by this department March 5, 1919 for burglary (committed several burglaries and was identified as the man that held up a jewelry store at 1604 N. Vermont Ave)."

Abe's arrest and conviction notices are in the *Los Angeles Times* of March 6, 1919, and January 14, 1920. The Majors pardon file (California State Archives) contains various trial documents, appeal notices, and commitment papers, but they shed little light on the crime. A number of letters relate to the various incidents, but all are for Abe's pardon applications and are, of course, favorable to him. The most interesting document is a November 9, 1920, letter from Warden Storrs, in which he tells of the Los Angeles County undersheriff's investigation of Abe's case.

An April 4, 1921, letter from Dwight S. Person verifies Abe's employment at the automotive repair shop. He reports Abe as "a clean-cut, trustworthy and dependable man."

Details of Abe's confrontations with the accusing jewelers and his later trial are in June Westerbeck's March 21, 1921, letter, and in attorney Schenck's April 3, 1921, letter. Both are in the Majors pardon file (California State Archives). Also in the file are a list of pardon application documents, including letters written from Yuma, Arizona by Ralph Wagner and his mother.

Abe's applications for prison gardening and road camp jobs are dated November 28, 1921, and May 5 and October 11, 1922. Charles

R. Burger, a member of the Los Angeles County Civil Service Commission, wrote on November 24, 1922, asking that Abe receive a road camp assignment. In an October 13, 1922, note, the warden turned down Abe's request, citing that he was ineligible for such positions as a third-termer. (Majors pardon file, California State Archives.)

Lucinda's sad letter to the State Prison Directors is dated March 24, 1921. She dictated it to a friend and her tortured signature clearly indicates her failing condition (Majors pardon file, California State Archives). Lucinda Wagner was buried on February 2, 1922, in the Forest Lawn Cemetery, Glendale, California. Her death certificate is from the California Department of Health Services, Office of the State Registrar of Vital Statistics, Sacramento.

Abe's five-page letter extolling his service in the prison tailor shop and asking he be given extra credits is not dated, but he obviously wrote it just prior to his release. An excerpt from the minutes of the California State Prison Board Meeting of January 12, 1924, notes Abe's parole with three months' additional credit for "meritorious services." (Majors pardon file, California State Archives.)

Abe's telegram to June Westerbeck may merely indicate a meeting with an old friend. In various letters noted previously, Westerbeck stated she was well acquainted with the family.

A death index in the California State Library, Sacramento, gives the date of Abe Majors' death. No newspaper obituary has been found.

SOURCES

Documents

Byram, Edward. Journals, notebooks, related memoranda and memorabilia. John Boessenecker collection, Foster City, California.

California, State of. Death certificate index, 1905–. California State Library, Sacramento, California.

California State Assembly. "Report of Committee Relative to the Condition and Management of the State Prison." In: Assembly Journal appendix, Document Number 26, 1855 session. Sacramento: B.R. Redding, State Printer, 1855.

California State Legislature. "Memorial from the Mechanics State Council in Reference to State Prison Labor." In: Legislative Journals appendix, 1874 session. Sacramento: State Printing Office, 1874.

California State Legislature. "Report of the Director of the California State Prison, Dec. 1, 1867." In: Legislative Journals appendix, 1868 session. Sacramento: State Printer, 1868.

California State Legislature. "Report of the Director of the State Prison Recommends the Pardon of Certain Criminals; Milton Harvey Lee." In: Legislative Journals appendix, 1868 session. Sacramento, California: 1868.

California State Legislature. "Report of the Directors of the California State Prison," July 1, 1871." In: Legislative Journals appendix, 1872 session. Sacramento: State Printing Office, 1872.

California State Legislature. "Report of the State Prison Committee of the Assembly." In: Legislative Journal appendix, 1866 session. Sacramento: State Printer, 1866.

California State Legislature. "Report on the State Prison by Joint Committee of Senate and Assembly," In: Legislative Journals appendix, 1856 session. Sacramento: James Allen, State Printer, 1856.

California State Legislature. "Report on the State Prison by the Joint

Committee of the Senate and Assembly." In: Legislative Journals appendix, 1872 session. Sacramento, California, 1872.
California State Senate. "Annual Report of the Board of State Prison Directors for the year 1858." In: Senate Journal appendix, 1858 session. Sacramento: State Printing Office, 1859.
California State Senate. "Annual Report of the State Prison Committee of the Assembly." In: Senate Journal appendix, 1866 session. Sacramento: State Printing Office, 1866.
California State Senate. "Report of Committee on Commitments, Statistical Reports." In: Senate Journal appendix, 1860 session. Sacramento: State Printing Office, 1860.
California State Superior Court, Fresno County. *California v. Harvey Lee*, etc., complaint, May 29, 1884. Justice's Court, Third Township, County of Fresno. Fresno County Clerk's Office, Fresno, California.
California State Superior Court, Fresno County. *California v. Milton Harvey Lee and John Herbert*, Number 188, September 1884. Fresno County Clerk's Office, Fresno, California.
California State Superior Court, San Bernardino County. *Indictment of James Lee for grand larceny*, case number 308. San Bernardino County Archives, San Bernardino, California.
California v. Rodundo. Trial Transcript, File No. 8783, California State Archives, Sacramento, California.
Couts, Cave. Manuscript Collection, Henry E. Huntington Library, San Marino, California.
Day, Eli (convict in Utah State Prison). Statement and sketch, 1889. Utah State Historical Society, Salt Lake City.
English, June. "W.D. Grady—Anti-Divisionist." Typescript in author's collection.
Fifth Judicial District of California. Henry J. Talbot Records, 1854. Mariposa County Courthouse, Mariposa, California.
Folsom State Prison, Represa, California. Registers. California State Archives, Sacramento, California.
Fresno City directories, 1907–1916, various publishers and locations. Fresno County Library, Fresno, California.
Gladden murder, reward petitions. Governor's Reward Files, California State Archives, Sacramento, California.
Golden family deaths, inquest record of. San Joaquin County Clerk's Office, Stockton, California.
Grand Jury Report on Henry J. Talbot, 1862. Second Judicial District of Nevada. Nevada State Library and Archives, Carson City,

Nevada.

"Investigation in the Jail Break, October 14, 1900," Typescript. In Governor Heber Wells' correspondence, 1895–1905. Utah State Archives, Salt Lake City, Utah.

"Jackson, George" (Milton Harvey Lee). In: Description of Convicts, 1897. Oregon State Prison, Oregon Department of Corrections, Salem, Oregon.

"Jackson, George" (Milton Harvey Lee). Pardon file. Secretary of State Papers, Oregon State Archives, Salem, Oregon.

"Jackson, George" (Milton Harvey Lee). Physical Examination Report, 1897. Oregon Department of Corrections, Salem, Oregon.

Latta, Frank F. Manuscripts. In Harold G. Schutt Collection, Special Collections, Henry Madden Library, California State University, Fresno.

Lee, Joseph D., superintendent. *Biennial Report of the Superintendent of the State Penitentiary to Hon. T.T. Geer, Governor of Oregon.* Salem, Oregon: State Printing Office, 1901.

"Lee, Milton Harvey." Death Certificate. Fresno County Recorder's Office, Fresno, California.

"Lee, Milton Harvey." Pardon file. Governor's Pardon Papers, California State Archives, Sacramento, California.

Letters Received, Fort Walla Walla, Washington Territory, April 13, 1862. National Archives, Washington, D.C.

List of Convicts on Register of State Prison at San Quentin. Sacramento: State Printing Office, 1889.

[Majors, Abe.] Pardon file. Governor's Pardon Papers, California State Archives, Sacramento, California.

[Majors, Abe.] Parole papers. Governor's Parole Papers, California State Archives, Sacramento, California.

Massachusetts, State of. Index to the Convict Register, 1840–1860. Massachusetts Archives at Columbia Point, Boston.

[Mortimer, Charles.] Pardon file. Governor's Pardon Papers, California State Archives, Sacramento, California.

Mountain View Cemetery Records, Fresno, California.

Oregon, State of. Circuit Court, Multnomah County. *State of Oregon vs. George Jackson,* etc., Commitment Papers, Multnomah County Courthouse, Portland, Oregon.

Oregon State Penitentiary. Convict Record. Oregon State Archives, Salem, Oregon.

Pine Grove Cemetery Records, Lynn, Massachusetts.

San Francisco Police Mug and Record Books, 1860. Christian de

Guignè collection, San Mateo, California.
San Quentin State Prison. Historic maps. San Quentin Museum Association, San Quentin, California.
San Quentin State Prison. Registers. California State Archives, Sacramento, California.
Sixth Judicial District of California. *California v. Charles Mortimer*, March 1873. California State Archives, Sacramento, California.
Second Judicial District of Nevada. Henry J. Talbot Records, 1861–65. Nevada State Library and Archives, Carson City, Nevada.
[Talbot, Henry J.] Pardon file. Governor's Pardon Papers, California State Archives, Sacramento, California.
Tuolumne County, California. Inquest Records, 1854. Tuolumne County Historical Society.
United States Census. Wilkes County, Georgia, Population Schedules, 1840.
United States Census. Wilkes County, Georgia, Population Schedules, 1850.
United States Census. Fresno County, California, Population Schedules, 1900.
United States Census. Los Angeles County, California, Population Schedules, 1860.
United States Census. Santa Clara County, California, Population Schedules, 1860.
United States Census. Santa Clara County, California, Population Schedules, 1880.
United States Census. Sonoma County, California, Population Schedules, 1870.
United States Census. Genoa, Utah Territory, Population Schedules, 1860.
United States Census. Walla Walla County, Washington Territory, Population Schedules, 1860.
Utah State Board of Corrections. *Biennial Report of the State Board of Corrections of the State of Utah, for the Years 1899 and 1900.* Salt Lake City, Utah: Deseret Evening News, 1901.
Utah State Board of Corrections. *Report of the State Board of Corrections of the State of Utah, for the Years 1899–1900.* Salt Lake City, Utah: Deseret Evening News, 1900.
Utah State Board of Corrections. *Report of the State Board of Corrections of the State of Utah, for the Years 1903–1904.* Salt Lake City, Utah: Star Printing Company, 1904.
Utah State Board of Corrections. *Report of the State Board of Corrections*

SOURCES 247

for the Years *1909–1910*. Salt Lake City, Utah: Tribune-Reporter, 1910.
"Wagner, Lucinda A." Death certificate. State of California, Sacramento, California.

Newspapers

Alameda (California) *Daily Argus*
Alameda County (California) *Gazette*
Argonaut (San Francisco)
Arizona Daily Star (Tucson)
Arizona Weekly Citizen (Tucson)
California Chronicle (San Francisco)
California Courier (San Francisco)
California Police Gazette (San Francisco)
Deseret Evening News (Salt Lake City, Utah)
Fresno (California) *Daily Evening Expositor*
Fresno (California) *Morning Republican*
Fresno (California) *Weekly Expositor*
Fresno (California) *Weekly Republican*
Los Angeles Star
Los Angeles Times
Mariposa (California) *Chronicle*
Monterey (California) *Sentinel*
Mountain Democrat (Placerville, California)
National Police Gazette (New York City)
Nevada Daily Gazette (Nevada City, Nevada)
Nevada Daily Silver Age (Carson City, Nevada)
Nevada State Journal (Reno)
New York Sun
Oakland (California) *Daily News*
Oakland (California) *Daily Transcript*
Ogden (Utah) *Standard*
Portland Morning Oregonian
Portland Oregonian
Red Bluff (California) *Beacon*
Riverside (California) *Daily Press*
Sacramento Bee
Sacramento Daily Record
Sacramento Daily Union

San Andreas (California) *Independent*
San Bernardino (California) *Guardian*
San Diego Union
San Francisco Alta California
San Francisco Chronicle
San Francisco Herald
San Francisco Evening Bulletin
San Francisco Examiner
San Francisco Morning Call
San Joaquin Republican (Stockton, California)
San Jose (California) *Daily Herald*
San Jose (California) *Mercury*
San Jose (California) *Mercury-Herald*
San Jose (California) *Morning Times*
San Jose (California) *Patriot*
Santa Cruz (California) *Sentinel*
Stockton (California) *Daily Independent*
Territorial Enterprise (Virginia City, Nevada)
Tulare Weekly Times (Visalia, California)
Visalia (California) *Weekly Delta*
Walla Walla (Washington) *Union-Bulletin*
Wallace (Idaho) *Press-Times*
Washington Standard (Olympia)
Washington Statesman (Walla Walla, Washington)
Weekly Mountaineer (The Dalles, Oregon)
Yreka (California) *Journal*
Yreka (California) *Semi-Weekly Union*
Yreka (California) *Union*

Books

Bailey, Robert. *River of No Return.* Lewiston, Idaho: R.G. Bailey, 1935.
Bancroft, Hubert H. *History of Nevada, Colorado and Wyoming.* San Francisco: The History Company, 1890.
Barker, John. *San Joaquin Vignettes: The Reminiscences of Captain John Barker.* Edited by William Harland Boyd and Glendon J. Rodgers. Bakersfield, California: Kern County Historical Society, 1955.
Beal, Merrill D. and Merle W. Wells. *History of Idaho.* New York: Lewis Historical Publishing Company, 1959.
Beers, George A. *Vasquez; or, the Hunted Bandits of the San Joaquin.* New

York: Robert M. DeWitt, 1875.
Bell, Horace. *Reminiscences of a Ranger.* Santa Barbara, California: Wallace Hebberd, 1927.
Berry, John J., editor. *Life of David Belden.* New York: Belden Brothers, 1891.
Black, Esther Bolton. *Rancho Cucamonga and Doña Merced.* Redlands, California: San Bernardino Museum Association, 1975.
Black, Jack. *You Can't Win.* New York: Macmillan, 1926.
Bowen, Eliza A. *The Story of Wilkes County, Georgia.* Marietta, Georgia: Continental Book Company, 1950.
Bowles, Samuel. *Our New West.* New York: Hartford Publishing Company, 1869.
Brewer, William. *Up and Down California in 1860–1864.* Edited by Francis P. Farquhar. New Haven, Connecticut: Yale University Press, 1930.
Browne, J. Ross. *J. Ross Browne: His Letters, Journals and Writings.* Edited by Lina Fergusson Browne. Albuquerque: University of New Mexico Press, 1969.
Buntline, Ned (Edward Zane Carroll Judson). *Red Dick, the Tiger of California.* New York: Street & Smith, 1890.
Corning, Howard M., editor. *Dictionary of Oregon History.* Portland, Oregon: Binford & Mort, 1989.
Cottle, Benjamin H., and Theodore F. Wright. *Directory of the City of San Jose, 1878.* San Jose, California: n.p., 1878.
Defenbach, Byron. *Idaho: The Place and Its People.* Volume I. New York: American Historical Society, 1933.
DeGroot, Henry. *The Comstock Papers.* Reno, Nevada: Grace Dangberg Foundation, Inc., 1985.
Del Castillo, Richard Griswold. *The Los Angeles Barrio, 1850-1890.* Berkeley and Los Angeles: University of California Press, 1979.
Doten, Alfred. *The Journals of Alfred Doten.* Edited by Walter Van Tilburg Clark. Reno: University of Nevada Press, 1973.
Drury, Wells. *An Editor on the Comstock Lode.* New York: Farrar & Rinehart, 1936.
Duke, Thomas. *Celebrated Criminal Cases of America.* San Francisco: James H. Barry, 1910.
Dullenty, Jim. *Harry Tracy: The Last Desperado.* Dubuque, Iowa: Kendall/Hunt, 1989.
Elsensohn, M. Alfreda. *Pioneer Days in Idaho County.* Cottonwood, Idaho: Idaho Corp. of Benedictine Sisters, 1978.
Flinn, Charles J. *Life and Career of the Most Skillful and Noted Criminal of*

His Day, Charles Mortimer... Sacramento: William H. Mills & Company, 1873.
Ford, Tirey L. *California State Prisons: Their History, Development and Management.* San Francisco: James H. Barry, 1910.
Giles, Rosena A. *Shasta County, California.* Oakland, California: Biobooks, 1949.
Goulder, William A. *Reminiscences.* Boise, Idaho: Timothy Regan, 1909.
Graves, Jackson A. *California Memories.* Los Angeles: Times-Mirror Press, 1930.
Greenwood, Robert, comp. *The California Outlaw, Tiburcio Vasquez.* Los Gatos, California: Talisman Press, 1960.
Guinn, J.M. *History of the State of California and Biographical Record of the Coast Counties of California.* Chicago: Chapman, 1904.
_____. *History of the State of California and Biographical Record of Oakland and Environs.* Los Angeles: Historic Record Company, 1907.
Hansen, Gladys. *San Francisco Almanac.* San Francisco: Chronicle Books, 1975.
Harrison, Fred. *Hell Holes and Hangings.* Clarendon, Texas: Clarendon Press, 1968.
Hart, James D. *A Companion to California.* New York: Oxford University Press, 1978.
Hawley, James H., editor. *History of Idaho.* Chicago: S.J. Clarke, 1920.
Hunt, Aurora. *The Army of the Pacific.* Glendale, California: Arthur H. Clark, 1951.
Issel, William and Robert W. Cherny. *San Francisco, 1865–1932.* Berkeley and Los Angeles: University of California Press, 1986.
Kelley, Joseph "Bunco." *Thirteen Years in the Oregon Penitentiary.* Portland, Oregon: Author, 1908.
Knuth, Priscilla. *Picturesque Frontier.* Portland: Oregon Historical Society, 1987.
Lamott, Kenneth. *Chronicles of San Quentin.* New York: McKay, 1961.
Langford, Nathaniel P. *Vigilante Days and Ways.* Chicago: A.C. McClurg, 1927.
Latta, Frank F. *Joaquin Murrieta and His Horse Gangs.* Santa Cruz, California: Bear State Books, 1980.
_____. *Saga of Rancho El Tejon.* Santa Cruz, California: Bear State Books, 1976.
Lyman, George D. *The Saga of the Comstock Lode.* New York: Charles Scribner's Sons, 1946.
Lyman, W.D. *History of Walla Walla County.* Chicago: S.J. Clarke, 1918.

SOURCES 251

McConnell, W.J. *Early History of Idaho*. Caldwell, Idaho: Caxton Printers, 1913.

Mighels, Ella Sterling Cummins. *The Story of the Files*. San Francisco: Co-operative Print Company, 1893.

Morrell, Ed. *The Twenty-fifth Man*. Montclair, New Jersey: New Era Publishing Company, 1924.

Newmark, Harris. *Sixty Years in Southern California, 1853–1913*. Boston: Houghton Mifflin, 1930.

Nichols, Nancy Ann. *San Quentin Inside the Walls*. San Quentin, California: San Quentin Museum Press, 1991.

Reinhart, Herman Francis. *The Golden Frontier: The Recollections of Herman Francis Reinhart, 1851–1869*. Edited by Doyce B. Nunis, Jr. Austin: University of Texas Press, 1962.

Orton, Richard H. *Records of Men in the War of the Rebellion, 1861–1867*. Sacramento: State Printing Office, 1890.

Perkins, William. *Three Years in California. William Perkins' Journal of Life at Sonora, 1849-1852*. Edited by Dale L. Morgan and James R. Scobie. Berkeley and Los Angeles: University of California Press, 1964.

Riddle, Jeff C. *The Indian History of the Modoc War*. Medford, Oregon: Pine Cone Publishers, 1973.

Rojas, Manuel. *Joaquin Murrieta, El Patrio*. Mexicali, Baja California, Mexico: El "Far West" Del Mexico, 1986.

Sawyer, Eugene T. *History of Santa Clara County, California*. Los Angeles: Historic Record Company, 1922.

———. *The Life and Career of Tiburcio Vasquez, the California Stage Robber*. San Jose, California, 1875; reprinted, Oakland, California: Biobooks, 1944.

Shinn, Charles Howard. *Graphic Description of Pacific Coast Outlaws*. Los Angeles: Westernlore Press, 1958.

Smith, Wallace. *Prodigal Sons: The Adventures of Christopher Evans and John Sontag*. Boston: Christopher Publishing House, 1951.

Snow, Horace. *"Dear Charlie" Letters*. Fresno, California: Mariposa County Historical Society, 1979.

Soulé, Frank, John H. Gihon, and James Nisbet. *The Annals of San Francisco*. New York: D. Appleton, 1854.

Talbot, Virgil. *The Talbots*. Colcord, Oklahoma: privately published, 1983.

Twain, Mark (Samuel Langhorne Clemens). *Clemens of the Call: Mark Twain in San Francisco*. Edited by Edgar Branch. Berkeley and Los Angeles: University of California Press, 1969.

_____. *Roughing It.* New York: Harper and Brothers, 1913.

_____. *The Selected Letters of Mark Twain.* Edited by Charles Neider. New York: Harper & Row, 1982.

Walker, Franklin. *San Francisco's Literary Frontier.* New York: Alfred A. Knopf, 1939.

Warren, Mary Bondurant. *Chronicles of Wilkes County, Georgia.* Danielsville, Georgia: Georgia Heritage Papers, 1978.

Wells, Harry L. *History of Siskiyou County, California.* Oakland, California: D.J. Stewart, 1881.

Winther, Oscar Osburn. *The Old Oregon Country: A History of Frontier Trade, Transportation, and Travel.* Lincoln, Nebraska: University of Nebraska Press, 1950.

Periodicals

McKanna, Clare V., Jr. "Crime and Punishment: The Hispanic Experience in San Quentin, 1851–1880." *Southern California Quarterly,* Spring 1990.

Parker, Paul. "The Roach-Belcher Feud." *California Historical Society Quarterly,* March 1950.

Secrest, William B. "Brave Len Harris Is Dead." *True West,* December 1992.

_____. "The Horrifying History of a Highwayman's Head." *The Californians,* November-December 1986.

Shinn, Millicent Washburn. "Cherokee Bob: The Original Jack Hamlin." *Overland Monthly,* July 1890.

Standart, Sister M. Collete, O.P. "The Sonoran Migration to California, 1848–1856; A Study in Prejudice." *Southern California Quarterly,* Fall 1976.

Timmen, Fritz. "Deadly Belle of the Ball." *True Frontier,* May 1970.

Walsh, George E. "The Life of a Barrel." *Scientific American,* January 21, 1905.

INDEX

Ada (girlfriend of Charles Mortimer) 50
Adams, Sheriff (Santa Clara County, California) 134
Agua Caliente stage station, California 139, 140
Alabama 4
Alameda, California 93, 99, 183
Alameda County, California 101, 102, 106, 108, 109, 120, 178; courthouse 116; jail 116, 178
Allison (attorney) 195
Alta California (San Francisco): see *San Francisco Alta California*
Alvarado, California 110
Andersonville military prison (Georgia) 134-135
Angelo House (Redwood City) 16, 17
Antioch, California 135
Arizona 128, 130, 133, 138, 208
Arizona Daily Star (Tucson), reports on Procopio's murder of Aurelio Cantabrana 128
Arkansas 132, 198
Arnett, John 112, 116
Asteanes, Jesus 105
Astoria, Oregon 28
Atkins, Saml. 5
Auburn, California 27
Aull, Charles 190
Australians 49, 148
Avery & Company hardware store (Portland, Oregon) 154

Bailey, Deputy Sheriff (Weber County, Utah) 191-192
Baker, Captain (San Francisco police) 68
Baker, J.E. 188
Bakersfield, California 122, 123
Baldwin, A.W. (boot and shoe manufacturer) 119
Bamberger, Simon T. 205
Bancroft, Hubert Howe 26
Barbary Coast (San Francisco) 53
Barcenas, Francisco ("Sancho") 115
Barry (Portland, Oregon, chief of police) 157
Barter, Richard A. ("Rattlesnake Dick") 55
Bates Station, California 144
Bean, Roy 18, 19
Beard, A.S. 18
Beauregard, P.T. 34
Bec, Henri 83, 91
Belcher, Lewis 20
Bell, Tom: see Hodges, Thomas
Belmont, California 60-62, 64, 73
Belnap, Joseph 191, 192, 194
Benson, Robt. 5
Bentley, George 187
Benton, Joseph 46
Beresford Hotel (San Francisco) 182
Berkeley, California 183
Bernal, Juanita Armida: see Bustamante, Juanita Armida Bernal
Bible 166
Big Oak Flat, California 8
Bishop (prison guard) 201
"Black Bart": see Boles, Charles E.
Black, Jack 198
Blackburn, John L. 26, 38
Blackwine, Mr. 83, 84
Blakely, S.W. 77, 90
Bliss' Ferry, California 138
Bob, Cherokee: see Talbot, Henry J.
Bohen, Ben 54, 116
Boise, Idaho (State, Territory, Washington Territory) 45
Bojorques, Narciso 107, 108, 109, 110, 112; portrait sketch of 109

253

Boles, Charles E. ("Black Bart") 101, 147
Boling, John 9, 10, 11; photograph of 11
Booth, Newton 98
Boston, Massachusetts 4, 36, 50, 52
Boulton, Tom 64, 65
Bovee, James 54
Bowen, John ("Black Jack") 58, 59, 60, 64; photograph of 59
Box Elder County, Utah 191, 192, 195
Branham, Benjamin 144
Brannigan, Mike 55, 56
Bridges, Madaline 206
Brigham City, Utah 191, 194
British Columbia, Canada 194
Broadway Street (Oakland) 84
Broadway Street (San Francisco) 53
"Brown of Calaveras" (Bret Harte short story) 48
Brown, Fielding 29
Brown, Officer (San Francisco police) 69
Brown, Sidney: see Bryant, Sidney
Brown, Thomas 8
Brown, William A. 191, 192, 194, 195, 196, 203, 209
Brownstone's Store (Grangeville, California) 121
Bryant, Sidney (alias Brown) 14
Bryte, Mike 91, 93
Buckley, James 34, 36
Budd, James H. 187, 188, 189
Bunker Hill Monument (Boston) 50
Buntline, Ned: see Judson, Edward Zane Carroll
Burgess, W.H. 18
Burke, E. 9
Burke, Martin 62
Burns, A.V. 67
Bustamante, Juanita Armida Bernal 130, 131
Bustamante, Margarita 130; photograph of 129
Bustamante, Tomás Procopio (alias Procopio, Tomás Rodundo, Red Dick): xiv, xv; birth, early years in Mexico and northern California, relationship to uncle Joaquín Murrieta, 101-103; moves to Sonora Town, Los Angeles, 103-104; early involvement with crime, murder of John Rains, 104-106; criminal activities in Livermore Valley, murder of Golding family, 106-107; arrest, trial and ; conviction for rustling, 108-110; first term at San Quentin, 110-112; continued rustling activities, riding with Vasquez gang, 112-115; again arrested, tried; convicted for rustling, 115-118; second term at San Quentin, 118-120; released, resumes rustling activities, 120-121; involvement in Grangeville, Caliente, and Hanford robberies, 121-123; kills posse member Sol Gladden, 123-127; flees to Mexico, further criminal activity there, 127-130; marriage, later life and death, 130-131; photographs of 100, 129
Bustamante, Vicenta Murrieta: see Valenzuela, Vicenta Murrieta Bustamante
Byram, Edward 99

C Street (Fresno, California) 149
Calaveras County, California 75
Calaveras stage road 142
Caliente, California 122, 127
California 4, 5, 6, 7, 10, 12, 22, 23, 24, 27, 29, 33, 37, 38, 46, 100, 101, 102, 104, 114, 115, 128, 130, 132, 134, 147, 148, 153, 162, 169, 170, 173, 174, 185, 194, 195, 196, 204, 205, 208
California Chronicle (San Francisco), reports on Cherokee Bob 10
California Courier (San Francisco), reports on Cherokee Bob 7
California gold rush 4, 102, 107, 133
California Powder Works (Portland, Oregon) 154
California Rangers 102
California Society for the Prevention of Cruelty to Children 187
California State Constitutional

INDEX

Convention (1878) 147
California State Insane Asylum
  (Stockton, California) 98
California State Legislature 102
California State Library
  (Sacramento) 209
California Volunteer Infantry, Fourth
  27, 28, 33
Californios 104, 120, 131
Camargo, Juan 112, 116, 118
Campbell (prosecutor) 91
Canada 176, 194
Cantabrana, Aurelio 128
Cantua Creek (Fresno County,
  California) 102-103
Cape Horn, California 144
Cardon, Sheriff (Box Elder County,
  Utah) 192, 194–195
Carlisle, Robert 105, 106
Carmel mission 16
Carr, Mary Ann 99
Carrico, Asa 15
Carrillo, Don Ramon 106
Carrisoso, Jose 130
Carson City, Nevada (Nevada
  Territory, Utah Territory) 25, 26,
  27, 38, 40
Carson Valley, Nevada 25
Carter (San Gabriel, California, resident) 20
Cascade Mountains 29, 32
Casey, J.W. 155, 156
Cerradel, Manuel 105, 106
Chamberlain, Fred 60
Chamberlain, George E. 169
Chappelle, Officer (San Francisco
  police) 28
Charleston, South Carolina 4
Charlestown, Massachusetts 52
Chellis, John 56
Cherokee Bob: see Talbot, Henry J.
"Cherokee Mary" (roadhouse owner)
  65, 67, 68
Cherokees 3, 6
Chicago, Illinois 194
Chileans 6, 8
Chinatown (San Francisco) 53
Chinese 8, 56, 66, 68, 128, 147
Chow, Mook 10
Church of Jesus Christ of Latter-Day

Saints: see Mormon Church
Cinematograph 170
Civil War 27, 46
Clarksville, Arkansas 132, 133
Clearwater River 38
Clemens, Samuel Langhorne: see
  Twain, Mark
Clune, Ella 187
Coast Range, California 123
Cody, Al 157
Coffee, John 81
Colonel Wright (steamer) 32
Colton, California 148
Columbia River 28-29, 31, 154, 167
"Comanche Jack" (Bret Harte fictional character based on
  Cherokee Bob) 48
Confederates 33
Connors, Bill 178
Connors, Frank 200, 202
Conrad, City Marshal (Oakland,
  California) 197
Constitutional Convention,
  California State (1878) 147
Contra Costa County, California 14
Coon, Henry 61
"Copper" credit bill (California State
  Legislature) 70
Copper Mountain Mine (Milford,
  Utah) 204
Corral Hollow, California 107
Cory, A.J. 136
Cotton, Lafayette 18
Cotton, W.W. 169
Council Bluffs, Iowa 173
Courts: Box Elder County (Utah)
  Superior 194, 195, 197; Fifth
  Judicial District (California) 9;
  Fresno County (California)
  Superior 145; Los Angeles
  (California) Superior 206;
  Multnomah County (Oregon)
  Circuit 160; Santa Clara County
  (California) Superior 177;
  Second Judicial District (Nevada)
  40; Sixth District (Sacramento,
  California) 91
Cowal (prisoner) 10
Crandall, J.B. 138-140
Creaner, Charles M. 9

Cremony, John 46
Crooks, A.D. 67-69
Cross, Manuel 94, 96
Crowley, Patrick 75
Cruelty to Children, California Society for the Prevention of 187
Cucamonga Ranch (San Bernardino County, California) 104
Cummings, C.C. 120
Cummings (jailer) 178
Cunningham, Jose 123
Curnow, Mrs. Dr. 179
Curry, Abe 40
Curtis, James F. 28
"Cynthia" (paramour of Cherokee Bob, William Mayfield) 40-44, 47

Dappello, John 144
Davidson, Dr. 168
Davis, Jefferson 34
Davis (robbery victim) 144
Davis, William 138
Dayton, Frank 200-202
de Groot, Henry 46
Delaney, Martin: see Morrell, Ed
Democrats 40
Denson, Samuel C. 92, 94, 97
Deseret Evening News (Salt Lake City); reports criticism of Abe Majors 202
Dick (friend of Charles Mortimer) 50
Dikes, Bill 123
Dimsdale, Thomas J. 46
Dixon, Maynard (sketch by) 193
Dixson, E.C. 26
Dole, Nick 88
Donnelly (cowboy) 138-139
Dorsey, Charles 147
Dougherty (rancher) 120
Douglass, Colin 14
Douglass, William 69
Dow, George 198
Downey, George 26
Draper, Theodore 125
Dunn, Kate 73-74
Dupont Street (San Francisco) 28, 80, 99
"Dutch Charley" 65, 67

Edgar, Captain John 148, 151
Edson, Juan 179
El Camino Real 20
"El Molacho": see Sanchez, Louis
Eldeo, Fermin 123
Elias, Miguel 123
Elk City, Idaho (Idaho Territory, Washington Territory) 41
Empire Street school (San Jose, California) 153
Encinas, Francisco 123
Estell, J.M. 12, 13, 14, 15
Eugenio, Tal 105
Europe 204
Evans, Charles 155
Evans, Chris 149-151
Ewing, William (alias of Cherokee Bob's brother) 7
Express Number Two (Oregon Railway and Navigation Railroad) 155

F Street (Fresno, California) 168
Fashion Stables (Portland, Oregon) 155, 157
Fellows, Dick 101
Ferrell, Frank B. 167
Ferry, Bob 65-68
Fifth Street (Oakland, California) 182
Firebaugh's Ferry, California 108, 120, 127, 131, 138
Fitzpatrick, James 71
"Flemming": see Talbot, Henry J.
Flinn, Charles J.: see Mortimer, Charles
Flinn, Edward 50, 94
Flinn family (Lynn, Massachusetts) 49, 94, 97
Flinn, Frank 50, 94, 98-99
Flinn, Louisa 50, 52
Flinn, Mary 50
Flinn, Thomas H. 50, 94, 97, 99
Flinn, William (alias Williams) 50, 94, 95-96, 99
Florence, Idaho (Idaho Territory, Washington Territory) 29, 38, 39, 41, 43, 46; photograph of 39
"Folensbee" (partner of Charles Mortimer) 76, 77

INDEX

Folsom, California 60
Folsom State Prison (Represa, California) 150, 151, 184, 185-188, 196, 204, 208-209; photograph of 184
Ford, Abe: see Majors, Abe
Forest House, (Siskiyou County) California 67
Fort Dalles, Oregon; photograph of 31
Fort Jones, California 66
Fort Lapwai, Washington Territory 38
Fort Smith, Arkansas 198
Fort Vancouver, Washington Territory 28
Fort Walla Walla, Washington Territory 33-34, 36
Foster, George: see Mortimer, Charles
Frederick, Pauline 204
"French Frank" 58
Fresno, California 121, 123, 127, 132, 144, 145, 149-150, 168, 170, 171, 172
Fresno Cooperage Company (Fresno, California) 132, 144, 170, 171, 172; photograph of 171
Fresno County (California) 102, 150; hospital 172; jail 144, 149
Fresno (California) *Morning Republican*; reports on Rose Lee's attempted suicide 168
Fresno Slough, California 138
Fresno (California) *Weekly Expositor*; reports on Procopio 127; reports on trial of Milton Harvey Lee and John Herbert 145; reports on Yosemite stage robbery by Milton Harvey Lee and John Herbert 144
Fresno (California) *Weekly Republican*; reports on Procopio's Hanford robbery 123

Gabriel, Pete 130
Gafney, Owen 80
Garcia, Anastacio 20
Gard, George 130
Garden, Mary 204

Gardner, Constable William 26
Genoa, Nevada (Nevada Territory, Utah Territory) 26-27
Georgia 3-4, 6, 10, 12, 46
Germans 53
Gibson, Mary 85, 86, 87-88, 89
Gilbert, Warden (Oregon State Prison) 163
Gilroy, California 112, 177
Girard's piano store (East Bay, California) 183
Gladden, Sol 123, 124, 127, 126
Gold Hill, Nevada (Nevada Territory, Utah Territory) 58, 60
Gold Rush, California 4, 102, 107, 133
Golden Gate (San Francisco) 28
Golding, Aaron 107-108
"Good time" bill (California State Legislature) 69
Goodwin bill (California State Legislature) 69
Goodwin, Pete 58
Grady, Walter D. 145, 149
Grangeville, California 121, 123
Gray, J.S. 45
Gray, John M. 15-16
Green, J.J. 71, 72
Greenfield, Massachusetts 52
Greenhorn Mountains 67
Grewell (crime victim) 114

Haight, Henry 137, 138
Hale, William E. 148, 151-152
Hamilton, James and Jenny (boardinghouse owners) 154, 157
Hamlin, Jack ("Comanche Jack"; Bret Harte fictional character based on Cherokee Bob) 48
Hampton, James 191
Hanford, California 123, 126-127, 180, 182
Harmon, Charles 56
Harrington, D.W. 136
Harris, Leonard ("Len") 84, 88, 89, 90; photograph of 89
Harrisville road (Utah) 191
Hart, Judge (Box Elder County, Utah) 195
Harte, [Francis] Bret 46, 48

Haworth, Nick 201-202
Hawthorn's stage station (California) 138
Hayes, Judge Benjamin 21-22, 105
Headquarters Saloon (San Gabriel, California) 18, 19
Healdsburg, California 76
Heninger, Captain 21
Herbert, John 142-145; photograph of 143
Hermosillo (Sonora, Mexico) 101, 115, 128, 130-131
Hill, S.H. 144, 145
Hines, Michael 14
Hispaños: see Mexicans
Hodges, Thomas (Tom Bell) 16, 41
Holy Cross Hospital (Salt Lake City, Utah) 202
Hornitos, California 8
Hot Springs (Utah) 191, 192
Hubbard, Ansil 34
Humane Society (children's welfare organization, San Francisco) 180, 182
Hume, James B. 160
The Hungry Heart (motion picture) 204
Hutchinson family 149
Hutchinson, Grace Lee 141, 149-150, 172
Hutchinson, Jim 149-150, 149
Hutchinson, Mr. 149

Idaho 27, 29, 38, 41; gold rush 27, 29
Ideal Radiator and Body Works (Los Angeles, California) 206
Illinois 173
Illinois lodging house (Nevada Territory) 58, 173
Indian Valley, California 134
Indians 8, 18, 58, 106, 108
Ingram, Frank 167
Ione, California 185
Iowa 173
Irish 128
Irwin, William 128

J Street (Sacramento) 88
Jacalitos Creek, California 125
Jackson Street (San Francisco) 28
Jackson, George: see Lee, Milton Harvey
Jacobs, Zebulon 200-202
Jamestown, California 8
Jewell, Joseph 174, 176, 196
Jibboom Street (Sacramento) 88
Jones, Billy 81-82
Jones, S.R.T. 167
Juanito, Tal 105, 108
Judson, Edward Zane Carroll ("Ned Buntline") 128
Julia (steamer) 29
Jury duty, horrors of 9

K Street (Sacramento) 88
Karcher, Matt 88
Kearny Street (San Francisco) 5, 53, 61, 73, 81
Keefer, George (alias Maguire) 66, 67
Kellett, John 8-9
Kelley, Joseph "Bunco" 163, 164, 166, 168
Kennedy, W.C. 116
King brothers 106
King, Tom 66, 67
Kings River, California 138
Klamath River, California 65
Knight's Landing, California 64
Kreyenhagen, Gus 125

La Libertad, California 125
La Lista Blanca (Sonora, Mexico) 131
La Poza, California 17
Lahr, Pete 178
Lake Bigler: see Lake Tahoe
Lake Tahoe 25
Langford, Nathaniel Pitt 42, 46
Lantzenhiser, John B. 34
Latta, Frank F. 102, 103, 115, 130
Layne, Sheriff (Weber County, Utah) 191-192
Lee, George 132-135, 145, 153
Lee, Grace: see Hutchinson, Grace Lee
Lee, Henry 36-37
Lee, James: see Lee, Milton Harvey
Lee, Jasper 132-135, 138
Lee, Joseph D. 164, 166, 169

INDEX

Lee, Mark 132-133
Lee, Milton Harvey (alias George Jackson, James Lee): xiv, xv-xvi; birth in Arkansas, moves to San Jose area with family, 132-134; early horse-stealing activities, arrested, tried and convicted, 134-135; first term at San Quentin, 135-138; resumes criminal career in southern California, again arrested, tried and convicted, 138-140; second term at San Quentin, 140-141; robs Yosemite stage, arrested, tried and convicted, 141-145; third term at San Quentin, 145-153; involvement with Ed Morrell, 148-151; travels to Portland, commits train robbery there, 153-158; arrested, tried and convicted for train robbery, 158-160; term at Oregon State Prison, 160-169; involvement with Harry Tracy's escape from prison, 166-168; release, final years in Fresno and death, 169-172; photographs of 143, 146, 161, 171
Lee, Nancy: see Naylor, Nancy Lee
Lee, Rose 141, 149-150, 168-169, 172
Lee, William 132-133
Lees, Isaiah 49, 62, 64, 116
Lemoore, California 127
Levy, Samuel 206
Lewiston, Idaho (Idaho Territory, Washington Territory) 27, 29, 38, 40
Lincoln, Abraham 33
Lincoln, Charles 114-115
Livermore and Livermore Valley, Alameda County, California 107-108, 112, 113, 118, 120, 121, 131; lithographic illustration of 113
Loewenberg-Going Company (foundry) 162
Lone Star Social Club 141
Longley, Dr. 67
Lord, Charles 160
Lorenzana, Mattias 114-115
Los Angeles, California 17-18, 19, 21, 103, 104, 105, 106, 108, 128, 130, 140, 145, 205-209
Los Angeles County, California 208; jail 206
Los Angeles Star 21, 104; reports discovery of John Rains' body 104; reports on Cherokee Bob's arrest 21; reports on Manuel Cerradel 105; reports on murder of John Rains 106; reports on Procopio's conviction 104; reports on stolen livestock 106
Los Angeles Times, reports on Abe Majors' arrest 205; reports on Procopio's suspected capture 130
Los Gatos, California 174, 177
Love, Harry 102
Low, Frederick F. 69, 136-137
Luna House hotel (Lewiston, Idaho) 40
Luttrell, James M. 66
Lynch, Jim 201-202
Lynn, Massachusetts 49, 94, 97, 99
Lynn (Massachusetts) *Semi-Weekly Reporter*, reports on Charles Mortimer 99

MacLease, Mr. 204
Madera, California 144
Maguire, George: see Keefer, George
Maher, Detective (Portland, Oregon police) 157, 158
Majors, Abraham ("Abe"; alias Abe Ford, James Morgan, James Wilson): xiv, xvi; birth, early years in San Jose, 173-179; criminal activities of father, Lloyd Majors, 174-179; years in San Francisco, Oakland and Hanford, 180-182; arrest, trial and conviction as "boy burglar," 181-186; first term at Folsom, attempts to gain release, 186-190; resumes criminal activities with brother Archie, shootout with lawmen in Utah, 190-194; arrested, tried, and convicted for murder, 194-195; sent to Utah State Prison, further attempts to obtain release, 195-198; attempted prison escape, 198-203; serves remainder of

term, finally released, 203-204; straight employment in Utah and California, 204-205; arrested, tried, and convicted for theft in Los Angeles, 205-206; final time at San Quentin and Folsom, 208-209; release and death, 209; photographs of 184, 207; portrait sketch of, 175
Majors, Archibald ("Archie") 174, 180, 185, 190-192, 194-196; portrait sketch of 175
Majors, Lena Stone (wife of Archibald Majors) 190
Majors, Lloyd 173-174, 176, 177, 178-179, 186, 196; photograph of 175
Majors, Lucinda: see Wagner, Lucinda Majors
Majors, Maud 179
Mare Island, California 15
Marin County, California 10, 137
Mariposa County, California 8-10, 12
Mariposa, California 9, 10, 12
Maron, Antonio 123
Martin, Ed: see Morrell, Ed
Martin (horse thief pursuer) 9
Martin, W.F. 130
Martinez, California 120-121
Mary Street (Fresno, California) 170
Marysville, California 5, 64
Massachusetts 49-50, 94, 97, 99
Massachusetts Cavalry, Second (Civil War) 134
Massachusetts State Prison (Charlestown) 52
Maxwell, Mr. (convict) 201
Mayes, T.A. 20
Mayfield, William H. 25-26, 38, 40-42
McAdams Creek, California 65
McChesney, Mrs. 188
McCrea, Mr. 134
McCullough, E.A. 66
McCullum, Ike 55, 60
McDougal, John 16
McGurley, A. 5
McIntyre, Archibald 176-178
McPherson, Doc 123, 126
McSkimmins brothers 141
Mechanics House (Sacramento) 85, 88

Melones, California 7
Merced County, California 145
Merrian & Cole (furniture manufacturers) 119
Merrill, David 166-167
Methodist church 174
Mexican War 102, 116
Mexicans 6, 18, 102, 103, 104, 107, 111, 115, 121, 122, 123, 125, 127, 131
Mexico 17, 18, 101, 102, 115, 123, 128, 133
Milford, Utah 204
Millerton, California 9
Miner, Bill 148
Ministerial Society (Salt Lake City, Utah) 197
Mission Nuestra Senora de la Soledad, California 17
Mission road (El Camino Real) 20
Mission San Carlos del Borromeo, California 16
Mission San Gabriel, California 19, 21; drawing of 19
Mission San Jose, California 108
Mission Santa Clara de Asis, California 133
Mission Viejo, California 105
Mission Woolen Mills (San Francisco) 137
Missouri 25, 41, 173-174
Mitchell, Ellen 55
Mitchell, Tom 58
Mitchner, Tom 8-9
Moirel, John 105
Mojave Desert, California 106
Molla Company (acting) 128
Monterey County, California 114, 127
Monterey, California 18, 21, 22, 103, 111, 112, 114
Monterey (California) *Sentinel*, reports on Cherokee Bob's arrival 22
Montgomery Street (San Francisco) 53, 76
Moore & Ryland (San Jose law firm) 137
Moore, A.A. 118
Moore, Mr. 112

INDEX

Moore (rancher) 139
Morales, Ignacio 118
Morehouse, L.C. 116
Morgan, James: see Majors, Abe
Morgan, John 150
Mormon Church 194
Mormons 194, 198
Morrell, Ed (Ed Martin, Martin Delaney) 148-152
Morse, Harry 106, 107, 108, 112, 116, 117; photograph of 117
Mortimer, Charles (Charles J. Flinn; alias George Foster): xiv-xv; birth, boyhood in Massachusetts, early criminal activity, 50-52; migrates to California, 52-53; involvement in San Francisco robbery, 53-54; sent to San Quentin, first term there, 54-58; escapades in Nevada, 58-60; further criminal activities in California, 60-61; robs Charley Wiggins and George Rose, 61-64; additional criminal activities in northern California, 64-66; capture, escape from Yreka jail, 66-68; tried, convicted, second term at San Quentin, 68-72; return to San Francisco, further criminal activity, 72-73; meets Carrie Spencer, 74-76; scheme to rob Santa Cruz County treasury, 76-77, 90-91; difficulties controlling Carrie Spencer, 77-80, 83-84; involvement in Caroline Prenel robbery/murder, 80-82; arrested, tried and convicted for pickpocketing, 82-83; drifts to Oakland and Sacramento with Carrie Spencer, 84-85; involvement in Mary Gibson robbery/murder, 85-88; arrest, trial and conviction for Mary Gibson murder, 88-94; betrayal by Carrie Spencer, 91-93; brother attempts to rescue from jail, 94-97; last days and execution, 98-99; photographs of 51, 89
Morton Street (San Francisco) 116
Mount Hamilton, California 144
Mount Hood Saloon (The Dalles, Oregon) 29

Mount Tamalpais, California 57
Mountain View Cemetery (Fresno, California) 172
Mulford, Prentice 46
Mullen, Ed 201-202
Murphy, Con 56
Murphy, Detective (Los Angeles police) 205
Murrieta, Joaquin 101-103, 107, 114, 127-128, 131
Murrieta, Rosa Feliz 101-102
Murrieta, Vicenta: see Valenzuela, Vicenta Murrieta Bustamante
Myers, Henry 62-63

Napa, California 64, 74
Nathan, Herman 121
National Police Gazette (New York), reports on Procopio 128
Naylor, Anna 133
Naylor, Archibald W. 133, 134
Naylor, Ellen 133
Naylor, Nancy Lee 133-138, 153
Naylor (prison guard) 201
Nevada County, California 147
Nevada (State, Territorial) Prison (Carson City) 40, 64
Nevada (state, territory) 24, 27, 40, 58, 60, 64, 76
Nevins, James 156, 157
New Jersey 4
New York 4, 52, 66, 107
Newhouse, Samuel 203-204
Newton, Adolph ("Dolph") 55
Nicaragua Saloon (Lewiston, Idaho) 38
Niles Canyon (Alameda County, California) 101-104, 107
Noble, Newton 138-140
North Ogden Road, Utah 191
Novelscope 170
Novelty Vaudeville Theater (Fresno, California) 170
Noyes Hotel (San Gabriel, California) 18
Nuenes (shooting victim) 108

Oakhurst, John (Bret Harte fictional character) 48
Oakland, California 84, 178, 180,

182-183, 190, 194, 197, 209; jail, 178
Oakland Hotel (Oakland, California) 209
Ogden (Utah) *Standard*, reports on Abe Majors trial 195
Ogden, Utah 191, 195
Oliver, Jack 32
Oregon 8, 27, 38, 65, 153, 154, 160, 161, 162, 164-168, 169
Oregon Boots 166
Oregon Express 169
Oregon Railway and Navigation Railroad 154
Oregon State Penitentiary (Salem) 160, 162, 164, 166-168; photograph of, 165
Orofino, Idaho (Idaho Territory, Washington Territory) 41
Ortega, Chano ("Chino") 107-108
"The Outcasts of Poker Flat" (Bret Harte story) 48
Overland Monthly (magazine) 46
Owen, Bill 7
Owsley, Barney 40, 42, 45
O'Brien, James P. 156-157

Pacheco Pass, California 138
The Pacific (religious newspaper, San Francisco) 46
Pacific (steamship) 28
Pacific Mail (steamship line) 52
Palace (Sacramento dive) 85
Panama 52
Parker House (San Francisco) 5
Parkinson, Mr. 20, 21
Pauly Company (prison builders) 198
Penglass, Jack 200
Pennsylvania 148
Perkins, William 6
Person, Dwight S. 206
Petaluma, California 54
Pfister, Conrad 51, 53, 54
Philadelphia, Pennsylvania 4
Phillips and Weinshench store (Hanford, California) 123
Pierce City, Idaho (Idaho Territory, Washington Territory) 41
Pinal County, Arizona 130

Pinckney Alley (San Francisco) 80
Pine Grove Cemetery (Lynn, Massachusetts) 49, 99
Pitman, Will 42
Placerville, California 24, 27
Placerville (California) *Mountain Democrat*, reports on rush to Nevada/Utah Territory silver mines 24
Plummer, Henry 38
Point San Quentin, California 10, 22, 54
Pope, Mr. 108
Porter, George 34
Portland, Oregon 28, 29, 30, 153, 154, 155, 156, 157, 158, 160
Portland Oregonian, comments on Milton Harvey Lee and Charles Williams' train robbery 158; reports on Idaho gold rush 29; reports on train holdup by Milton Harvey Lee and Charles Williams 157
Portsmouth Square (San Francisco) 5
Posa Chane, California 125, 127
Powers, William 14
Prenel, Caroline 80, 81, 82, 84, 91
Prescott, Lydia 187, 188
Presidio (San Francisco) 27
Preston School of Industry (Ione, California) 185
Prison ships 10
Pulgas Rancho (San Mateo County, California) 16
Pullen, B.F. 13, 14
Puttman, George 196

R Street (Fresno, California) 170
Rains, John 104, 105, 106, 108; photograph of 109
Rancho del Chino (southern California) 105
Rand, Jasper 45
"Rattlesnake Dick": see Barter, Richard A.
Ream, Dr. 68
Reardan, T.B. 92, 94
Red Bluff (California) *Beacon*, reports on conditions at San Quentin 54

INDEX

Red Bluff, California 54, 68
"Red Dick": see Bustamante, Tomás Procopio
Red Dick, the Tiger of California (Ned Buntline dime novel) 128
Redwood City, California 16
Reeves (rancher) 66
Reilly, Joe 157, 159; photograph of 159
Reinhart, Herman 27, 33, 38
Renowden, William P. 174, 176, 177
Rialto theater (Salt Lake City, Utah) 204
Richardson, Bill 65, 66
Rio de Janeiro, Brazil 52
Riverside, California 148
Riverview Cemetery (Portland, Oregon) 158
Roach-Belcher feud (Monterey County, California) 19, 20
Roach, William 20
Robbins, Orlando ("Rube") 43, 44-45
Roberts, Mr. 186
Robinson, "Three-fingered" 58
Rodriguez, Antonio 104, 111
Rodundo, Tomás: see Bustamante, Tomás Procopio
Roman, Anton 46
Rose, George 62-64, 68-69, 72-73
Roseborough, Alexander M. 66, 68
Ross Landing, California 57
Ross (prison guard) 167
Rucker, Mr. 8
Ruiz, Bessena 123
Ruiz, Ike 168

Sacramento, California 5, 24, 27, 53, 55, 60, 68, 75, 84, 85, 86, 87, 91, 92, 97, 98, 99, 190; jail 99
Sacramento County jail 94
Sacramento Daily Bee; describes Charles Mortimer on trial 92
Salem, Massachusetts 52
Salem, Oregon 162, 168
Salinas, California 112
Salinas Valley, California 17
Salmon River, Idaho (Idaho Territory, Washington Territory) 29, 38, 41
Salt Lake City Telephone Company 204

Salt Lake City, Utah 72, 194-195, 198, 202-205
Salt Lake City Woman's Club 197
Salt Lake Theater (Salt Lake City) 204
Salvation Army 190
San Benito County, California 122
San Bernardino, California 138, 140, 141
San Bernardino County, California 104, 140; jail 140
San Bernardino (California) *Guardian*; reports on capture of Milton Harvey Lee and J.B. Crandall 140
San Diego, California 18, 105, 133
San Francisco Alta California, 22; reports on appearance of Charles Mortimer 72; reports on Charles Mortimer in city jail 68; reports on Cherokee Bob Talbot 5; reports on murder of Tal Juanito 108; reports on San Quentin escape (1854) 14; reports on San Quentin "mush break" (1866) 72; reports on San Quentin prison break rumors (1855) 15
San Francisco Bay 10, 16
San Francisco Bulletin, reports on Procopio 114; reports on Procopio's arrest (1872) 116; reports on Procopio's conviction (1872) 118
San Francisco, California 10, 12, 14, 15, 16, 17, 22, 24, 25, 27, 34, 46, 49, 51, 52, 53, 54, 58, 60, 61, 63, 64, 68, 69, 72, 73, 75, 76, 77, 79, 108, 111, 114, 115, 116, 118, 120, 133, 137, 140, 142, 145, 148, 152, 153, 154, 155, 160, 180, 182, 183, 194, 197, 205; City Hall 76-77; City Hall cornerstone-laying, photograph of 79; City Hall prison 68; city prison of 72; police mug-book photographs 51, 79
San Francisco Call, reports on Charles Mortimer 19; reports on efforts to overturn Abe Majors' conviction in Utah 197; reports on killing/capture of Majors brothers in Utah 194; reports on

Majors family troubles 182
San Francisco Chronicle, 84; reports on arrests of Abe Majors and Bert Willmore 183; reports on San Quentin jute mill strike 152
San Francisco Evening Bulletin, reports on departure of California Volunteers 27
San Francisco Herald 15
San Francisquito Canyon, California 105
San Gabriel, California 17-18, 20; drawing of 19
San Gabriel Canyon, California 105
San Gabriel mission 21; drawing of 19
San Joaquin River, California 9, 138
San Joaquin Valley, California 104, 106, 108, 121, 131, 132, 138, 149, 170, 180
San Jose (California) *Argus,* reports on Milton Harvey Lee's pardon application 136
San Jose, California 14, 16, 58, 73, 116, 120, 134, 135, 136, 141, 142, 144, 153, 173, 174, 178, 179, 181, 187; jail 135; photograph of 181
San Jose de Guadalupe (Sonora, Mexico) 101, 133-135
San Jose (California) *Herald*, comments on Lloyd Majors' execution 178; reports on Lloyd Majors' attempted escape 179; reports on Lucinda Majors' grief 179; reports on McSkimmins brothers mystery 141
San Jose (California) *Mercury;* reports arrest of Milton Harvey Lee and John Herbert 144; reports on Milton Harvey Lee's arrest 134
San Leandro, California 110; jail 116
San Luis Obispo, California 17, 127
San Mateo, California 180
San Miguel, California 17
San Pedro, California 140
San Quentin State Prison, California 9, 10-16, 20, 22, 23, 24, 38, 41, 54-59, 63, 66, 68-72, 84, 89, 93, 106, 110-112, 113, 116, 118-120, 127, 132, 135-138, 140-141, 145-149,

151-153, 162, 177, 207, 208; breaks at: in 1854 12-14; in 1855 15-16; in 1862 57-58, 111; in 1864 111; in 1866 ("mush break") 70-72; cell at, photograph 59; descriptions of: in 1850s 10-16; in 1860s 54-58, 69-72, 110-111, 135, 137-138; in 1870s 118-120, 140-141; in 1880s 145-149; in 1890s 151-153; drawing of 11; founding of 10; jute mill at, and strike 147, 151-153; photograph of 113; "Rose Bowl" (cistern) 70; "The Stones" (early cellblock and offices) 10, 55, 69, 110
San Rafael, California 57
Sanchez estate 20
Sanchez, Louis ("El Molacho") 105
Sanford, Mrs. 182
Santa Barbara, California 17, 20, 21
Santa Clara County, California 133, 137, 144, 145, 177, 179, 181; courthouse, photograph of 181
Santa Clara mission 133
Santa Clara, California 63, 64
Santa Cruz, California 75, 76, 77, 90, 91, 94, 114, 115
Santa Cruz (California) *Sentinel,* reports on manhunt for Tiburcio Vasquez gang 115
Saranac (military ship) 62
Saulard, Leon 205
Savannah, Georgia 4
Schell, Frank M. 16, 17, 21
Schenck, Paul 206, 208
Sciad Creek, California 66
Scott Bar, California 65, 66
Scott's Valley, California 65, 67
Sea Bird (ship) 22
Sears, A.F. 169
Seattle, Washington 190
Second Street (Sacramento) 88
Senator (steamer) 106
Seventh Street (Portland, Oregon) 154
Shanks (partner of Charles Mortimer) 64-65
Shasta, California 64
Shasta County, California 27
Shaw, Alice 187

INDEX

Shearer, Bill 93, 98
Sherman, Jesse 67
Sherwood, Charles 163
Shinn, George 147
Shinn, Millicent Washburn 46; on Cherokee Bob 5
Showers, John 174, 176-177, 196
Shurtleff, Dr. 98
Sibley, George 62
Sierra Nevada 24, 27
Skinner, Cyrus 41, 42
Smith, Elias 202
Smith, James 14
Smith, Jim 55
Smith, J.J. 208
Smith, Will 149
Smith's dance hall (California) 118
Snook, Charles 190
Snow, Horace 9
Soap Lake, California 112
Soledad Canyon, California 106
Soledad mission 17
Sonora, California 6, 7, 8
Sonora (province, Mexico) 101
Sonora Town (Los Angeles barrio) 103-104
Sontag, John 149
Soto, Juan 112
South America 52
South Carolina 4
Speck, Alex. 5
Spencer, Carrie 74-88, 90-93; photograph of 79
St. Nicholas Saloon (Carson City) 26, 38
Standifer, William 138
Staples, Captain 33
Stapleton, Jack 166
State Insane Asylum (Stockton, California) 98
Steel, John S. 10
Stephens, William D. 204
Stewart, James (rancher) 138
Stewart, James (San Quentin convict) 13
Stockton, California 5, 24, 53, 98, 107
Stockton (California) *Independent*; reports on Aaron Golding murder 107

Stockton Rancho (San Mateo County, California) 73
Stone and Hayden (saddle & harness making firm) 119
Stone, Appleton 116
Stone, Lena: see Majors, Lena Stone
Stoneman, George 178
"The Stones": see San Quentin State Prison
Storrs, George 204, 205, 208
Strawberry Flat, California 24
Summers, Jack 139
Sunol Valley, California 112

Talbot (brother of Henry J. "Cherokee Bob) 7–8, 25, 27, 37–38, 45, 46
Talbot, Henry J. (alias Cherokee Bob, Flemming): xiv; birth, boyhood in Georgia, 3-4; migrates to California, gambling and criminal activities, 4-8; description of, 5-6; arrest, trial and conviction for horse thievery, 8-10; term at San Quentin, 10-16; escape attempts from San Quentin, 12-14, 15-16; flight from San Quentin to San Gabriel, 16-20; arrest, examination on murder charge, 20-22; returned to San Quentin, 22-24; journeys to Nevada, activities there, 24-27; accompanies California Volunteers to Pacific Northwest, 27-29; travels to The Dalles, gambling activities there, 29-32; embarks for Walla Walla, involvement in Civil War factional riot there, 32-38; leaves for Lewiston in Idaho mining country, activities there, 38-40; involvement with "Cynthia," 40-41, 42-45; moves to Florence in Idaho mining country, activities there, 41-44; gunfight with Jacob Williams and Orlando Robbins and resulting death, 44-45; literary remembrances of, 45-48; photograph of grave 47
Tehachapi Mountains, California 122

Tejon Mountains, California 122
Tejon Road (California) 105
Ten Mile House (Siskiyou County, California) 65, 67
Tenino (steamer) 32
Terhune, Tolman 142
Tesca, Avelino 120, 121
Texas 190, 191
Thais (motion picture) 204
The Dalles, Oregon 29, 31, 33, 40; photograph of 31
Thompson, John 13
Thompson, Tommy 121
Tiffany, B.F. 167
Toomstrap, Julian 121
Towle, James 72
Tracy & Company's Express 29
Tracy, Harry 166-168
Trafford, Officer 105
Tres Pinos, California 127
Trinity Express 55
Tucson, Arizona 130
Tucson Arizona Weekly Citizen, reports Procopio's purported arrest 130
Tulare County, California 107, 130
Tuolumne County, California 5, 148
Turner, Smith 20
Twain, Mark (Samuel Langhorne Clemens), comments on Charles Mortimer's lenient sentence 54; describes Special Detective George Rose 72; on early Carson City 25; reports on Charles Mortimer 49; reports on condition of Detective Rose 64
Tyler, George 73, 91

Uhrig (street inspector, San Francisco) 80, 82
"Uncle Bill" (thief) 78
United States Navy 52
University of Michigan 173
Ures (Sonora, Mexico) 101
Urilda (steamer) 15
Utah State Board of Corrections 202, 203, 205
Utah State Prison (Salt Lake City) 166, 190-191, 194-195, 197-198, 199, 205; photograph of 199
Utah (State, Territory) 24, 73, 166,
190, 191, 193, 194, 195, 197, 198, 199, 202, 203, 205, 208

Valencia, José 9
Valenzuela, Francisco 103, 104
Valenzuela, Vicenta Murrieta Bustamante 101, 102-104, 114
Vallejo, California 120
Vancouver, Washington Territory 32
Vanderlip, Edward 56, 57
Varnum, George D. 206
Vasquez, Tiburcio 101, 111, 112, 114, 115, 122, 127
Velasquez (gambler) 8
Vermont 50
Vigilante Days and Ways (Langford) 46
The Vigilantes of Montana (Dimsdale) 46
Virginia 4
Virginia City, Nevada (Nevada Territory, Utah Territory) 24, 25, 58, 60
Visalia, California 112, 122, 127, 138, 149, 150
Visalia (California) *Delta*, reports on bungling in posse's search for Procopio 127
Visalia stage 112
Visalia (California) *Weekly Delta*, reports on Procopio's Grangeville robbery 122
Volunteer Infantry, Fourth California 27

Wabau (state prison ship) 10
Waddell, Harry 198, 200-202
Wagner, Joseph A. 180, 182
Wagner, Lucinda Majors 173-174, 179, 180, 182, 183, 185, 186-190, 191, 194, 195-196, 197, 203-204, 205, 208
Wagner, Ralph 205, 208
Wall, Isaac B. 20, 21, 22
Walla Walla, Washington Territory 29, 33, 35, 36-38, 198; photograph of 35
Wallula, Washington Territory 32
Walters, R.T. 206
Warrens, Idaho (Idaho Territory,

INDEX

Washington Territory) 41
Washington Statesman (Walla Walla, Washington), reports on citizen-soldier fight in town 36; reports on Salmon River mines 41
Washington Street (Oakland, California) 182
Washington Street (San Francisco) 81
Washington (State, Territory) 27, 28, 33, 36, 38, 41, 44, 154, 167, 190, 198
Washington, Georgia 4
Washoe country, Nevada (Nevada Territory, Utah Territory) 24
Watkins (San Quentin convict) 14
Weller, John B. 22, 24
Wells, Fargo and Company 143, 145, 160; mugbook photograph 143
Wells, Heber M. 202
Westboro, Massachusetts 50
Westerbeck, June 209
Westlake district (Los Angeles) 205
Wetzler, Mrs. 83
Whatcom, Washington, gold rush 154
White, Bill 15, 16
White, Samuel 8, 9, 10
Whitesides, Jon 123, 125
Whitman, Elias 35, 36; sketch portrait of 35
Wiggins, Charley L. 61-62, 72, 73
Wilcken, David 201-202
Wilkes County, Georgia 3-4
Wilkes, Marion P. 155
Willamette River, Oregon 154
"Williams": see Flinn, William
Williams family 105
Williams, Charles 153-156, 158, 160, 162, 163; photograph of 159
Williams, Jacob ("Jakey") 40, 42, 43, 44, 45
Wilshire district (Los Angeles) 205
Wilson, James: see Majors, Abe
Williamson, Thomas 20, 21, 22
Willman, John 154
Willmore family 182
Willmore, Bert 180, 182, 183, 184, 185, 190, 189, 197; photograph of 184

Willmore, Ina 180, 185, 197
Willmore, Mrs. 180, 183, 185
Willoughby, Bill 43-45
Winchester rifle 126
Wingate, George 72
Witthouse, Gus 144
Women's Christian Temperance Union (Salt Lake City) 197
Wood, O.B. 110, 127
Woodland, California 64
Woods, Detective (Los Angeles police) 205, 206
Worcester, Massachusetts 50
Workingmen's Party (California) 147
Wright, Cockey 58
Wyoming 167

Yacatecas (Zacatecas, Mexico) 128
"Yank" (crime victim) 78, 80
Yguerria brothers 125
York, Waldo 185, 190
Yosemite stage road 142, 144-145
Yosemite Valley 142
Young, Dr. A.C. 202
Yreka, California 64, 65, 66, 67, 68
Yreka (California) *Semi-Weekly Union*, reports on Tom Boulton's arrest 65
Yreka (California) *Weekly Union*, reports on Charles Mortimer 68
Yuma, Arizona 208

Zacatecas (province, Mexico) 128

ABOUT THE AUTHOR

William B. Secrest has for many years chronicled the little-known stories of early Californians. He has long maintained that "Wild West" history ignores California, and he has set out to correct the record in a long list of magazine articles, monographs, and books. His work has appeared in *True West, Old West, The Californians, Westways, American West*, and many others. His book, *Lawmen & Desperadoes: A Compendium of Noted, Early California Peace Officers, Badmen, and Outlaws*, appeared in 1994.

Secrest is a commercial artist and art director for a Fresno, California, advertising agency and a member of the editorial board of the Fresno City and County Historical Society.